Homeless
in America

Homeless in America

CAROL L. M. CATON

New York   Oxford
OXFORD UNIVERSITY PRESS
1990

Oxford University Press

Oxford   New York   Toronto
Delhi   Bombay   Calcutta   Madras   Karachi
Petaling Jaya   Singapore   Hong Kong   Tokyo
Nairobi   Dar es Salaam   Cape Town
Melbourne   Auckland

and associated companies in
Berlin   Ibadan

Published by Oxford University Press, Inc.,
200 Madison Avenue, New York, New York 10016

Oxford is a registered trademark of Oxford University Press

Library of Congress Cataloging-in-Publication Data
Caton, Carol L. M.
    Homeless in America / Carol L. M. Caton.
      p.   cm.
    Includes bibliographical references.
    ISBN 0–19-503918-1
    1. Homelessness—United States.   2. Homeless persons—
Services for—United States.   I. Title.
  HV4505.C37   1990
  362.5'8'0973—dc20   89-16259   CIP

9 8 7 6 5 4 3 2 1

Printed in the United States of America
on acid-free paper

To Lisa
My Beloved Daughter
and the Daughters and Sons of Her Generation
Whose Help Will Be Needed to Bring an End
To Homelessness in America

82747

Foreword

Every spring, beginning on Mother's Day, my guild, the American Psychiatric Association (APA), holds its annual scientific meeting. This year ten thousand of us left our comfortable hotels to convene at the San Francisco Convention Center. To get there most of us hurried past small groups of ragged people holding posters and passing out blurred leaflets with various slogans: Psychiatry Uses Drugs That Kill, ECT Destroys the Brain, Save Your Pet from Animal Researchers!

Inside the Convention Center, we entered halls filled with television monitors and well-dressed colleagues discussing the day's activities. We grabbed free pens from pharmaceutical companies promoting their newer and better medications while trying to keep their older ones alive. Private psychiatric hospitals told us why we should send them patients who need their special care. Rooms were packed with attentive members and guests learning from each other about the cocaine epidemic, AIDS, and a plethora of facts and theories, which could not be digested in a lifetime, much less four days. By tradition the president of the APA picks his own theme for the meeting, and in 1989 it was "overcoming stigma."

On leaving the Convention Center in the early evening, we saw that the protesters, who had energetically called attention to their concerns that morning, were gone. Only their leaflets remained, strewn over the pavement. The streets had been abandoned to others who were protesting not with signs held high but rather with outstretched hands. We stepped around them without acknowledging their existence. We were afraid, embarrassed, and shamed by them. We had made them the stars of the show inside the Convention Center, but outside we passed them by. They were the homeless mentally ill.

Thirty years ago, today's homeless mentally ill would have lived in large psychiatric institutions, but based on the conviction that these institutions were horrible places (and they were indescribably awful), we closed them. Psychiatrists and other mental health workers were promised community-based treatment and housing programs and, in turn, we promised to staff them. Few programs ever emerged and, in fact, we did not have adequate scientific knowledge to provide these services.

In the 1980s, literally thousands of homeless mentally ill, fearful of shelters, have lived on the streets of major urban centers. The visibility of their plight has spurred programmatic efforts, such as New York City's Project Help, to get the homeless off the streets. But public concern often pressures communities to ''do something'' before science can test how to achieve the desired goals. A brief case history of Project Help's attempts to help one homeless person, Joyce Brown, illustrates the complexity of this task.

Joyce Brown lived with her family and was employed as a secretary until she was 37 years old. In 1984 her behavior changed, and in 1985 her sisters brought her to an emergency room. They said she was aggressive and potentially assaultive. She also had a history of substance abuse. Ms. Brown was hospitalized and, while there, was placed in seclusion and in four-point restraints. During her hospitalization, she was diagnosed as having an atypical psychosis with the possibility of paranoid schizophrenia (a diagnosis which requires evidence of being ill for at least six months). She was treated with moderately high doses of Thorazine and after 15 days was no longer considered threatening or dangerous. She was discharged and given a diagnosis of paranoid personality disorder.

In December 1986, Ms. Putnam, a psychiatric social worker and coordinator of Project Help, first met Ms. Brown, who was living on a hot-air vent in Manhattan. Ms. Putnam had received many calls from people in the community who were concerned about Ms. Brown's welfare. They said she appeared dirty, disheveled, and inadequately clothed for winter. When Project Help workers offered to help, Ms. Brown shouted obscenities at them. Her behavior was noted to have become worse over the winter. In May 1987, Ms. Putnam saw Ms. Brown, who is black, shouting racial epithets at black males making a delivery across the street from her vent. Ms. Putnam was concerned that Ms. Brown's behavior placed her in danger of being assaulted. As time went on, Ms. Putnam saw fecal matter on the sheets in which Ms. Brown wrapped herself, and on at least one occasion she saw her urinating and defecating on the street.

In July 1987, Dr. Hess, a psychiatrist working with Project Help, observed that Ms. Brown was disheveled and twirling an open umbrella (it was not raining). He heard her speaking in rhymes with a sexual content relating to him and Ms. Brown's genitals. Dr. Hess felt she was speaking in a confusing manner typical of individuals with schizophrenia.

Five days later, Dr. Hess observed that Ms. Brown's clothes were more dirty and torn. She cursed him, exposed her nude buttocks toward him, and made reference to his genitals. Her affect was flat. Two months later, Dr. Hess noted that her clothes were now so torn that large portions of her torso were exposed. She smelled of urine and feces. Torn up currency was piled in neat stacks on the street, and she appeared to have urinated on them. She cursed and shouted obscenities at Dr. Hess. He offered her food that at first she refused. She later accepted the food only to throw it at him, and then she chased him around the corner. A month later, the scene was essentially the same. Again, there was torn up currency that appeared to have been urinated on. She repeatedly asked Dr. Hess, "What is my name?" Dr. Hess believed her condition had deteriorated and her aggressive behavior had escalated.

Ms. Brown was taken to Bellevue Hospital and involuntarily admitted. She told the admitting psychiatrist that she had run into traffic and had the right to do so. She said that if she got hurt it was no one's business but her own. She also said that she urinated and defecated in her clothing. She was given a neuroleptic, apparently only for a short time. On her second hospital day, another psychiatrist, Dr. Mahon, saw her but did not speak to her since she used threatening gestures and was hostile. The next day Dr. Mahon was able to talk with Ms. Brown for 30 minutes. She told Dr. Mahon a number of things about herself which turned out to be untrue, but her condition continued to improve over the next few days.

Ms. Brown, who felt that she was a professional street person and a survivor, however, initiated a court challenge protesting her involuntary confinement. Despite the Appellate Court's decision to continue her hospitalization, Ms. Brown was released from Bellevue in January 1988. Apparently barred from forcing her to take medication, her psychiatrists felt they could do little for her. She was released to the Travelers Hotel, a temporary residence for women trying to re-enter society.

Ms. Brown was elated to have her freedom back and instantly became a national media celebrity, appearing on *60 Minutes* and the *Donahue* show. She addressed law schools, including Harvard, and at each appearance she was cogent. Subsequently she received eight book and movie offers and six job offers.

By March 1988, Ms. Brown was still living at the hotel but was again panhandling, screaming loudly at black people, and yelling aloud to herself. Her family insisted she was regressing.

In September 1988, Ms. Brown was arrested in a Harlem housing project, charged with possession of hypodermic needles and heroin. She was conditionally discharged after pleading guilty to disorderly conduct.

Today, despite the notice that federal, state, and local governments— as well as the private sector—have taken of the homeless, there is little scientifically based knowledge that can be used to help them. At best, the problem has been addressed with descriptions and head counts because, as a society, we have not seen the need to treat our social problems with the same scientific rigor required of medical science. Social ideas compete in political and legal arenas, not on the pages of refereed journals, where every statement requires support and replication by experimentation. While we spend over 100 million dollars to test a new drug's efficacy and safety before allowing patients to use it, we are unwilling to subject our social policies to similar scrutiny, though they often affect much larger numbers of individuals and have a far greater impact on the way we live.

The social problem of homelessness is finally and thoroughly confronted in *Homeless in America*. Indeed, as the book points out, only a portion of the homeless are mentally ill, and the problem as a whole is much greater than previously acknowledged. Beginning with a valuable history of how communities have lived with endemic homelessness, the book examines how homelessness becomes epidemic as an aftermath of wars, economic turbulence, pestilence, migration, and a host of other social ills. Homelessness in America today is such an epidemic, and Dr. Caton and her colleagues write about it from their own experience with the homeless. They provide moving, often tragic, vignettes of individuals, and they outline the homeless problem, shading it in with what we know about its extent.

Though the reasons for the epidemic are only partially understood, a persuasive argument is made that a failure to provide low-income housing is a substantial factor. Aside from the ethical issues, can we afford to build low-income housing? It is reasonable to assume that when the cost of crime, ill health, morbidity, and loss of productivity of the homeless and their children are considered, the cost to our nation is very high. Providing low-income housing could prove less expensive than allowing the condition of homelessness to perpetuate, but creating housing is not all that must be done. Our social scientists, through well-designed studies, must advance our knowledge of how best to remedy the situation.

This book is a first step. Clearly written, *Homeless in America* makes it easy for the interested reader to learn about homelessness. More important, it is an excellent text for those who can and will do something about the problem. The book is a landmark by which to judge ourselves as a society. If, by the second edition of *Homeless in America*, we have not decreased the anguish of the homeless, we will have robbed ourselves of the opportunity to make our nation a better one.

Washington, D.C.   Richard Jed Wyatt, M.D.
October 1989   Chief, Neuropsychiatry Branch
                                            National Institute of Mental Health

Preface

The complacency of everyday life in contemporary America has been jarred in recent years by the growing presence of people without homes. It is unsettling to find, wandering in city streets, sleeping in doorways or depots, the tired, hungry, and sometimes insane members of our society, yet they are becoming all the more numerous. It is ironic that as modern industrial society has embarked on a space age, sóme of its citizens should be confronted with homelessness, a problem that has plagued humankind from the beginning of our existence on this planet. Perhaps homelessness is endemic to human civilization, associated as it is with the consequences of war, natural disaster, impoverishment, illness, and disability. The fact that homelessness is still experienced by even a small minority of the population fifty years after the Great Depression issued in a wave of social and economic reform suggests that current remedies are ineffective.

In recent months a number of articles and books has heightened public awareness of the plight of the homeless and has gnawed at our collective conscience. It is a problem that up to now has defied solution. Is it that up to now we have not understood the nature of homelessness? As a first step, we must examine its causes and consequences because only then can we suggest program initiatives. We have written *Homeless in America* in this spirit—as a guide for students, service providers, policymakers, and advocates who wish to understand and change the fate of our homeless.

New York City   C. L. M. C.
October 1989

Contents

Homeless
in America

1 | Homelessness in Historical Perspective

CAROL L. M. CATON

The situation of homelessness, with its physical and psychological challenges, has been endemic in the human family from the beginning of civilization. Often the result of natural disasters, war, and economic failure, homelessness has been experienced over the centuries by a great variety of people. However, the destitute, disabled, and antisocial have typically made up the core of those for whom homelessness has been a way of life. In preindustrial society, slaves and prostitutes were also among these outcast groups (Hotten, 1860; Ribton-Turner, 1887; Aydelotte, 1913; Smith, 1970; Pound, 1971; Grice, 1977). When the Industrial Revolution encouraged migration from rural to urban areas and across continents, the ranks of the homeless were swelled by seasonal laborers and migratory workers (Culver, 1933; Cross and Cross, 1937). New opportunities to obtain work as sailors, miners, or loggers demanded that men be uprooted from their families, isolating them from familiar social worlds (Bahr, 1970).

The archetypal images of the homeless recalled in literature range from the vulnerable, mentally disabled "Toms-o-Bedlam"[1] of Shakespeare's *King Lear*[2] to the adventurous wanderers depicted by Jack London in *The Road*. Policy on the homeless problem has often been dependent on the vicissitudes of public attitudes toward those who deviate from society's mainstream.

Early attempts to control the problem of homelessness have focused on distinguishing the "worthy poor" from a criminal or irresponsible element. In general, the disabled or truly impoverished have been viewed with greater compassion than the able-bodied wanderers with no permanent home or employment. An English law of 1388 required that all persons moving from place to place, including the destitute poor, laborers in search of work, members of religious orders, and university scholars, obtain letters from town officials to authorize their travel. The absence of papers was punished by imprisonment or involuntary return to one's birthplace (Wallace, 1965, p. 4). In the centuries that followed, there were numerous legislative attempts to impose increasingly severe penalties on "vagrants," defined as able-bodied, unemployed wanderers. A statute of 1530–31 licensed the aged, the poor, and the disabled to beg. Those considered the deserving poor were provided with lodging at the expense of the town (Wallace, 1965). All others were subject to "whipping" and "ear lopping." Anyone found guilty of giving money or shelter to an unlicensed beggar were fined or imprisoned. In 1547, Edward VI ordered that all persons loitering, wandering, and not seeking work be taken before a justice of the peace, branded with a "V," and placed with a master to work. One-time escapees could be taken back by their masters, but refusal by master meant return to one's birthplace to be a slave of the town. Those who escaped twice were executed. Some unwanted vagrants were deported to Ireland, Scotland, Wales, or the New World.

Despite harsh punishments, the problem of vagrancy did not disappear. The punitive measures of Edward VI were overturned by the Poor Law Act of 1601, which called for the return of all homeless persons to their place of birth. Taxes were levied for the relief of helpless and needy persons. Overseers of the poor were appointed to ensure the proper administration of relief. Work was provided for the able-bodied, but those who refused to work were imprisoned.

Only rarely in history has public policy been directed at a cause of homelessness. In 1619, Charles II devised a unique policy to ameliorate the problem of population uprooted by war. Legislation was enacted to facilitate the reintegration of about 50,000 soldiers into civil society by permitting them to exercise trades without apprenticeships (Wallace, 1965, p. 8). Although this measure demonstrated that effective employment policies could prevent destitution and homelessness, policies based on rational principles did not become widespread until centuries later.

The American Experience with Homelessness

The Colonial Era

The first wave of immigration to the New World occurred in the mid-1600s and included many "unworthy" poor—the criminals, unwed mothers, and vagrants sent by the English government as indentured servants. It was probably from this pool of individuals that the first homeless emerged, unable as they were to cope with the harsh demands of Colonial life (Martin, 1987; Golden, 1988).

Early English attitudes toward poor and dependent persons were transported by English colonists to the New World. The Elizabethan Poor Law Act of 1601, which provided the model for poor relief in the American colonies, formalized the practice of placing the support of dependent persons in the hands of the local community (Deutsch, 1937; Grob, 1973). However, many communities avoided supporting the poor by making it difficult for beggars, vagabonds, and other nonworking persons to settle within their boundaries. The financial status of strangers was closely checked before they were allowed to settle in a community. A term of "quiet and undisturbed" residence in a locality, lasting from three to twelve months, was required before the status of legal resident was conferred, which carried with it the town's obligation to provide support in the event of need.

This community reluctance to welcome the poor was manifest when the poor were "warned out" of the town's borders. If a person dared to return to a locality after such an experience, he or she was frequently whipped before being driven out a second time. The mentally ill and other dependent persons were often spirited out of town in the dead of night and placed in or near a neighboring town in the hope that another community would assume responsibility for their care. As a consequence, a cadre of homeless wanderers emerged among the destitute and disabled in the American colonies (Deutsch, 1937, pp. 39–54).

Institutions for the homeless began to appear in the eighteenth century. From 1725 to 1750 houses of correction, workhouses, and almshouses sprang up in the larger towns. One of the first was the "Poor-House, Work-House, and House of Correction of New York City," established in 1736. Paupers and petty offenders were treated alike in the workhouse, and thus it served as a combination poorhouse and jail. The mildly to moderately mentally disturbed were put to work side by side with common paupers and criminals picking oakum, spinning wool and flax, knitting and sewing. The equivalent of the workhouse in rural districts was the custom of bidding for the insane at the auction block, a practice which had gradually evolved toward the end of the Colonial Era. The able-bodied insane, along with other dependent persons, were put to work on farms and given food, clothing, and shelter in return (Deutsch, 1937, Ch. 5).

The Early to Mid-Nineteenth Century

Although institutionalization of the care of disabled and dependent persons became more widespread in the nineteenth century (Rothman, 1971), the problem of the homeless continued to grow. The first soup kitchen in New York was set up in 1802, and the first shelter in New York, the Sailors Snug Harbor, was established in 1814 (Wallace, 1965, p. 11). As the century progressed, services and programs for the homeless were in increasingly short supply, forcing many to be lodged in police stations.

Station house lodging—crisis housing to shelter the homeless in the absence of more adequate facilities—was generally crowded and dirty. Cities were urged to end this practice and set up more permanent lodging houses for the "worthy poor," defined as those willing to work and not charged with vagrancy. Reformers such as Josephine Shaw Lowell spoke out against lodging houses, contending that they destroyed people's incentive to work by enabling them to live so cheaply. An alternative, the wayfarers lodge, was proposed, where the homeless could receive food and lodging in exchange for work (Ringenbach, 1973).

The almshouses became the centers of "indoor" poor relief (lodging in public institutions) in the nineteenth century, particularly for those rendered ineligible for government payment of room and board in a home setting ("outdoor" relief). By 1835, most counties in New York State had almshouses, and by mid-century, the inmate population of almshouses was nearly 10,000 (Rothman, 1987, p. 12). During this period, one-fourth of the almshouse inmates were children, and many suffered from mental illness or retardation, physical disabilities (deafness, blindness, loss of a limb), or were filthy and diseased (Rothman, 1971, pp. 198–99). Crowded and unsanitary conditions were commonplace.

Throughout the late 1800s, the unemployed homeless were found in a variety of settings. Some were taken in as boarders for which homeowners charged the local government for room and board, while others were lodged in jails or county institutions. Some were put to work, while others were not.

The Post-Civil War Era

The economic crises of 1819 and 1837 left many able-bodied men un-employed and vulnerable to homelessness (Ringenbach, 1973). However, homelessness did not become a significant national problem until after the Civil War, which uprooted many persons and rendered them destitute. In addition, waves of immigrants came to the United States in the post-Civil War era. Some had low cash reserves and quickly slipped into homelessness in times of economic adversity. A committee of the New York State Charities Aid Association reported that during 1874–75, over 435,000 persons were lodged by the police in station houses in New York City (Ringenbach, 1973, p. 11). This count may, however, by inaccurate since the same persons were sent from one station house to another during the same period.

While care was provided to the destitute, disabled, and unemployable, harsh measures were instituted to control the vagrant population, including those who drank to excess and were involved in crime. At an 1877 conference of the New York Board of Public Charities, it was advocated that national legislation be established to make it a criminal offense to beg, wander aimlessly, and solicit alms. This would have allowed authorities to jail vagrants and put them to work at hard labor (Ringenbach, 1973, p. 22).

The Rhode Island Tramps Act of 1880, which served as a model for other states, established a special office whose job was to aid in arresting and securing the conviction of tramps and beggars, who were then sent to workhouses for a specified time. "An Act Concerning Tramps" defined a tramp as "one living without labor or visible means of support and roving from place to place, begging" (Ringenbach, 1973, p. 22).

In opposition to this view, Kansas Populist governor Lorenzo D. Lewelling stated that the debate over which homeless were deserving or undeserving was academic and disputed the contention that being unemployed was a crime. He attacked the Kansas vagrancy statute of 1889, which assumed that there were always jobs available for those able and willing to work (Ringenbach, 1973, p. 38).

The post-Civil War era, also witnessed the development of "skid rows," named for Seattle's Skid Road, a street along which horses skidded logs to a sawmill. Skid Road was inhabited by lumberjacks who lived in the flophouses lining the street and who frequented its saloons and brothels. After the Panic of 1873, skid rows sprang up in many American cities. The thousands of men who lost their jobs during that economic depression were forced to move from town to town searching for temporary jobs as loggers, miners, farmhands, or construction workers. Without families, the hub of their work and social ties revolved around their existence in skid rows (Leepson, 1982; Siegal and Inciardi, 1982).

The mercantile failures of 1873 ("Black September") resulted in an unemployment rate of 30 and even 40 percent, establishing vagrancy as a national welfare problem of the first rank (Wallace, 1965, p. 15). There was no national policy directed at the homeless problem, but voluntary organizations, such as the Salvation Army and the Young Men's Christian Association, provided relief for the unemployed. In 1873, the Young Men's Christian Association established a facility in New York's Bowery, and between 1891 and 1903, the Salvation Army built four hotels in that location (Wallace, 1965, p. 16). Both of these organization emphasized the importance of work and family ties. Other proposed solutions to unemployment encouraged the development of Western lands and discouraged migration to the cities. Employment bureaus and labor exchanges were set up in urban skid rows to recruit employees for new jobs in frontier areas.

As the economy improved, in the 1880s, the homeless problem diminished. Indeed, shelters such as the Night Refuge Association Lodge in New York City, established in 1876 to take the pressure off police station lodging, closed because they were no longer needed. However, as economic hard times re-emerged in the 1880s and 1890s, so did the homeless problem. At the height of the Panic of 1893, on Industrial Black Friday (May 5, 1893), the number of unemployed was estimated between 900,000 (Broadstreet) and three million (Samuel Gompers; see Ringenbach, 1973, p. 38). Thus, the homeless problem persisted and continued to be a topic of controversy.

The Early Twentieth Century

As the twentieth century approached, reports on the homeless problem became more descriptive. In 1893, J. J. McCook surveyed 1,349 tramps, most of whom were native-born Americans. He found that 60 percent had some type of skill and had initially started to wander in order to seek employment. While three out of five were intemperate, McCook concluded that tramping was a consequence of unemployment, not of drunkenness.

One of the first major twentieth-century studies of the homeless was carried out by Alice Solenberger (Solenberger, 1911), who reviewed the cases of 1,000 male subjects who applied to the Chicago Bureau of Charities for assistance during the years 1900 to 1903. Although some of the subjects were runaway boys, criminals, or deserting husbands, the majority were unattached single men who lived in cheap lodging houses. Nearly two-thirds were native-born Americans, mostly white. About half were between the ages of 25 and 49 years, and one-fourth were 24 years of age or younger. Only 1 out of 20 men was illiterate, and most had attended school.

An important finding from this study was that nearly two-thirds of the men had a major health problem. More than one-quarter suffered from a serious physical disability such as blindness, deafness, or crippling. About one in ten suffered from tuberculosis. Nearly 11 percent suffered from insanity (about 5 percent), feeblemindedness, epilepsy, or another type of nervous disorder. Of those who were insane, nearly half had left home after having been diagnosed as such and before proper arrangements could be made for them to be treated. However, Solenberger hypothesized that some of the subjects became insane as a result of the stresses of homelessness.

With the Depression of 1913–15, the number of homeless increased again. New York City's Municipal Lodging Houses provided 253,406 lodgings (approximately 1,400 per night) during the first half of 1915, and the population of the Bowery—New York City's infamous skid row— was estimated at from 26,000 and 75,000 persons (Wallace, 1965, p. 19).

The pre-World War I era produced another large-scale study of homeless men, this one carried out in the Municipal Lodging House of New York City. Two thousand men were given a medical examination, in which it was determined that nine out of ten were physically able to work, with fully 62 percent considered capable of hard manual labor (Advisory Social Service Committee of the Municipal Lodging House, September 1915).

The problem of homelessness persisted after the end of World War I. In a classic study, Anderson (1923) interviewed 400 homeless men on freight trains en route from Salt Lake City to Chicago in the summer of 1921. A major finding was that 41 had physical defects that would noticeably hinder their working capacity. Nearly all the men were migratory workers or hobos.

Anderson also documented the skid row area of Chicago in the twenties. Calling it "hobohemia," he described its function as a labor exchange for migratory workers and a place where low-cost housing could be found. Anderson also described "jungles"—those areas outside the central city where homeless men gathered and that were in close proximity to a railroad division point. Anderson concluded that men leave home and live in hobohemia in order to do seasonal or migratory work. They end up jobless and homeless because they are industrially inadequate, have personality defects, or serious family problems.

The percentage of homeless remained relatively constant until 1927–29, when wages began to decline and the Great Depression hit the nation. Roseman (1935) reported that from October 1, 1930, to September 30, 1931, the number of lodgings provided in Chicago reached 1 million (2,740 lodgings per night); from October 1, 1931, to September 30, 1932, there were 3.25 million (8,904 lodgings per night); and from October 1, 1932, to September 30, 1933, there were 4.25 million (11, 644 lodgings per night). In 1933–34, there were 4,228,356 lodgings provided in Chicago alone (11,585 lodgings per night) (Roseman, 1935). A 1933 census conducted by the Federal Transient Bureau estimated the number of transient and homeless persons in the United States to be between 1 and 1.25 million (Reed, 1934). Nels Anderson, a social scientist (U.S. Senate Subcommittee, 1933), estimated that there were 1.5 million homeless, a conservative estimate since others ranged from 2 to 5 million.

Despite the development of new institutions to care for the sick and disabled, such as the municipal hospital system and state mental hospitals, almshouses remained a part of American life until World War II. The almshouse population in the twentieth century was composed primarily of the elderly (a 1930 New York State Commission report identified that nearly 90 percent were over age 50; 42 percent were age 70 or older). The majority had once worked as unskilled laborers, but had become demented, intemperate, ill, or disabled (Rothman, 1987). Many of the public facilities had physically deteriorated or were inadequate and unsafe for the care of older people. Finally, however, as welfare benefits were expanded to include old-age pensions and health-care and unemployment insurance, the almshouse disappeared.

Post-World War II Years

With the recovery of 1936 and the advent of World War II, the skid row populations in the United States nearly disappeared, reaching a low point in 1944, when the New York City Municipal Lodging House reported an average of only 550 lodgings per day, compared with 18,000 in 1935 (New York City Welfare Council, 1949). Such social welfare programs for veterans as the G. I. Bill of Rights, the Veteran's Administration, and a series of benefits ranging from education to psychiatric treatment enabled most World War II returning servicemen to reenter society, unlike the aftermath of other wars, and few ended up on skid row. An estimate made in 1950 placed the number of skid rowers in 41 cities at less than 100,000 (Bogue, 1963).

In the 1950s and early 1960s large-scale action-oriented surveys of skid row residents were taken in cities such as Sacramento (McEntire, 1952), Minneapolis (Caplow, Lovald, and Wallace, 1958), Philadelphia (Blumberg, 1961), Chicago (Bogue, 1961), and New York (Bahr, 1968). Stimulated by federal policy toward urban renewal in major metropolitan areas, these studies provided descriptions of skid row neighborhoods and the men who lived there. As geographically distinct areas within older commercial districts, skid rows contained rooming houses, inexpensive residential hotels and restaurants, employment bureaus, bars, missions, and social service agencies. Skid row residents were typically drawn to the area because of its low living costs, opportunities for companionship with other single men, and many bars and drinking establishments. These neighborhoods also functioned as employment centers for unskilled and daily laborers.

Studies conducted in this era reported that most men arrived in skid row areas when they were in their late thirties or early forties, and health problems were common among them. For example, Bogue's study of 613 Chicago men interviewed in 1957 and 1958 revealed that about 7 in 10 had some form of disability or physical handicap. Only one man in ten was unable to engage in gainful work. Nearly one-half were handicapped by excessive alcohol use. Bogue found the death rate among homeless men in Chicago to be 70 per 1,000, which was 6.5 times the national average (Bogue, 1961).

In 1968, Bahr compared two groups of homeless men to a control group of domiciled men. Two hundred three residents of New York City's Bowery were compared to 198 residents of a camp for homeless men in the Catskill Mountains of New York State, and 125 residents of the Park Slope neighborhood of Brooklyn. All three groups had median ages in the fifties, but the camp group was substantially older, with a median age of 59 years, in contrast to 52 years for the Bowery sample and 50 years for the Brooklynites. Less than one-third of study subjects were black, and blacks were not overrepresented on skid row. Most men were American-born Protestants or Catholics of Northern European descent. While the level of education of all three groups was similar, skid row and camp men had been very poor for most of their adult lives. The gap between their occupational statuses and those of control respondents increased as they got older. In addition to a lower standard of living, skid row and camp men were more likely to have had a poor work history, marital difficulties, health problems, heavy use of alcohol, and repeated arrests both for drunkenness *and* more serious crimes, as compared to domiciled Brooklyn men.

Homelessness in the 1980s

Beginning in the late 1970s, observers of the American social scene began to note with increasing frequency the presence of people without homes, wandering city streets and sleeping in doorways and depots (Klerman, 1977; Segal, Baumohl, and Johnson, 1977; Reich and Siegel, 1978; Talbott, 1979; Baxter and Hopper, 1981). Some were obviously mentally ill (Baxter and Hopper, 1981), people who "were dirty, wore torn or inappropriate clothing, hallucinated or shouted to others, and in general acted in a strange or bizarre way" (Talbott, 1979). Others were the unemployed who had exhausted their relief benefits and experienced loss of rental housing or foreclosure on their homes (Cuomo, 1983); some were welfare mothers and their children unable to find affordable rental housing on a relief allotment (Carmody, 1984); Salerno, Hopper, and Baxter, 1984). First apparent in large cities, in this decade homelessness has penetrated rural and suburban areas from coast to coast and across the heartland.

The unrelenting increase in the number of homeless people in the United States has marked homelessness as a serious social problem of the eighties. Although there are no annual national statistics, in New York City the number of single people in shelters has grown considerably in recent years, from about 5,000 in December 1983 to about 9,000 in January 1988. A similar trend has been observed for homeless families seeking shelter (Barbanel, 1988).

What has caused this problem to reappear with such force in the 1980s? To date, the genesis of homelessness remains poorly understood, and it is not clear the extent to which homelessness is primarily an economic problem, a housing problem, a problem secondary to changes in institutional care of the deviant and disordered, or a problem aggravated by inadequacies in social welfare policies (Rossi et al., 1987). Nor is it known how much of the problem can be attributed to family issues, psychiatric disorder, substance abuse, criminality, or a combination of these individual and social system factors. The recent literature on homelessness, however, has attributed the condition to economic and social policy failure, as the following discussion details.

Economic Recession

In the early 1980s, when the problem of homelessness began to accelerate, economic recession was endemic, producing the worst levels of unemployment since the 1930s. In mid-1984, 8.5 million were jobless (Joint Economic Committee, Congress of the United States, June 15, 1984). During 1982 and 1983, the national unemployment rate exceeded 10 percent for a period of ten months. At the worst point in the recession (November 1982), nearly 12 million people—or 10.7 percent of the workforce—were unemployed. This represents a 40 percent increase in unemployment over a period of two years. It is notable that at least one-fourth of all persons in the labor force were touched by this phenomenon. Significant unemployment occurred at a time when double-digit inflation had markedly reduced the buying power of the dollar, an occurrence particularly harmful to those on fixed incomes but affecting all whose incomes did not keep pace with inflation.

Unemployment, which led to a considerable increase in home mortgage foreclosures, significantly affected homelessness. The Mortgage Bankers Association reported that 130,000 Americans lost their homes due to foreclosure in 1982. Midwestern farming regions were especially hard hit, with rates of foreclosure markedly higher than the national average. In Illinois, foreclosures rose 25–30 percent in 1982 and 1983, reflecting the state's persistent high rate of unemployment. In Wisconsin, in 1983 farm foreclosures were at their highest level since the Great Depression (Cuomo, 1983, pp. 38–39).

More recently, the drop in the unemployment rate to below 6 percent in 1987–88 would seem to augur well for the homeless problem. It is not clear at this time how an improved economy affects homelessness or who of the homeless might benefit, and why. For more detail on this issue, see Peter Marcuse, Chapter 7.

Decline in Housing for the Poor

In contrast to the previous recessions of the post-World War II era, the economic downturn of the 1980s coincided with a sharp decline in the availability of low-cost housing. Although incomes in general rose during the decade between 1970 and 1980, as evidenced by a 53 percent drop in the number of renter households with incomes below $3,000 per year (from 5.8 to 2.7 million), the number of rental units which would be affordable (requiring only one-third of the annual income) to those households in this income range dropped by 76 percent, from about 5.1 to 1.2 million (Low Income Housing Information Service, 1984). The median rent paid by households in the lowest income group increased from $72 per month in 1970 to $179 per month in 1980. This means that for those in the very lowest income group, nearly three-quarters of an annual income goes for rent, leaving very little for the rest of life's essentials.

Housing stock for the poor declined largely for two reasons. First, many urban metropolitan centers, particularly those in the Northeastern and North Central States, have undergone extensive urban renewal and "gentrification." In many instances, the skid rows or areas of the city with low-cost residential hotels and rooming houses have been virtually eliminated to make room for luxury housing (Kasinitz, 1984). For example, in the period from January 1975 to April 1981, New York City experienced a 62 percent decline in single room occupancy and low-priced hotel rooms (Kasinitz, 1984, p. 13). In a similar period of time, San Francisco lost one-third of its residential hotel units through conversions, while Detroit lost 17.7 percent between 1980 and 1982. Loss of low-cost residential hotel housing has occurred in other cities as well (Cuomo, 1983, pp. 37–38).

The Census Bureau's Annual Survey of Housing found that in 1982, the number of households with two or more related families sharing space rose from 1.2 million units to 1.9 million units, a 58 percent increase. Doubling up families, a situation very close to homelessness, has been termed "pre-homelessness" because the strains of overcrowding often break through as guest families are evicted by their own kin into the streets (National Governor's Association Task Force on the Homeless, 1983). For a more thorough discussion of this issue, see Peter Marcuse, Chapter 7.

Recently, municipalities have made a deliberate attempt to provide housing alternatives both for single adults and for families (Barbanel, 1988). Information is not yet available on the effectiveness of such programs to guide future policy and program development.

Reforms in the Social Security Disability Insurance Program

Another factor suspected of contributing to the homeless problem was the federal government's effort in the early 1980s to reform the Social Security Disability Insurance Program. Under this program, those who are physically or mentally unable to perform in any kind of job for which they are qualified, regardless of job availability, receive benefits. Following a report by the General Accounting Office that as many as 20 percent of the beneficiaries might be ineligible, an extensive review of this program was initiated in March 1981. Between 150,000 and 200,000 people lost their benefits (a total of 3.8 million disabled workers and their dependents received benefits in 1983) before the controversial procedure was halted in April 1984. It has been contended that some of those pared from the disability rolls were truly disabled, some being so mentally ill that they could not respond to notices that their benefits had been terminated. In May 1984, a federal court ruled that nearly 4,000 mentally ill people dropped from this program receive shares of an 8-million-dollar settlement with the Social Security Administration (*New York Times,* May 27, 1984, p. 46). However, the federal government subsequently dropped new rules to liberalize the criteria for awarding Social Security Disability Insurance benefits to people with severe mental disabilities (*New York Times,* September 15, 1984, p. 1, and December 9, 1984, p. 1).

How changes in this policy have influenced homelessness is not clear. The only data have been anecdotal reports directly connecting the termination of disability benefits with loss of housing and homelessness. Restoration of benefits did not reduce the number of homeless adults seeking shelter, at least in municipalities where data on shelter use trends are available (Barbanel, 1988).

Deinstitutionalization of Health and Social Welfare Systems

The post-World War II era has witnessed major changes in systems of care for dependent and disabled persons. The century-and-a-half old methods of institutional care, such as orphan asylums for homeless children, hospitals for the mentally ill, and jails and prisons for criminals and delinquents, which emerged in the 1820s as the population in cities and towns grew larger (Rothman, 1971), have given way to programs anchored in the community-at-large. A multiplicity of factors have contributed to this development, including heightened concern for the civil liberties of incarcerated persons and a belief that care in large, understaffed, and overcrowded institutions had negative effects on a person's social identity and level of adjustment. Moreover, the rising dollar costs of providing institutional care motivated exploration of outpatient and community-based methods of management that promised to be less expensive.

Deinstitutionalization of state and county mental hospitals is the most commonly cited example of this phenomenon. Beginning in the mid-1960s, deinstitutionalization became the most significant public mental health policy in most states. The goal of this policy has been the phasing out of the state mental hospital as the primary locus of care of the chronically mentally ill in favor of community-based treatment. Deinstitutionalization has been carried out by discharging long-term patients from state mental hospitals and tightly controlling the admission of new patients, which has resulted in a 70 percent drop in the inmate population in state and county mental hospitals, from 559,000 in 1955 to 150,000 in 1980 (Department of Health and Human Services Steering Committee, 1980). It is well known that the deinstitutionalization movement was poorly planned and that many patients were released from hospitals that did not adequately prepare appropriate postdischarge living arrangements and outpatient psychiatric care for them (Arnhoff, 1975; Klerman, 1977; Talbott, 1979; Lamb, 1984; Goldman and Morrissey, 1985; Bassuk and Lamb, 1986). Surveys of the adult homeless in the United States have established that a portion of the homeless on the streets and in shelters are suffering from psychiatric disorders (see Paula Eagle and Carol L. M. Caton, Chapter 4).

A policy of deinstitutionalization is also apparent in the child welfare system, which has developed programs such as foster care (Bryant, 1981) to provide children with a more familylike living setting. Even when institutional care is provided, its duration is more limited, as welfare agencies have been encouraged to have natural parents involved as much as possible in their children's upbringing. Some children placed in the care of the child welfare system experience multiple changes in their living arrangements as they revolve among family living settings and foster care placements. In a New York City study of 118 runaway and homeless youth between the ages of 12 and 17, approximately half had histories of foster care placement, while none were recent discharges from state or county mental hospitals (Shaffer and Caton, 1984).

The prison system has also been influenced by deinstitutionalization to some degree, making greater use of rehabilitation concepts and early parole. It is possible that gaps in the adequacy of release planning and community placement are responsible for the fact that nearly half of adult shelter residents have been in prison or jail (Hoffman, 1982; Bassuk, Rubin, and Lauriat, 1984; Crystal and Goldstein, 1984; Rossi, Fisher, and Willis, 1986).

Homelessness: A Serious Social Problem of the 1980s

While the roots of homelessness are still being debated (Holden, 1986), there is a growing concensus that the problem is increasing in the United States. The National Coalition for the Homeless has estimated that there were 2.5 million homeless in 1983, an increase of 500,000 over the preceding year. Perhaps the most compelling evidence that homelessness has increased in recent years is the growth in the number of public shelters. In New York City, for example, 25 new public shelters have been opened since 1980. In addition, more than 60 small shelters sponsored by churches and synagogues provide hundreds of lodgings per night. Other major cities have markedly increased their shelter capacity to accommodate the growing numbers of people seeking a bed for the night.

A historical overview of homelessness reveals that neither the problem itself nor some of the proposed solutions are new or radical. What is promising, however, is the response to homelessness in the 1980s in both lay and professional circles. Thoughtful people, deeply troubled by what they have observed, have sought information and understanding. A new genre of research has emerged to record efforts to learn who is homeless and why, and what can be done to bring about solutions. Aspects of this literature will be presented in the chapters to follow. A more scientific understanding of the nature of contemporary homelessness may bring about more long-lasting and effective remedies to this age-old problem.

Notes

1. Patients discharged from London's Hospital of St. Mary of Bethlehem (founded in 1247), who roamed the countryside as homeless beggars (Deutsch, 1937; Henry, 1941).

2. "Poor Tom, that eats the swimming frog, the toad, the tadpole, the wall-newt and the water; that in the fury of his heart, when the foul fiend rages, eats cow-dung for sallets, the old rat and the ditch-dog, drinks the green mantle of the standing pool; who is whipped from tithing to tithing, and stock-punished and imprisoned . . ." (*King Lear* III, 4).

2 | The Epidemiology of Homelessness

CAROL L. M. CATON

A central issue in the public concern for the homeless has been estimating the size of the homeless population. A national census to determine this population in the United States has not yet been carried out. At present, there is little information on the incidence of new cases of homelessness in a given time, nor are there accurate statistics on the total number of Americans who have ever experienced an episode of homelessness. Because homelessness is often intermittent, interspersed with episodes of living in low-cost transient, institutional, or family settings, the number of people homeless on a single night will be considerably lower than the number of people who experience homelessness at some time over an entire year. While this seems self-evident, there has been great confusion about the meaning of figures that estimate the number of homeless and how they were derived. Advocates for the homeless state that there are as many as two or three million homeless people in the United States. In 1980, the Community for Creative Non-Violence concluded that 1 percent of the population, or 2.2 million people, lacked shelter (Hombs and Snyder, 1982). This figure was a rough estimate based on information received from about 100 agencies and organizations in 25 cities and states.

Problems in methodology is a major reason for the lack of adequate data in this area. While housed persons can be counted during a specified period, it is extremely difficult to get an accurate assessment of the numbers of persons sleeping in transportation depots, in public parks, or other outdoor locations. Moreover, any assessment is highly dependent on one's definition of homelessness. If it is defined as being without shelter, the number of people homeless on a given night would be quite different from the number with unstable family support (or no family at all), those without a stable or permanent living setting, or those doubling up with others in public or low-cost housing units.

Defining Homelessness

Any study enumerating the size of a specific population must define the groups under study, but over the decades, the definition of homelessness has varied considerably. Wallace has noted that historically state vagrancy statutes have defined a homeless person as one who wanders about and lodges in taverns, groceries, alehouses, watch or station houses, out-houses, marketplaces, sheds, stables, barns, uninhabited buildings, or out in the open and who does not give a good account of him or herself (Wallace, 1965, p. 90). Solenberger (1911) defined homeless men in her study in Chicago as those living in rooming houses and low-cost residential hotels who sought assistance from a local office of the Chicago Board of Charities. Some of the men she studied had lived in these places for years. Numerous studies of skid row men have focused on those living in flophouses, missions, and low-cost residential hotels located in specific sections of the central city (Bogue, 1961; Bahr, 1968). Those homeless who find shelter outside the skid row areas were not studied, such as those found in transportation depots and outdoor locations. Wallace defined a skid rower as someone who was isolated and without kin, and did not "bathe, eat regularly, dress respectably, marry or raise children, attend school, vote, own property, or regularly live in the same place" (Wallace, 1965, p. 144). Bahr has defined homelessness as disaffiliation, a condition of detachment from society as evidenced by the absence of affiliative bonds "that link settled persons to a network of interconnected social structures." (Bahr, 1973, p. 17).

Contemporary surveys of the homeless have tended to define the phenomenon in purely pragmatic terms. "Homelessness" refers to people who have no fixed abode or nighttime shelter other than that provided by a private or public agency. Rossi et al (1987) have termed this "literal" homelessness. Homeless people are thus distinguished from those who have permanent shelters even though that shelter may be physically inadequate (U.S. Department of Housing and Urban Development, 1984, Ch. 2) or unstable and precarious (Rossi et al., 1987). Psychosocial conceptions of homelessness as disaffiliation or estrangement from family or kin are not considered.

The homeless are also distinguished from those living in overcrowded conditions, such as people who have lost their homes or apartments and are forced to double up with friends and relatives, which frequently results in overcrowding and physically inadequate living settings. While it often happens that tensions resulting from such living arrangements often result in evictions, unless or until such an event takes place, the people involved do have a roof over their heads and are not homeless. The most comprehensive count of the homeless, the U.S. Housing and Urban Development study (1984), counted a person as homeless if his or her nighttime residence is in public or private emergency shelters, which take a variety of forms—such as armories, schools, church basements, government buildings, former firehouses, and temporary placement in hotels, apartments, or boarding homes paid for by vouchers provided by private and public agencies. The study also counted the homeless in streets, parks, subways, bus terminals, railroad stations, airports, under bridges or aqueducts, abandoned buildings without utilities, cars, trucks, or any other public or private space not designed for shelter (USHUD, 1984, Ch. 2). A similar definition was used in Rossi et al.'s (1987) study of the Chicago homeless. (For a thoughtful consideration of the need to expand the definition of homelessness beyond the literal one, see Peter Marcuse, Chapter 7.)

Definitions of homelessness must also deal with its duration. Some people are chronically homeless, while others are homeless only on a short-term or temporary basis. Any investigation of the number of people homeless on a specific night reveals prevalence at that point in time and does not represent the incidence of new cases of homelessness over a given period or the total number of people who experience homelessness at any time during a year.

Unfortunately, there is virtually no literature on the phenomenon of homelessness among minors in the United States, although a small number of studies have examined the incidence of runaway behavior and the characteristics of the young people involved in it. A possible factor in the reluctance to label anyone 17 years old and younger as homeless is that, from a legal perspective, no youth is homeless. Those who cannot live with a natural parent are the responsibility of the child welfare system until they come of age.

Defining homelessness and runaway behavior and distinguishing between the two is important. Chapter 722 of the August 7, 1978, New

York State Social Services Appropriation defines a *runaway* youth as "a person under the age of 18 years who is absent from his legal residence without the consent of his parents, legal guardian, or custodian" and a *homeless* youth as one "who is in need of services and is without a place of shelter where supervision and care are available." These definitions imply that a runaway child has somewhere to go where he or she would be cared for, whereas a homeless child does not, although the psychological reality of whether all runaways do indeed have a place to return to is debatable. Those definitional issues were explored in a study of runaway and homeless children in New York City conducted by Shaffer and Caton (1984). Of the 118 subjects, ages 12 through 17, admitted to youth shelters who were interviewed, none had a parent, biological or adoptive, who was currently homeless. Only seven youths (6 percent) did not know the whereabouts of either parent. When asked where they intended to go upon leaving the shelter, 24 percent revealed that they planned to return to their families, 17 percent to foster care, and 20 percent to independent living. Thirty-nine percent did not know where they intended to go. Moreover, 46 percent stated that they could not go home to live, and 60 percent stated that they did not want to live at home. Twenty percent stated that they had no home, and about 14 percent felt the youth shelter was home, which yields a homeless rate of about 34 percent. When asked whether they defined themselves as runaway or homeless, 44 percent classified themselves as runaways, 34 percent as homeless, and 22 percent indicated that they were both runaway and homeless.

Previous researchers have defined runaway behavior in terms of the youth's intent (Shellow et al., 1967) or as a period when the youth is absent from home without the permission of a parent or guardian (Leventhal, 1963; National Center for Health Statistics, 1975), with or without a time qualification. Some have felt that the period of absence should be at least two hours (Opinion Research Corporation, 1976), eight hours (Behavioral Research and Evaluation Corporation, 1975), overnight (Robins and O'Neal, 1959; Roberts, 1982; BREC, 1975; Stierlin, 1973; Opinion Research Corporation, 1976), or at least 24 hours (Riemer, 1940). Workable definitions of homelessness that take into account stimulus and duration of time have been lacking.

A National Estimate: The USHUD Study

The most comprehensive attempt to marshal systematic evidence on the number of homeless comes from the U.S. Department of Housing and

Urban Development (USHUD). In this report (1984), four approaches, which rely on a variety of information sources and procedures, are presented. Each approach has its strengths and weaknesses in estimating this elusive and often hidden population. But taken together, they sketch out a clearer approximation of the homeless in the United States than any previous study. The four approaches include: (1) using published local estimates; (2) interviewing local observers in a nationwide sample of 60 metropolitan areas; (3) interviewing a nationwide sampling of shelter managers; and (4) using a combination of shelter and street counts.

Extrapolation from Highest Published Local Estimates

The first method of estimating the number of homeless in the nation is based on the highest published estimates in 37 urban centers. The figures were taken from newspaper articles, studies, congressional hearings, and task force reports, including the Report to the National Governor's Association Task Force on the Homeless (Cuomo, 1983). Some estimates were made in 1981, but most were from 1982 and 1983. Figures represented the total number of homeless persons at any particular point in time. A straight extrapolation from these 37 cities to the nation as a whole assumes a constant rate of homelessness in all areas of the country, whether it be New York City or a rural county. Such a method is bound to produce an overly high estimate, since statistics on the homeless generally emerge from places where the problem is likely to be most severe. Moreover, the extent of homelessness in small towns and rural areas is not as high as in metropolitan areas. Thus the majority of facilities for the homeless, such as shelters, soup kitchens, and welfare agencies, are concentrated in central cities rather than rural or suburban areas. The suburbs do not provide many sleeping places outside of shelters, such as abandoned buildings, heating grates, transportation depots, and so forth, where the homeless could stay, and so also have a lower homeless population. Using the highest local estimates, the overall homeless rate is .25 percent, or 25 persons per 10,000 population. A straight extrapolation of this rate to the nation as a whole produces a figure of 586,000 homeless, an estimate on the high side (see Table 2.1).

Interviews with Local Experts in a National Sample of Metropolitan Communities

In attempting to resolve some of the problems of relying only on published local estimates of the number of homeless, a nationwide sample of

Table 2.1   Summary of four approaches to estimating number of homeless persons nationwide (USHUD, 1984)

Approach 1	Extrapolation from highest published estimates	586,000
Approach 2	Extrapolation from estimates in 60 metropolitan areas, obtained in 500+ local interviews	254,000
Approach 3	Extrapolation of estimates from national sample of 125 shelter operators	353,000
Approach 4	Shelter population and local area street count	192,000
	Shelter population and 1980 census street count	267,000
	Most reliable range: 250,000–350,000	

60 metropolitan areas (of varying sizes and from different regions) was selected so that the estimated national total is not based only on cities where the homeless problem is severe or where published information exists. Over 500 telephone interviews were conducted with local experts during the winter of 1984 to elicit their assessment of the size of the homeless population in their areas, the reliability of which was assessed by the USHUD team. This more systematic procedure used the same definition of homelessness from city to city. The number of estimates obtained varied depending on the size of the metropolitan areas: three to five for smaller metropolitan areas, four to seven for medium-sized metropolitan areas, and eight to twelve for large metropolitan areas (separate estimates were obtained for the central city and surrounding jurisdictions). A single estimate for each metropolitan area was derived by averaging, which weighted the reliability of each estimate (e.g., estimates derived from street counts and shelter bed statistics received more weight than mere impressions). In extrapolating from the sample to the population as a whole, it was assumed that the rate of homelessness in small towns and rural areas was equal to that for the small metropolitan areas. This approach yielded an estimate of 254,000 homeless nationwide.

Estimates Provided by Shelter Operators

The national sample surveys cited earlier included estimates given by shelter operators. When their estimate alone is extrapolated to the nation as a whole, the total national estimate is 353,000 homeless. As in the previous approach, this figure represents the average number of homeless persons on any given night in December 1983 or January 1984.

Street and Shelter Counts

A fourth approach was to estimate the number of homeless found either in shelters or on the streets on any given night. The USHUD survey permits a reasonably certain estimate of the size of the sheltered population. On any given day in January 1984, an average of 69,000 people were given shelter—57,000 in metropolitan areas and 12,000 in nonmetropolitan areas.

The group living on the streets is very difficult to count for a variety of reasons. First, those whose personal appearance and behavior are not unusual might be overlooked in a search of people living on the streets. Second, although some people without homes seek refuge in public locations such as transportation depots or church steps, others sleep in concealed or isolated places for fear of being harassed or victimized. Actual attempts to count the number of homeless have yielded very low numbers. A 24-hour count conducted in 1982 by the Baltimore City Planning Department, using police officers as enumerators, located only 29 homeless individuals, even though the Greater Baltimore Shelter Network estimates that there are about 600 homeless at any one time. News reporters searched the downtown area in Richmond, Virginia and discovered only 16 homeless, even though local experts estimated the homeless population to be between 50 and 125 persons.

In assessing the number of homeless on the streets, two sources of data were used: the casual count from the 1980 Census (Bureau of Census, 1982) and locally done street counts in Boston, Pittsburgh, and Phoenix. To include those transient persons usually not counted using traditional procedures, a ''casual count'' was mounted in connection with the 1980 Census, which considered homeless persons in places such as employment and welfare offices, transportation depots, food stamp centers, pool halls, and street corners. The 23,237 individuals found in this way cannot be considered a national census of street people, since it was conducted in urban census districts representing only 12 percent of the population. Adjusting for the fact that the street count was conducted in those districts where the homeless population is higher, and the impression of local experts that the numbers of homeless have increased an average of about 10 percent a year, the estimate of the number of homeless people in the streets in 1984 is 198,000.

In 1983, three cities conducted systematic surveys of the homeless population in fairly mild weather when people were out on the streets: Phoenix in March 1983, Pittsburgh in June 1983, and Boston in October. In all three cities, more people were found in the streets than in the shelters. For every 100 persons in shelters in Boston, there were 129 persons in the street. In Phoenix, there were 273 people on the street for every 100 in shelters, and in Pittsburgh the figure is 130. Taken together, the average street-to-shelter ratio for the three cities is 178:100. Using the estimate of 69,000 in shelters nationally, the street-to-shelter ratio extrapolated nationally would yield a street population of 123,000. Depending on which method is used to calculate the number of homeless people on the streets, the total number of homeless derived from this approach ranges from 192,000 to 267,000. The figure derived from interviews with local observers (254,000) is within that range. Table 2.1 summarizes the four approaches used by USHUD to enumerate the homeless in the United States; the combined study yields a range of 250,000 to 350,000 persons.

The Department of Housing and Urban Development study also revealed some interesting geographic differences. Contrary to the popular opinion that the problem of homelessness is greatest in the Northeast, the USHUD study found greater concentrations of the homeless in the West. Nearly one-third of all homeless people in metropolitan areas are in the West, despite the fact that this region of the country contains only 19 percent of the national population. The South, Northeast, and North Central states, more populous than the West, have roughly the same share of homeless, between 22 and 24 percent. The greater homelessness in the West probably results from the large migration of people there seeking job opportunities and a more temperate climate. While urban renewal in the Northeast and North Central states has sharply reduced the availability of low-cost housing, the West has very little older housing that could be converted into housing for the poor.

The majority of the homeless (about 60 percent) are found in large metropolitan areas with populations in excess of one million. The ratio of homeless to the total population in cities over 250,000 is 13 persons for every 10,000 population. However, in smaller metropolitan areas (50,000 to 250,000 population) the ratio drops to 6.5 persons per 10,000. The reason for greater numbers of homeless in central cities and large metropolitan areas is probably because people are drawn there seeking job opportunities. Shelters, soup kitchens, social services, and low-cost housing, essential services for the needy, are also more available in urban centers.

A Local Estimate: The Chicago Homeless Study

More recently, Rossi et al. (1987) have reported their effort to estimate the composition and size of the homeless population of Chicago. Focusing on the "literal homeless," those who clearly have no access to a conventional dwelling, an attempt was made to enumerate the population living in shelters and on the streets. Two distinct but complementary samples of shelters and street dwellers were taken at two different times— one spanning a two-week period in late September and early October 1985, and the other carried out over a two-week period in late February and early March 1986. The two samplings enable an examination of seasonal effects on the size and composition of the homeless population. The shelter surveys were conducted in all Chicago shelters that provide sleeping accommodations for homeless persons—22 shelters in the fall and 27 shelters in the winter. Teams of interviewers counted all present in the shelters, assumed to be among the literal homeless, on the nights of the study. The street surveys were based on stratified random samples of 168 blocks in the fall and 245 in the winter, drawn from among Chicago's 19,409 census blocks. Blocks were stratified by the expected number of homeless to be found there, determined through consultation with the Chicago Police Department as to how many homeless persons could be expected on that block in nighttime hours. This resulted in a list of blocks expected to have high concentrations of homeless. The street surveys were carried out by teams of interviewers accompanied by off-duty policemen. All places on each sample block to which the study team could gain access, such as all-night businesses, alleys, hallways, roofs and basements, abandoned buildings, and parked cars and trucks were searched. Persons encountered in such searches were queried to determine whether or not they could be counted among the literal homeless.

This study was designed to produce statistically unbiased estimates of the number of literal homeless in Chicago. The estimated average number of such persons each night was $2,344 \pm 735$ in fall 1985, and $2,022 \pm 275$ in winter 1986 (see Table 2.2). The difference in these figures is not statistically significant. In the fall the number of literal homeless found in the streets outnumbers those in shelters, while the opposite holds true in winter.

The median duration of homelessness in this study was 7.6 months (mode, 1 month), indicating the extent to which there is turnover within the population of literal homeless. Using such information, Rossi et al.

Table 2.2   Estimates (± standard errors) of the prevalence of literal homelessness in Chicago. Estimates are based on probability samples of shelter residents and homeless persons on the streets and public access places in fall 1985 and winter 1986.

Survey component	Fall 1985	Winter 1986
Point prevalence estimates		
Average daily homeless		
Shelter residents	961 ± 13	1,492 ± 55
On streets or in public places	1,383 ± 735	528 ± 269
TOTAL	2,344 ± 735	2,020 ± 275
Annual prevalence estimates [a]		
Number ever homeless		
annually, street and shelter		
combined	6,962 ± 1,881	5,051 ± 505

[a] Annual prevalence estimates are based on conservative assumptions concerning the average length of time spent homeless. Alternative assumptions produce estimates that vary by almost one magnitude from those shown here.

estimate that about 6,000 Chicagoans experience an episode of literal homelessness in a one-year period—about 0.2 percent of Chicago's population of 3 million.

The sampling method used in Chicago can serve as a model for similar studies in other locations. Although Rossi et al. defined homelessness similar to the way USHUD did, their method of counting nights for two separate fourteen-day periods provides a more stable estimate of the number sheltered each night than the one-night count used in the USHUD study. Moreover, Rossi et al.'s innovative procedure for obtaining a count of the homeless in streets and public places provides a unique estimate of this segment of the homeless population in Chicago.

Fearing that their method might have excluded several important groups of homeless persons, such as dependent children, those residing temporarily in rented rooms or the homes of friends, inmates in hospitals, prisons, or other institutions, and those in specialized shelters excluded from the larger study (such as those for battered women, the chronically mentally ill, and substance abusers), Rossi et al. provide estimates of the likely number of subjects in these groups. They derive a final estimate of 2,722 Chicagoans literally homeless on an average night (Rossi et al., 1987, p. 1,340).

Estimating the Number of Homeless Youth

Shelters for youth were not included in either the USHUD study or the Chicago Homeless Study. Estimates of the extent of homelessness among youths (those 17 years old and younger) are sketchy. The most reliable estimates of the size of the problem of runaway behavior comes from a nationwide study carried out by the Opinion Research Corporation (1976), consisting of a telephone survey of a probability sample of 62,895 households, of which 13,942 included a youth between the ages of 10 and 17. This survey indicated the annual incidence of overnight runaway behavior to be 1.7 percent of those aged 10–17, or between 519,000 and 635,000 individual runaways per year nationally. No comparable data are available on the incidence of homelessness. However, estimates based on Shaffer and Caton's (1984) data indicate that approximately 0.5 percent of New York City youths between the ages of 12 and 17 years use shelters in a one-year period.

But not all who run away or are homeless make use of community services. Many seek shelter with relatives or friends, never coming to the attention of public authorities or service agencies.

The Social Characteristics of the Homeless

Examining the burgeoning ranks of the homeless in the late 1980s reveals a heterogeneous group of children and adults who share this one condition in common but have very different needs, depending on gender, age, mental health and health status, and work potential. In many locales the homeless have already been divided into specific subgroups for the purpose of providing shelter. There are separate shelters for single adult females, single adult males, runaway and homeless youth, and family groups. Among adults of both sexes, the mentally ill homeless have been singled out for specialized mental health programs (see Paula Eagle and Carol L. M. Caton, Chapter 4). As the homeless problem began to escalate in the early 1980s, policymakers and epidemiologists began to ask, "Who are the homeless?" and "Why are they so?" Considerable information has since been obtained on the adult homeless; minors and homeless families have been studied to a lesser degree.

The Department of Housing and Urban Development's (1984) nationwide study of sheltered homeless adults, based on information obtained from shelter directors in 60 cities, provides descriptive data on a large segment of the adult homeless population. In addition, at least 14 local surveys of this group provide more detailed information on the psychiatric, medical, and social conditions of the homeless. These studies have been carried out in such urban metropolitan areas as New York City, Philadelphia, Boston, Chicago, St. Louis, and Los Angeles, where the homeless problem has been most acute. One study covered the entire state of Ohio (Roth and Bean, 1986). While much research has dealt only with the homeless in shelters, some investigators have also studied those living in streets (Rossi, Fisher, and Willis, 1986; Roth and Bean, 1986), in transient settings such as inexpensive hotels (Roth and Bean, 1986), and users of day centers and meal programs in skid row (Farr, Koegel, and Burnam, 1986).

Homeless Adults

Unlike the typical "skid row" homeless person of the 1950s, who was a white, American-born male in his early fifties likely to be suffering from alcoholism, the current population of homeless includes a growing number of women.[1] Although two out of three homeless are single adult men, single women make up about 13 percent of the homeless population and family members about 21 percent (USHUD, 1984, p. 28).

The average age of homeless adults today is in the mid-thirties, considerably younger than in the past. Only a small percentage are elderly, probably because older people are not suited to a treacherous life on unprotected streets or crowded shelters, particularly if they are frail or disabled. The underrepresentation of the elderly among the homeless may be accounted for by the benefits for which the elderly are eligible, such as Social Security, Medicare, and food stamps, which buffer the boundary between poverty and destitution.

Although most of the adult homeless are white, minorities are overrepresented in this population and their percentage is increasing. According to the national shelter survey (USHUD, 1984), 44 percent of the shelter population is black, Hispanic, or Native American—minority groups that make up about 20 percent of the population as a whole. Blacks predominate in the metropolitan centers of the East and Midwest, while Hispanics are found in greater numbers in the cities of California and the Southwest.

Surprisingly, from 20 to 25 percent of the homeless are employed, usually on a part-time or irregular basis. Many have experienced long-term unemployment and have encountered great difficulty in attempting to re-enter the job market. About one out of three receives some form of public assistance. The remainder, about half, survive by begging, foraging in refuse containers, selling blood, collecting redeemable beverage cans, or receiving handouts (USHUD, 1984). The average monthly income of a homeless person in Chicago is about $168 (Rossi et al., 1986). Indeed, many rely heavily on the food, shelter, and clothing provided by public or charitable agencies. Without this assistance, they would confront starvation and exposure (Rossi et al., 1986).

Homeless adults are somewhat less educated than the population at large (Farr et al., 1986). Although the proportion of high school graduates is roughly comparable in both populations, fewer of the homeless have attended college (Rossi et al., 1986). About one man in three has served in the Armed Forces, a proportion similar to that found in the general population.

Approximately three out of five homeless adults have never been married. Of those who have married, the majority are either separated or divorced. Even though few have married, the majority have had children. However, most homeless adults, particularly men, are alone in their homelessness despite the fact that many of their children are not yet grown.

When people end up in shelters or on the streets, it is because the safety net of supportive family and friends has failed. Social isolation is very high among homeless adults. Surveys report that as many as half have no contact with family or friends (Crystal et al., 1982; Farr et al., 1986; Fischer et al., 1986; Roth and Bean, 1986; and others). The study by Rossi et al. (1986) found that both men and women aged 40 and older are likely to have entered the homeless condition from a solitary living arrangement. In contrast, more than half the homeless women under age 40 were in a family living setting prior to homelessness, but few expressed any desire to return home. Although fewer men in this age group lived in a family setting before becoming homeless, about half felt returning home was an appealing idea.

Patterns of Homelessness

There is considerable variation in the duration of an episode of homelessness. In Roth and Bean's (1986) statewide survey, the *median* length of homelessness was 60 days. Rossi et al.'s (1986) study of the Chicago homeless found that the *median* length of homelessness was 7.6 months. More than one-third of study subjects had been homeless for a year or more, and the *mean* length of homelessness was 21.9 months. Very long episodes of homelessness have also been reported among men in New York City shelters (Crystal and Goldstein, 1984). Farr et al. (1986) found that the majority of their skid row subjects experienced episodes of homelessness interspersed with periods of relative stability, in which they managed to support a place of their own or live with family or friends. When life was bad, they were homeless again and the cycle repeated.

At present, there is very little understanding of how homelessness evolves out of an individual's life experience or how it is related to personal characteristics and larger social and economic issues. Surveys have revealed that psychiatric and medical illness afflicts a considerable proportion of homeless single adults (see Paula Eagle and Carol L. M. Caton, Chapter 4, and Arnold Drapkin, Chapter 5). However, few hold their disabilities accountable for their homelessness. When asked why they are homeless, the majority cite economic problems such as unemployment and difficulty paying rent (Rossi et al., 1986, Roth and Bean, 1986). Many also list personal crises, such as being evicted from an apartment or home, being released from hospital or jail with nowhere to live, family discord or violence, or a recent separation, as precipitants of homelessness (USHUD, 1984; Roth and Bean, 1986; and others). Indeed, people give many reasons, which they often see as interrelated, for the loss of a home.

Differences in Sheltered and Street Homeless

Despite the widespread availability of crisis shelters in most urban metropolitan areas, many homeless do not use them. In Rossi et al.'s (1986) study of the Chicago homeless, a total of 55 percent slept in shelters. In the warmer autumn season, only 39 percent used shelters, and even in the middle of winter, only 74 percent chose to sleep in a shelter. Although nearly half of all homeless believe that shelters are dangerous, those who prefer life on the streets to a shelter generally have more negative attitudes about shelters.

In the study by Rossi et al. (1986), it was found that street subjects spent an average of less than five nights per week on the streets. They occasionally used shelters, rented rooms, or stayed in someone's home. In contrast, shelter subjects were less likely to seek alternative sleeping arrangements. The researchers conducted a multivariate analysis of characteristics of homeless people that might explain why they lived in shelters, on the streets or in other public places, or in the homes of others. They found that women spent less time on the streets or in other public places than men, and that younger people spent more time in someone else's home. Street people were more often rated by interviewers as shabby, dirty, unkempt, incoherent, or confused. Moreover, they scored higher on symptoms of depression than sheltered homeless. These findings are similar to those of Roth and Bean (1986), who reported that street people were more disturbed behaviorally than sheltered subjects. The Rossi et al. (1986) study also found that homeless people who avoid shelters are less likely to have used either detoxification or inpatient psychiatric care, perhaps reflecting a tendency of street people to avoid the service system altogether.

Runaway and Homeless Youth

Earlier research on the issue of homelessness among youth focused specifically on runaways. Running away from home occurs with almost equal frequency among males and females (Opinion Research Corporation, 1976; Shellow, et al., 1967), as does the use of shelters (Shaffer and Caton, 1984). Although runaway behavior often occurs before puberty (National Center for Health Statistics, 1975), most runaway episodes have been reported to take place in mid-adolescence (Opinion Research Corporation, 1976; Shellow et al., 1967). Runaways are more likely to define themselves as homeless as they get older (Shaffer and Caton, 1984). The Opinion Research Corporation's (1976) national household survey revealed that runaway episodes occur in families of all social class backgrounds and ethnic groups. However, a study of users of New York City youth shelters revealed that 44 percent had mothers who were on public assistance (Shaffer and Caton, 1984). Among shelter users, whites are somewhat underrepresented and blacks overrepresented (Bureau of the Census, 1982).

Shellow et al. (1967) and Shaffer and Caton (1984) found that repeat runaway episodes are common, and noted correlations between this phenomenon and school attendance difficulties and family problems. Shaffer and Caton (1984) found that approximately 40 percent of the 118 New York City youth they studied had been admitted to a youth shelter previously. Recidivism was associated with a history of foster care placement, looser connections to home backgrounds, and greater involvement in antisocial behavior. Approximately one-half had histories of foster care placement, but less than one in ten had ever been admitted to a psychiatric hospital.

Family conflict, ranging from communication problems and relationship difficulties (Wolk and Brandon, 1977; Williams, 1979) to allegations of sexual and physical abuse (Gullotta, 1979), has been implicated as a precipitating force for leaving home among adolescents. Shaffer and Caton (1984) uncovered considerable family pathology in their study of sheltered New York City youth; three out of five had a parent with a history of drug or alcohol abuse or criminality. Moreover, about half indicated that a parent had physically abused them to such a degree injuries were sustained.

So far studies have identified four major areas of behavioral difficulty among runaway and homeless youth: school problems, antisocial behavior, depression, and suicide attempts. The Opinion Research Corporation (1976) noted that runaways had worse relationships with teachers and lower academic aspirations than other students. Adams and Munro (1979) report the existence of difficulties in school before the first episode of running away.

In Shaffer and Caton's 1984 study of sheltered New York City youth, approximately half had repeated a grade in school, and nearly three out of five were more than one standard deviation behind on reading achievement tests. Seventy-one percent of boys and 44 percent of girls had been suspended or expelled from school.

In a long-term follow-up of runaways who had attended a child psychiatric clinic, Robins and O'Neal (1959) found that over the course of time they had high juvenile arrest rates. Shaffer and Caton (1984) found that antisocial behavior was common both in the parents of runaway and homeless youth and in the youth themselves.

A number of studies identified psychological difficulties—depression and low self-esteem (Beyer, 1974), neurotic anxiety (Williams, 1979), and interpersonal difficulties—as prevalent in runaway youth. Shaffer and Caton (1984) found that both depression and suicidal thoughts, as well as suicide attempts, were common among the youth they studied. Notably, psychosis is rare in this population.

Homeless Mothers and Children

Nationwide data on the characteristics of homeless families are lacking, but a Boston study (Bassuk, Rubin, and Lauriat, 1986) strongly suggests that these families considerably overlap with "multi-problem" welfare families (Leavitt, 1981; Phillips et al., 1981; Simpson, Kilduff, and Blewett, 1984). In the Boston study, 80 homeless mothers and 151 children living in 14 Massachusetts' family shelters (two-thirds of such facilities in the state) were interviewed. The median age of mothers, 45 percent of whom were single and 45 percent of whom were separated, divorced, or widowed, was 27 years. About half were black and from the Boston area; the other half were white and more often resided outside of Boston. Each mother had an average of 2.4 children, most of whom were living with her in the shelter. Nine out of ten of these female-headed families were recipients of Aid for Dependent Children (AFDC). Only three out of five had ever finished high school, and only one out of three had any work experience lasting for more than one month.

Homeless mothers commonly experienced family disorganization in childhood. Two out of three reported a major family disruption, such as separation, divorce, death of a parent, or out-of-home placement. No less than one out of three mothers ever knew her own father, and a similar proportion reported abuse by a parent or another adult during childhood or adolescence. Nearly one-fourth of the mothers studied were involved with social service professionals as a result of probable abuse or neglect to their own children.

Two out of five mothers came to the shelter from shared, overcrowded living arrangements. The majority cited eviction, nonpayment of rent, overcrowding, and housing conversion as primary reasons for homelessness. Problems with other household members were also important in the loss of a living arrangement.

Unfortunately, there are no systematic data on runaway and homeless youth or homeless mothers who choose to live on the streets rather than in shelters. Nor is it known how homelessness in youth is related to adult homelessness. Such issues deserve to be addressed in future studies in the area.

A fuller understanding of homeless people can be gained by examining their lives in more detail. The following chapter looks at specific case studies of homeless men and women as well as runaway youth.

Note

1. Some would contend that women have always figured prominently among the homeless, as hobos, wanderers, and inmates of almshouses (Martin, 1987; Golden, 1988).

3 | The Homeless of the 1980s: Case Reports from Clinicians' Notebooks

PART ONE: HOMELESS MEN

JEFFREY GRUNBERG

Case 1: Hsuan-Li

Hsuan-Li, as I shall call him, was born in 1949 in Hunan Province, which is located in the central part of mainland China. His father, a municipal judge, and his mother had high expectations for him and his six brothers and sisters. All seven obtained college degrees. The oldest, a woman currently residing in China, received a doctorate in drama and literature from an American University. The others, except for one still in school, received master's degrees. One is now in Europe working as a business lawyer. Another is a professional printer living in the American Midwest.

When Hsuan-Li was 14 years old, he left home to enroll in the Chinese navy. He traveled to many ports in the China Sea during his three-month stint and all the while, he now recalls, he was aware of a growing need for more privacy than the society he lived in permitted. He resented the grouping together of people. He just wanted to be alone and, whenever possible, he was.

After those three months, he entered the army where, after reaching the level of sergeant in four years, he was approached by the government to enter advanced military training school, where he could become a general. He declined. Immediately, he was transferred back to the navy, where he was forced to start from scratch. Working as a male nurse, he reached the level of sergeant again in three years.

At the age of 22, he left military service and went to a Chinese college away from his home, where for the first time he lived alone. He worked in a government-sponsored program in order to maintain a small income.

During these years, whenever he was by himself, he developed a taste for rice wine. He does not remember experiencing any difficulties regarding this practice of combining wine with solitude.

After graduating at the age of 26, he traveled to Japan, again as part of a program, where he helped train workers on the art of building tunnels. He lived there for one and one-half years in a dormitory, made no friends, and usually sat alone in his room drinking sake. Following this, he spent another one and one-half years in Hong Kong, where he worked as an advisor/trainer for those in the business of building civil structures. Here he first tasted American wine and whiskey.

He then traveled to the United States, where he attended a New England university, and lived alone in a neighboring town in a small one-room apartment. He had won an assistantship and did not drink at all during those two years. He felt less pressure, could be alone whenever he wanted, and, being new to the country, dared not risk losing what he had.

Upon graduating in 1980, now a 30-year-old with a master's degree in industrial engineering, he was offered a position as engineer with a New York City-based construction firm at a salary of $20,000 per year.

I was given the most boring job there. Maybe because I am Oriental. All they wanted me to do was deal with the numbers and the blueprints. All I did was sit alone in the office while everybody else was out there working. They never asked me to help them build anything.

He did not talk to anyone about this. He drank once in awhile but was much more interested in saving money and, after one and one-half years with the firm, he had saved $3,000.

His social life was negligible. He ate lunch alone. He slept alone. There was nobody to telephone. Up until this time, around July of 1982, he had only approached one girl for a date, a girl he did not want to go out with that much. When she accepted, he just stayed home and stood her up. Later, however, he met a woman whom he loved. He asked her out, but, he says, "She rejected me. She refused me."

This disappointment seemed to combine with his growing sense that he was being taken advantage of at the office. His old feelings of needing privacy gained momentum. He began to feel that people might want to hurt him. So, he decided, it was best to keep to himself.

> I was alone and lonely. I didn't have any friends. One day, I thought I heard voices that were warning me of something. So, I quit my job and went to my apartment.

He stayed there for three months, without leaving it even once. He ran out of food in two months and ate nothing the third. He had neither television nor radio. There was only the noise of the streets to listen to.

> One day, a power or something pushed me out. I left my apartment with my bankcard. I locked the door and threw away the key. For three days I walked. I began to eat then, but only liquids at first.

He went straight to the bank and withdrew, over strategically planned intervals of time, his entire savings account.

He headed south. The first complete stop he made was in Louisiana. Then he continued through Mississippi and Texas, making only short stops. When he reached South Carolina one evening, he laid down on the street to sleep. He was awakened by a police officer, who brought him to a state mental hospital where he stayed for two months.

When he was discharged, the hospital made an appointment for him to report to the outpatient clinic. Instead, he went to Atlanta, Georgia, where he worked parking cars in a garage for two months. He remembers drinking very little during that period, even though he had much of his money left. He still thought he was hearing voices. Sometimes, they asked him to hurt other people. He refused to listen to them. He quit his job, traveled to southern Georgia, and worked as a farm laborer.

It was not long before he quit and went to California. Again, he slept on the street. Again, he was taken to a hospital by a city policeman. This time, he was a patient for eight months. He was given medication, kept to himself, and began to relax. Upon release, he spent six months in a mission, where he mostly read novels and newspapers.

He then traveled to New York. This time, his sleeping on the streets brought him a stay in the shelter system. Before then, he had been treated by several different city hospital emergency rooms "just for nerves. They never asked me to stay. But they would talk to me and make me feel better."

Upon entering a shelter, he was seen talking to himself while eating alone at breakfast time. He was approached by a social worker who was making assigned rounds. Inquiries were made into his condition and Hsuan-Li stated that he wanted to see a doctor.

> The doctor was an Indian man. He didn't ask me too many questions, so I stayed pretty quiet. He decided to send me to this program [the one Hsuan-Li is currently in]. I think it's okay. I feel better.

The program to which he refers is geared to helping the mentally ill homeless. He is a regular attendee and divides his time between its work program, social activities, and poetry workshops. His poems are well written and usually talk of suicide and loneliness. He keeps mostly to himself, yet goes out in the evening with several drinking buddies.

Asked to rate his life at present, Hsuan-Li hesitates only briefly. "Okay, not too bad." The reference points for this simple statement are the late sixties and early seventies, when he remembers being very depressed and feeling very alone. "I didn't tell anybody because they were my private feelings. It was not for the public." Any affiliations Hsuan-Li has had mostly resulted from situations structured by others or were under the confinement of strict rules. He has had few friendships and has never dated anyone.

Case 2: Eduardo

"My father disowned me. My mother died when she had me." This is how Eduardo began his reply as to why he felt he was now homeless. As he went on:

> My father was visiting my mother at the hospital just after I was born. He looked at me and yelled, "He is not my son." My mother got so upset that her condition got very bad. She bled too much and she died. So my grandfather and grandmother took me home to live with them and their three sons.

In the middle of winter 1933, Eduardo was born to a black Hispanic father and white mother, both of whom had spent their lives in Puerto Rico. Just after Eduardo's birth, he was taken to live in a small, northern city, a poor town whose main industry was the cutting of sugar cane.

By the time he entered the first grade, he was already very good at baseball. He carried a ball around wherever he went, always trying to teach people how to play the game. He remembers being known for that and for attending school and church regularly. When he was in the third grade, both grandparents died within months. "From then on," he reports, "it was always, 'What are we going to do about Eddie?' "

He began to work almost immediately, selling papers to buy shoes or picking avocadoes to help pay for food. When he was in the eighth grade, he quit school to work full-time for a ceramic tile factory. He worked there for 4 years until he was 18 years old. He quit his job so that he could be home more often. By then, he had had a baby with his 16-year-old girlfriend with whom he lived in a nearby town. His girlfriend spent most of her time raising the child and keeping house while Eduardo worked odd jobs in the community.

At the age of 22, he traveled alone to the American mainland and found a job. In nine months' time, he sent for his girlfriend and son and settled in Manhattan. He commuted to New Jersey where, for several years, he worked in a factory making Christmas tree decorations. From the years 1961 to 1965, he and his common-law wife had four children, two of whom died soon after birth. Well before his second child was born, however, Eduardo became involved with heroin, encouraged to experiment with it by his friends. Almost immediately, he had run-ins with the New York City police department. He was arrested in 1958 and sent to Riker's Island prison for one year. But he resumed his drug habit upon his release. To maintain himself financially, he forged checks, for which he was arrested in 1961. He was sent to federal prison for one year. In 1964, after becoming involved in many fights, "during which either I would get stabbed or I would stab someone," he was arrested for assault while under the influence of drugs. "Everybody on the street carried knives and would always start slashing away as soon as a fight began. Usually they would be on drugs as well." He was sent to a state hospital for the criminally insane, where he stayed for eight months.

Between 1965 and 1971, he was jailed six times, never for more than six months at a time. In 1971, he entered his first methadone maintenance program, and in 1978, after many more jailings and many more methadone programs, "I finally stopped shooting up and stopped taking methadone. I never went to jail since."

Since 1978, whenever he has felt the urge to take something to calm himself down, he has gone to an outpatient psychiatric clinic, reported his anxiety and depression, and received some medication. Then, on his own, he would stop taking it. Once he grew so depressed that he tried to commit suicide by taking a whole bottle of Thorazine. His stomach was pumped in an emergency-room clinic and he was released. As for income over the last twenty-five years:

> I have been on welfare many times, maybe one dozen times. I have received food stamps, and on three occasions, I have received social security disability benefits. I have also worked all over the city, sometimes at a Chinese fruit stand, or for some store owner doing clean-up work two days at a time, three days maybe.

In early 1984, he came to the municipal shelter system.

> I didn't have an address so I could not get welfare. Also, it was hard to find work. I was willing to work but nobody would hire me. So, I came to the shelter.

When asked when, in his eyes, things were going the worst for him, he replied:

> Maybe nobody would believe this, but one day, I was sitting in my apartment and my girl said, ''Papi, I'm thirsty. You want to get me a soda?'' I said, ''Okay Mami.'' I went outside, it was rainy, and I saw a picture face down. I was curious. I looked at it. It was my first girlfriend. I couldn't believe it. I ran back up to my live-in woman and showed it to her. She said for me to get rid of it. I got rid of it immediately. But ever since then, things have gone down. She died one month later.

That experience precipitated his worsening depression and his suicide attempt.

At present, he knows where one of the uncles who raised him lives. He also knows where two of his nieces live. He will wait before looking them up.

> I changed too much. My features look different. I don't dress good. I look terrible. Maybe when I get my teeth back. I lost them a few years ago.

He also knows where his children live, but he will wait before looking them up as well.

Eduardo is usually very neatly dressed. He is a quiet man, convinced that one day, if he can reactivate his disability benefits and find a room, he will be on his own again. He would like to meet a woman. Currently, he suffers from diabetes. He has just recovered from pneumonia, and his physicians are on the lookout for AIDS. Eduardo feels that there is no one he can talk to as he trusts nobody. "A lot of people would bother me if they could."

Recently he mistakenly took Librium for an antibiotic, which made him dizzy and drowsy. He had slurred speech and constricted pupils for the entire day, and slept through several meals, dangerous for a diabetic. At this writing, Eduardo has lived in the shelter for 14 months. Except for his bout with pneumonia, which landed him in a city hospital, he has rarely left the building.

Case 3: Warren

Warren was 21 years old and no stranger to New York when he entered his shelter system early in the summer of 1982. Born to working-class, black, common-law parents in the Dade County, Florida "projects," he never learned more than the age and name of his father, who dropped out of sight when Warren turned three. At age four, Warren and his mother moved to Brooklyn into a building where one of her sisters already lived. His mother found a job in a local laundromat and left her son to be raised by his aunt. Two years later, his mother met a man who soon moved in to help raise the family, which grew by three more children over the years.

In fifth grade, due to such classroom behavior as "shooting paper clips, putting tacks in the teachers' chairs, and hanging out with a crowd that did whatever we wanted to do," Warren was thrown out of public school and forced to attend a special school. There the teachers were

> allowed to hit you if you don't do what the teachers say. They take their belts off and make you lean with your hands on the blackboard. If they didn't have a belt they would use a bamboo pole.

He stayed there for three years and was allowed, after graduating, to re-enter the public school system, where he finished the ninth grade.

During these public school years, he and his school friends took part in a scam to avoid attending classes. With store-bought program cards, they forged the appropriate signatures so as to convince their parents of their perfect school attendance records. School days were spent on the subways, drinking beer, smoking marijuana, and hanging out, using carfare and lunch money. They would be home by 3:30, with nobody the wiser. When starting tenth grade, he went the first day of school, sized up each teacher's method of signing off on the cards, and stayed absent for three months straight. At the beginning of the fourth month, he was caught by his mother and stepfather, who beat him and monitored him for several weeks.

While in high school, he found a part-time job in a supermarket, where he earned upwards of $80 per week. He remembers:

> On our breaks from work, on the weekends, we would throw bricks at passing buses and then run away. I might have hurt people but I really don't remember. I did not try to hurt anyone, but we really didn't think about that.

During his off-school hours, he hung out with Ted, an 18-year-old who was apparently involved with organized crime.

> He was in the twelfth grade. He always had two or three thousand dollars in his pocket from hurting or killing someone for his bosses. He wanted me to join him but I knew that if I joined, I might never get out.

Ted held parties in his Harlem apartment, often inviting three or four girls and several male friends.

> Rum, beer, and reefers would be all over the place. If the girls didn't want to go along, Ted would slip some Spanish fly in their drink and then everybody's clothes would come off. There would be ten or more of us naked.

When he was 17 years old, Warren's family moved South. He refused to go with them, choosing to remain in New York.

In the twelfth grade, he quit school and was fired from his job "for coming to work late." Immediately, he landed another job in a factory where, during his first week, he came to work late only once. During the second week he came to work late and was fired.

After this experience he went South to join his family. He did not feel like working right away.

> I was having too much fun. In Georgia, if you are from New York, you are like a celebrity. I had a radio and women just came to me. I didn't have a girlfriend because I wanted all of them. I just couldn't make my mind decide, so I had them all. I didn't live with my parents then. I had my own room for $20 per week.

Warren eventually took a job working "off the books" just long enough to earn carfare back to New York. There he got a job and moved into his own apartment. After four months, a girlfriend moved in with him. Her welfare payments now had an address to come to which proved fortunate because, three months later, he had an argument with his boss and lost his job. He returned to work at the same supermarket he had worked in as a child in school. Again, he was fired for tardiness and attitude. Warren said of his boss, "He would always be picking on me. His wife didn't want kids so he would be angry at me."

Warren then moved back to Georgia and took a job with his stepfather as a laborer, installing windows into makeshift, tin houses. He tired of that job within one month and quit. Soon he found a position loading watermelons onto trucks, which paid him over $100 a day, seven days a week. It lasted only two weeks due to its seasonal nature. After this job ended, he obtained a similar job as an apple picker. But after three days, upon finding out that after room and board he had only several dollars left, he quit.

> I just left one day. I turned from the foot of the ladder I had been working on and just walked down the highway. I had no suitcase and no money.

He hitched a ride to a local town and applied for welfare. He received, through Traveler's Aid, a bus ticket to New York City. In New York, he found a factory job. He took a one-room apartment and found a woman with whom to live.

> She was 33 years old and she didn't want to have sex. So, after two weeks, I told her to get me a bottle of vodka from the bootlegger on the corner. When she came back, she found her suitcase on the sidewalk. I snatched the vodka and slammed the door in her face.

Though he stayed at the factory job for nearly one year, he was eventually fired for continued lateness and for arguing with the boss's son. Warren received unemployment benefits and, instead of paying rent, spent it on movies, food, and clothing. "I could have paid rent but I didn't put my mind to it." After being evicted from his apartment, he lived for three months on the F train, a Manhattan–Brooklyn subway line.

> I would hang out until 11:30 or 12:00 with some guys I'd meet, getting high. Then, without telling them, I would board the train like I was going home. I

would ride from one end to the other, from 179th Street to Coney Island and back. Sometimes, at 179th Street, the police would take me off the train and put me on the Third Street bus [a special bus the city operates to take the homeless to the main referral center]. I would go down to the Bowery and stay around there for the night in some hotel. Once in a while, I got a summons for "attempting to jostle others." During rush hour only they would give me these. I would just be standing there, minding my own business, with a can of beer or rum in my pocket, and they would give me a ticket. A lot of times there would be warrants, too.

It was then that Warren entered the shelter system full time. For the first half year he was in a shelter, he participated in a work program that supplemented his unemployment benefits. However, he was arrested for sneaking onto a subway train. The arresting officer checked the computer and made note of outstanding warrants. Warren was sent to Rikers Island prison for six months under the charge of "jostling others."

It was okay there because I saw about 200 different people I knew from where I grew up. Some were there for murder, others were going upstate for something. Some of them said that they would rather be in Rikers than at a shelter because they got bigger portions of food there.

When he was released, he "toured" the shelter system, getting welfare benefits through the emergency program of each of the social service departments. "They had no way of knowing, because I would use different names and social security numbers and dates of birth."

He received welfare payments five different times. One check each time "just to help me get by. Then, I would miss the next appointment and they would cut me off. So I would go to another shelter in a different borough."

During the period between the summers of 1983 and 1984, Warren had four jobs. The first two involved picking potatoes in North Carolina. He went in a van with 15 others going South to work on various farms. In both times, he did not like the conditions and quit after several days. "I left because the outdoor bathrooms were cold and there was no toilet paper or soap." The other two jobs were in factories, found with the assistance of shelter social workers. Each lasted only three days.

I quit the first factory job because they had rules like I couldn't go to the bathroom between breaks. And, if you were late, they would send you home for the day.

The second job lasted for such a short time because he and the boss fought over his being late his first two days there. On the third day, "I realized I would be late so I got there and started arguing with him. And he fired me."

At present, Warren is unable to get welfare for several more months. He would like to find work. He describes an incident that reflects his attitude about living in a shelter for homeless men.

I was hanging out in the park with some girls I had seen around. We were drinking some rum and having a good time. This guy who knows me from the shelter approached and said to me, "Hey, don't you have to get back to the shelter and sign in for your bed?" I turned to him and told him to cool it but by the time I got back to this girl, she was walking away. You can't let the women know where you are staying. You have to let them know you are working and living on your own.

PART TWO: HOMELESS WOMEN

LOIS C. WOLF

Case 1: Conchita

Conchita is a 59-year-old, single Hispanic woman who became homeless when she returned to her three-room apartment one day and found that she had been evicted. All the contents of her apartment—furniture, clothing, papers—had disappeared. For the following year, until a room in a single room occupancy hotel was located, she was an inhabitant of the public shelter system in New York City.

Conchita had not been able to pay her rent in the months before the eviction. She had felt unable to work as a seamstress, a job she had done for over 15 years, after developing a spastic colon, a debilitating condition which, as she reports, necessitated her staying home. As Conchita had only worked in sweatshops, there were no benefits to see her through an illness when she got sick. Although she undoubtedly received notices concerning the nonpayment of rent, her basic attitude and understanding of life did not include the impersonal forces of legal rights and responsibilities, fair trade, and economic exchange. Conchita's view of herself was that she was a good person who had fallen into hard times. It was only right that she should be taken care of.

Conchita was born and grew up in Honduras. An only child, she was raised by her mother and never knew her father. Her mother died when Conchita was only five years old. Conchita has no memories of her mother. After her mother's death, she was taken in by a neighbor who raised her along with her own children.

When she was in her early twenties Conchita was sent to Costa Rica by her foster mother to care for a sick uncle. Conchita is vague and unspecific about her experiences during this period, but while in Costa Rica she worked as a housekeeper for an American family. It is a time she looks back on fondly. She was very attached to this family, who brought her to the United States with them. Conchita becomes attached in a childlike way to the people who help her and gives complete devotion in return for her expectation of complete and magical care.

After Conchita came to this country, she continued to work as housekeeper for the American family. As the years went by, however, she moved into the larger world by going to work as a seamstress in the factory owned by this employer. Conchita got her Green Card, which gave her legal status, but she never became a citizen.

She worked for this employer for as long as he lived. When he died in 1971 she went to work for a series of sweatshops. She belonged to the union only once, for a brief time, claiming bitterly that "they did nothing for me." In this manner, like so many frightened and uneducated immigrants, she kept herself out of any mainstream labor force, unprotected and ignored.

Prior to her recent illness, Conchita had worked two jobs, from 8 o'clock in the morning until 10 o'clock at night, so that she could afford to both rent and furnish an apartment in Washington Heights. When her television was stolen, she went out and bought another one for $1,700, a fact she recounts with bitterness, albeit with pride that she could afford it.

Some time after she was evicted (no doubt after ignoring the warning notices), Conchita was referred to a day program for the homeless along with several other homeless women staying at a women's shelter. During the time she was homeless, she was mugged and robbed and lost all of her papers, including her Green Card, the proof of her legal alien status. The director of the program helped her replace the Green Card and then found a room for her in a nearby single room occupancy hotel. She became extremely attached to the director and felt bitter when this director left the agency. She has since become fiercely devoted to the current director and to the staff.

Conchita is familyless except for a stepsister who lives in New York City. She has very infrequent contact with her stepsister and only a friend or two whom she sees on rare occasions. Her world is bounded by the few people she looks up to, the church, and her home.

Conchita has reconstructed her life through clear and tight boundaries. Church is primary; Conchita goes to church every day. Her tiny room is her own sanctuary, replete with candles and small statuettes of the Virgin on her dresser. When Conchita was asked about the likelihood of the church helping her out when she was destitute, she angrily asserted, ''I give to the church. The church cannot give to me!''

Second in importance, after the church, is the thrift shop run by the day treatment agency where Conchita has been working three afternoons a week. She does all of the sewing and repairs on clothes—fur coats, carpets, and upholstery. She has become very attached to the manager of the shop. Like the other client workers, she receives a small stipend for her work. This bit of money supplements her welfare benefits.

The third structuring element of her life is her involvement in the day treatment program. Conchita generally comes to the program about three afternoons a week. She attends a meeting of the thrift shop staff. She sits by herself on the outside of the circle. She makes the coffee, even though she doesn't drink it. She hardly says a word. She visits with program staff and occasionally converses briefly with clients she has known for a long time.

It must be noted that Conchita, although not suffering any major mental illness, has nevertheless come to her homeless state because of her basic isolation and lack of social networks—family, friends, services. She depends upon the nurturance of one or two people whom she idealizes. When these people disappoint her in any way, she is devastated. Her demands therefore become ultimately impossible to fulfill. When frustration or disappointment come her way, her thinking distorts into magical, vengeful grandiosity. ''They'll see what I can do!'' ''They won't get away with that. I have my ways!'' These said with a menacing tone, a screwed-up face, a malevolent stare.

The central set of symptoms that Conchita exhibits is physical—all kinds of aches and pains in the back, head, abdomen, eyes, and feet. In this way she can probably justify being on welfare and not working anymore. She has done her share; now she can suffer the ills of aging. Conchita has, in her terms, earned the right to be cared for as she never was as a child.

Because her thinking about the world is childlike, she is always terrified that there will be dire consequences, as indeed there were when she was evicted, or robbed, or dropped from welfare. She's terrified, therefore, to make any changes in her life, whether they be toward part-time work or housing or medical services. Homelessness looms like a specter. She will never chance that nightmare again.

The primary element to bring Conchita's life back together has been to find her housing. After more than a year and a half in the single room occupancy hotel room, Conchita was slowly persuaded to be housed in an apartment rented and supervised by the agency. This meant living with a roommate and sharing a kitchen and living room, although each would have her own bedroom. Her first roommate was also Hispanic and someone Conchita had known for over four months. However, Conchita was outraged when her roommate drank beer and brought men up to her room. To make matters worse, her roommate did not do her share of cleaning and never bought any food, but instead helped herself to Conchita's! Conchita scolded and threatened day in and day out. One night she heard her roommate screaming and wailing and unable to recognize Conchita. Conchita called the agency's emergency number, and her roommate was taken to an emergency room and admitted to a psychiatric unit.

Once her roommate was gone, Conchita showed her compassion. She inquired about her roommate's welfare and progress, but did not want to live with her or anyone else. However, community-supported housing for the chronic mentally ill will not provide the luxury of a four-room apartment for a single person. So Conchita was soon joined by a new roommate. Again Conchita lived through a turbulent situation with a mentally ill person who was unable to properly care for herself. Her new roommate barely cleaned, cooked, or shopped. She helped herself to Conchita's food. Although she was a quiet, decent person, she could not function on a level of normalcy or ever come up to Conchita's standards. Conchita was again constantly enraged, railing continuously against her roommate's failings. Her roommate responded by removing herself from the situation, sleeping at her mother's and coming home only to bathe and dress.

At this time, Conchita is about to move into a supervised residence where she will have her own small studio. Although she will not be obliged to share an apartment, she will have to be a responsible member of this therapeutic community. Since she loves to bake and share her cooking with others, Conchita will be encouraged in this area.

Although Conchita expresses no understanding of the agency's programs and goals, she is, in her own way, obedient. She attends support group and community group meetings on a daily basis, and interacts with staff and members. In spite of herself, she has been brought into this therapeutic community. These involvements, together with her part-time work and her church participation, provide her with the most stability and solidity that she has ever had.

Case 2: Mary

Mary is a 48-year-old white, single woman of German-Irish Catholic background. She has never married and has no children. She has a younger brother who moved to California in early adulthood and has since married and raised a family there. Mary grew up in a blue-collar ethnic neighborhood, where she attended parochial schools. She dropped out in tenth grade because "my father didn't see why I needed any more education." She worked sporadically in factories and banks until, and even after, the onset of her mental illness. Her father died in 1972, after which her mother moved to California to be near Mary's brother. An aunt and uncle moved upstate. Only one cousin remains in the old Queens neighborhood of New York.

The onset and course of Mary's illness is completely obscure. She is guarded, denying, and confused about her psychiatric history and current status. Whenever the subject arises, she moves from a calm and positive mood to one of agitation and wailing complaints, blaming all those who have disappointed her, "stonewalling" the interviewer until the subject is dropped and attempts are made to help her relax and pull herself together.

One can reconstruct some picture of how Mary came to be homeless. The immediate precipitant was her eviction from her small apartment in a two-family house because, as she claims, "the landlord wanted it for himself." Knowing Mary, her tenacity, her inability to take any realistic perspective on events, her suspiciousness and need to blame external forces, she must have held on as long as she possibly could. She remembers her sewing machine, family pictures, pieces of furniture. She doesn't know what happened. She's talked of going back to find her belongings.

Mary was referred to the day program by a young and caring priest.

At that time she was sleeping at a Harlem church shelter, the last stop in a two-year series of stays on the shelter circuit from Flushing in Queens to Lexington Avenue in Manhattan. The Harlem church limit of stay was three weeks; Mary had been there for three months. Her hope to live and work at the church shelter did not materialize.

Like many homeless people, Mary came to the day program without any records. Sources of information about her included the priest who referred her to the program. Father Peter knew little about Mary. He had met her one day when she was praying in a chapel at St. Christopher's, his church in midtown Manhattan. He referred her to the Harlem mission and then to the day program.

The second source of information was a psychiatrist at the mental health clinic Mary had attended in Queens. Mary had been seeing this doctor for the past two years. She had harassed him with her accusations, her fears of persecution, her complaints of past and present abuse. When she called him at his home, he threatened to stop seeing her. He knew little factual data of her psychiatric background, but filled in impressions of family background and recent behaviors. Because of her paranoid suspicions, he prescribed a low dose of antipsychotic medication, which Mary refused to take.

Mary talks nonstop. In the beginning, her ramblings fused past and present; causality related solely to her presence and her being; stories had no beginnings and no endings. Complaints merged one with the next. One "theme" marked those who did her wrong—parents, teachers, doctors, psychiatrists, social workers, and nuns; another "theme" marked events responsible for dislodging her from life's main track—an appendectomy at 15, a fall in the street, the loss of her small apartment.

It seems likely that Mary has been ill with schizophrenia for approximately 25 years, that is, from her late teens. She has been hospitalized, been treated with shock therapy, and currently sees a psychiatrist for her small dose of medication. Over the years, her family supports have become eroded.

Mary's need for attention and immediate gratification was and still can be insatiable. Her insistent complaints of abuse by people and events demand from her listeners instant support, starting from the beginning when her parents were mean to her until the moment before her litany began. Relationships remain tenuous. As intensity builds, they end.

Mary initially came to our day program from her bed at the Harlem mission. Each day she told stories of the nuns and other homeless people being abusive. This continued for two months. Just as she was given final notice at the shelter, we were notified of a room in a neighboring hotel. It looked as if Mary's troubles were over.

We couldn't have been more wrong. The dislocation of Mary from shelter life, a state to which she had become accustomed, and to being settled into her own room, alone, no others immediately visible, none to watch over her, was full of stress for her. In her frightened state, Mary perceived her social worker to be her worst enemy. In fact, this worker had been tireless in her efforts to find an appropriate room for Mary at a nearby single room occupancy hotel. The move itself was accomplished amidst Mary's rasping cries of "Danger," begun at the agency and continuing all through the taxi ride as she and her social worker drove to the hotel, where Mary was met at the door by the hotel manager and a social worker on his staff. Although she lived there for a year and a half, the first months were marked by her paranoid thinking about her social worker, who served as her advocate and general case manager. She become obsessed by this social worker's "evil" ways. She warned everyone against this person, whom she felt was conspiring to harm her. Mary watched with hatred in her eyes when her social worker was near; she whispered maliciously within earshot of the hapless worker.

Mary very gradually settled down. About a year after she moved in, she asked her social worker, no longer her enemy, to visit her room. Mary's room was neat and cheerfully decorated with care and style—with bedspread, a doily on the dresser, pictures on the wall, and a small table and chair obtained from the thrift shop operated by the program. For the first time in years she had made a little home for herself.

In spite of her mental illness, Mary has considerable strengths. She is able, even in the worst of times, to do handicraft work such as drawing, crocheting, and knitting. In the thrift shop, she has sorted and displayed merchandise. She is able to concentrate, to plan, and then to evaluate her work. This mastery of work processes, along with her general sociability, provide the basis for her move toward stability.

The day program offered Mary the chance to develop and maintain stability in daily life through attachment to people and things. We were able to house Mary—first in a hotel room and later in a supportive community residence apartment. For the two years prior to entry into our program, she had been rootless, nomadic, moving from shelter to shelter, from nuns to social workers and back again. Now, for the first time in years, she had an external stabilizing force to replace the inner chaos which had been her sole governor.

Mary was taken in without a history, on inadequate medication, with broken family relationships, and no friend or institutional ties except for Father Peter. We listened to her confused digressive psychotic talk and helped her turn to structured activities. We got her into daily routines and provided the milieu within which she could come together with the same people each day. Although finding her a room had the short-term effect of disorienting her and channeling her aggression into a rage at her social worker, she ultimately responded by progressing to a higher level of functioning.

After almost three years in the day program, Mary has re-established relations, through letters, to her mother, now in a California nursing home. She has also corresponded with her brother's family, a cousin in Queens, and an aunt and uncle in Florida. She invites other day program participants to her home for special occasions. She has become active in an East Harlem church as a member of their hospitality committee. In addition, Mary has done volunteer work in an infant nursery in a large teaching hospital and continues her steady work in the thrift shop. Her small income, disability payments, and a token amount for her thrift shop work seem to cover her basic needs.

Case 3: Audrey

Audrey is an attractive, 28-year-old black single mother of five who has resided for the past ten months in a two-room suite at the Martinique Hotel in Manhattan. A native New Yorker, the present episode of homelessness began ten and a half months ago when she was evicted from her four-room walk-up apartment in the Bronx for nonpayment of rent. Recently separated from her common-law husband, Audrey didn't have enough from her welfare allotment for housing ($310 per month) to pay the $485 needed for rent. The mother of Audrey's common-law husband had given Audrey and her family a house in the Bronx. After it was destroyed by fire, Audrey and her live-in partner separated, necessitating her move to an apartment and eventually a two-week hospitalization in the psychiatric ward of a local municipal hospital. According to Audrey, she "just couldn't function any more." During this initial psychiatric treatment episode, she stated that she heard voices other people did not hear and was treated with psychoactive drugs. She denies ever having taken excessive amounts of alcohol or street drugs. She still sees a therapist in the outpatient clinic where she was hospitalized, and prides herself on the fact that despite confronting homelessness, she has not had another "nervous breakdown." Indeed, she has tried to be strong for "the sake of my children."

Audrey states that the experience of homelessness has imposed severe hardship on herself and her children. Immediately after eviction from her apartment, Audrey and her children were housed in a makeshift shelter in a large gymnasium, along with other homeless families, for a period of two weeks. She reported that she and her family got very little sleep because the gymnasium was crowded and noisy, and babies cried through the night. She also noted that there were only two bathrooms, one for men and the other for women, which were usually dirty and overcrowded.

Audrey was relieved to be placed in a large (400 unit) welfare hotel in mid-Manhattan, where she and her children were given a small two-room suite with a private bath. Although there are no kitchen facilities, Audrey has a hot plate, which she uses to prepare dishes such as fried chicken and spaghetti. Because of the limited menu possible with such cooking facilities, a family treat is being invited to her former common-law husband's mother's home in the Bronx for a home-cooked meal. Her children's grandmother has been a major source of support for her during this period of homelessness. The grandmother often invites the children over to care for them and provide them with a safe place to play.

At the welfare hotel, described in a recent newspaper account as rat- and roach-infested, children play in the refuse-strewn halls or on the busy thoroughfare outside the building. Audrey has forbidden her children to associate with some people (children and adults) who apparently deal in and use crack and other street drugs and engage in criminal activities. So far Audrey does not think her children have been influenced by the people at the welfare hotel, but she knows other mothers who have been heartbroken when their children begin to follow a pattern of truancy from school, stealing, and drug use following residence at the hotel.

Audrey's children, three boys and two girls, range in age from three to twelve. Her eldest, a son, is an excellent student in school. However, her second oldest, another boy, has done poorly in school and has, according to his teachers, a learning disability. The three oldest children are enrolled in public schools in the district of the welfare hotel. The two younger children, both girls, participate in a local Head Start program.

Audrey is hopeful that her children will remain in school until graduating from high school.

Audrey dropped out when she became pregnant with her first child at age 16. Recently, she completed her GED (high school equivalency) and is planning to attend technical college in the fall to study pattern-making and clothing design. Audrey wants to get a job in the garment industry. She is looking forward to attending college and making something of herself. She reported that her former common-law husband is currently attending school and living with his father in the Bronx. She regards her biggest mistake in life as not finishing high school.

Audrey has been discouraged by the difficulty she has experienced in finding an adequate apartment. She is willing to live in any of the New York City boroughs, but would prefer her home borough of the Bronx. She has been unable to find an apartment she can afford. Currently, she is wait-listed for Section 8, a federal housing program in which the government would pay half of her housing costs. She has been wait-listed for three years. Audrey states that her sister chides her for not being aggressive enough to get what she wants and has told her that when a welfare worker does not seem to be doing enough to help her, Audrey should demand to see the supervisor. Audrey said that she is so frustrated that she has contacted a Bronx political leader for help in getting access to a federally sponsored housing support program. Audrey feels that once she gets this support, she will not have difficulty in finding a good apartment.

It is noteworthy that none of Audrey's siblings or close relatives have experienced homelessness. She does not want to mingle with women in the welfare hotel (the woman next door is an alcoholic and belligerent, often arguing far into the night), preferring to socialize with her sisters, mother, or ex-common-law husband's mother. She states that her children's father visits them occasionally and "does his best" to contribute money, food, and clothing for their support. Audrey dates occasionally but does not have a steady boyfriend. When she goes out, she likes to go to a restaurant for a good meal. She is not religious and does not belong to any community organization.

A meaningful experience was living in Holland for two years with her ex-common-law husband, who was stationed there while he was in the armed services. He had invited Audrey and the children to travel to Europe to live with him during his stay there. She says that experience was a highlight in her life, which she looks back on wistfully.

PART THREE: RUNAWAY AND HOMELESS YOUTH*

DAVID SHAFFER, M.D.
CAROL L. M. CATON

Case 1: John

John is a 16-year-old youth who was admitted to a shelter after running away from home for the second time. Both the current runaway episode and the previous one two years ago were precipitated by an argument between John and his parents.

John dresses sloppily and is poorly groomed and overweight. However, he is thoughtful and has a fine sense of humor. Occasionally his humor is self-disparaging. John attends special education classes for neurologically impaired/emotionally handicapped children at a Manhattan public high school. He is interested in acting as a career, and admires macho-type actors like Al Pacino and Robert De Niro.

Family life is quite stressful for John. One problem is that his father drinks a great deal and when drunk is verbally abusive. Religion is an area of conflict between John and his parents. His Catholic parents do not permit him to practice the Baptist religion he espouses.

School has also been stressful. John is teased for being in special classes, and for being overweight and unattractive. He thinks incessantly about girls, but does not date. He feels that one day he will outgrow his "adolescent awkwardness" (his term) and have lots of girlfriends.

At present, John is lonely and occasionally depressed. He feels that no one, except his acting teacher and his best friend, understands him. John admitted to one instance each of auditory and visual hallucinations. Both episodes occurred over a year ago and have not recurred. John has made one suicidal gesture; he swallowed some liquid soap after an argument with his father. He has never had any psychiatric help and says that he does not want any. He feels that he will "grow out of" his problems.

*Case examples were edited from David Shaffer, M.D., and Carol L. M. Caton, Ph. D., *Runaway and Homeless Youth in New York City,* A Report to the Ittleson Foundation, New York City, Division of Child Psychiatry, New York State Psychiatric Institute and Columbia University College of Physicians and Surgeons, January 1984, pp. 80–82.

Despite his resistance to counseling, he responded well to the interview and seemed pleased and relieved to discuss his situation.

Case 2: Richard

Richard is a 16½-year-old Texas-born Hispanic who was experiencing his first shelter admission, even though his first runaway episode was at age 14. He has a history of many different living arrangements in both family and institutional settings, including a group home, a residential school, and a detention center. Most recently, he was living with his grandfather because he does not get along with his mother. Richard went to a youth shelter when his grandfather decided to return to Puerto Rico.

Richard has a long history of antisocial behavior, including car theft and vandalism. He also has a history of heavy alcohol use, during which he drank daily, beginning in the morning. However, he denies that alcohol is a problem now. Other than a girlfriend whom he met while in a group, Richard states that he has no close friends. He admits to being depressed occasionally, but never for more than three days at a time. Richard has thoughts about suicide, but he has never planned it in any way. Despite the unhappiness he has experienced, he is very concerned about making something of himself. His standard reading score is above average, and he states that he likes school and wants to attend college to study computer technology.

Case 3: Donna

Donna is an attractive, pleasant 16-year-old who ran away from her parents' home because she was afraid of what her father's response would be when he learned that she was pregnant. This was her second runaway episode. She ran away two years previously when her father made unwanted sexual demands on her while he was intoxicated. As Donna expected that her father would behave in a violent manner when he found out about her pregnancy, she went to a youth shelter.

Donna was calm while reporting the details of her history. She said that her best friend was the 21-year-old boyfriend who was the father of her baby. She had seen him twice since she was admitted to the youth shelter.

Donna was well organized in her thinking. She is a good tenth-grade student with reading scores just under twelfth-grade level. Her only no-ticeable impairment in functioning during the past three months was re-lated to her concerns over her pregnancy and her father's reaction to it. She wants to be sent to a maternity shelter, have her baby, and hopefully go on to finish high school and attend college. She would like to become a social worker, because ''I know what I've been through and it would be very interesting to help others with these problems.''

4 | Homelessness and Mental Illness

PAULA F. EAGLE, M.D.
CAROL L. M. CATON

Homelessness is not a new phenomenon in the United States, where skid rows have often existed in major urban centers. However, over the past 20 years dramatic changes have occurred in the composition of the homeless population. Specifically, while the numbers of homeless have steadily increased, the numbers of homeless who are mentally ill have grown at a much higher rate. This situation has received a great deal of attention from the media, government officials, the public, and the medical profession, all expressing concern over the inhumane quality of life of these mentally ill people who have now become a painful and common sight in most American cities.

Considerable controversey has surrounded attempts to understand homelessness and its causes. Difficulties in defining homelessness and measuring psychopathology, as well as differing political or ideological orientations, have confounded many of the issues regarding the homeless. For example, those who view homelessness solely in terms of faulty economics or a lack of a home will see the problem and its solution differently from those who see homelessness as the profound deterioration of social and psychological functioning.

In addition, conflicting societal values of wanting to care for the sick and disabled, while being opposed to coercive measures such as the involuntary commitment of the mentally ill, have hampered the development of cohesive and constructive policies in dealing with the homeless mentally ill. At the same time, there are those who oppose the ''medicalization" of the problem of homeless mentally ill for fear that the blame and the burden of the solution of the problem will fall on the medical (and psychiatric) establishment, to the neglect of economic and political causes of homelessness. These political and philosophical factors are important and should be taken into consideration when we try to understand what has been written on the subject. In this chapter, we will focus on a subpopulation of the homeless, those who are mentally ill. We will explore who they are and how they came to be homeless.

Surveys of the Homeless

Since 1982, in an attempt to ascertain the mental health characteristics of the homeless, there have been 16 major surveys of the homeless in the United States (Crystal et al., 1982; Hoffman et al., 1982; Arce et al., 1983; Lipton, Sabatini, and Katz, 1983; Bassuk, Rubin, and Lauriat, 1984; Crystal and Goldstein, 1984; Shaffer and Caton, 1984; Bassuk, Rubin, and Lauriat, 1986; Crystal, Ladner, and Towber, 1986; Farr, Koegel, and Burnam, 1986; Fischer et al., 1986; Morse and Calsyn, 1986; Rossi, Fisher, and Willis, 1986; Roth and Bean, 1986; Snow, Baker, and Anderson, 1986; Struening, 1986).

One study dealt with the homeless admitted to a psychiatric emergency room (Lipton et al., 1983), three focused on homeless adults in both street and shelter locations (Rossi et al., 1986; Roth and Bean, 1986; Snow et al., 1986), and one study selected adults from shelters, meal programs, and day centers for the homeless (Farr et al., 1986). The majority of studies, then, focused on the sheltered homeless, usually adults (Crystal et al., 1982; Hoffman et al., 1982; Arce et al., 1983; Lipton et al., 1983; Crystal and Goldstein, 1984; Crystal et al., 1986; Fischer et al., 1986; Morse and Calsyn, 1986; Struening, 1986). In addition, one study dealt with homeless youth (Shaffer and Caton, 1984), another with children and adults of both sexes (Bassuk et al., 1984), and a third with homeless mothers and their children (Bassuk, Rubin, and Lauriat, 1986).

Sample sizes ranged from 51 subjects to 8,061, with the average being about 220 subjects. All studies employed random or systematic selection procedures or studied all available subjects over a specified time period. Most of the studies were carried out in large cities (New York, Chicago, Boston, Los Angeles, Philadelphia, Baltimore, St. Louis), and one study selected subjects from rural and urban areas across an entire state (Roth and Bean, 1986). Although two studies focused exclusively on males and one exclusively on females, the majority of the studies had markedly higher proportions of males, reflecting the fact that among adults, homelessness is far more common among males than females.

History of Psychiatric Hospitalization

One reliable indicator of mental disorder is a history of treatment in a psychiatric hospital. Thirteen studies have explored this issue (see Table 4.1). Not surprisingly, the sample with the highest rate of previous hospitalizations, 97 percent, was found in that selected from a psychiatric emergency room (Lipton et al., 1983). Lowest rates were found among homeless mothers and children, 7 percent (Bassuk et al., 1986), and homeless youth, 8 percent (Shaffer and Caton, 1984). Psychosis in these subgroups was rare, and hospitalizations were frequently the consequence of suicide attempts.

In both shelter and street samples of adult homeless, from 10 to 36 percent had a history of previous psychiatric hospitalizations. It should be noted that in eight studies the proportion of subjects with prior psychiatric hospitalizations ranged from about one-fourth to one-third.

Current Psychopathology

The relative consistency of findings concerning the hospitalization histories of the homeless contrasts with the marked unevenness of findings from studies examining current psychiatric disorder. This is the result, at least in part, of the fact that widely varying techniques have been used to determine the extent of psychiatric disorder among the homeless (see Table 4.2).

The earliest studies in this area employed a general approach: a clinical assessment of the presence of a psychiatric problem. Studies employing this technique have reported from 22 percent (Hoffman et al., 1982) to 36 percent (Crystal et al., 1982) of their subjects displayed psychiatric symptoms, but were not necessarily diagnosable as mentally ill. In a later study, Crystal and Goldstein (1984) determined the prevalence of psychiatric disorder using a clinician's assessment of current disorder and/or a history of prior hospitalization. They found that 22 percent of the men and 47 percent of the women had some psychiatric symptoms, which, again, did not necessarily indicate a diagnosable mental illness. For ex-

Table 4.1 History of psychiatric hospitalization among the homeless

Investigators	Where sample chosen	Sample selection	Age group	Sex	Sample size	% with psychiatric hospital history
Hoffman et al., 1982	Shelter	Random	Adults	Males only	107	33%
Crystal and Goldstein, 1984	Shelter	Systematic	Adults	Both sexes	922	33%
Crystal et al., 1982	Shelter	Systematic	Adults	Males only	128	33%
Arce et al., 1983	Shelter	Universe of admissions—two months	Adults	78% Male 22% Female	193	
Lipton et al., 1983	Psychiatric E.R.	Systematic	Adults	75% Male 25% Female	90	97%
Bassuk et al., 1984	Shelter	All available 5 nights	Children Adults	83% Male 17% Female	78	33%
Shaffer and Caton, 1984	Shelter	Systematic	Youths	50% Male 50% Female	118	8%
Morse and Calsyn, 1986	Shelter	Random	Adults	50% Male 50% Female	248	25%
Crystal et al., 1986	Shelter	Systematic	Adults	Both sexes	8,061	
Farr et al., 1986	Shelters Meal programs Day centers	Random	Adults	96% Male	379	36%
Roth and Bean, 1986	Shelter Street	Random	Adults	81% Male	979	30%
Fischer et al., 1986	Shelter	Random	Adults	94% Male	51	33%
Bassuk et al., 1986	Shelter	Systematic	Adults	100% Female	80	7%
Snow et al., 1986	Shelter Street	Random Convenience	Adults	95% Male	911	10%
Rossi et al., 1986	Shelter Street	Random	Adults	76% Male	722	22.5%
Struening, 1986	Shelter	Random	Adults	75% Male	1,172	19%

Table 4.2 Psychiatric problems among the homeless

Investigators	Where sample chosen	Sample selection	Age group	Sex	Sample size	Method of assessment in psychiatric disorder	Prevalence of psychiatric disorder
Hoffman et al., 1982	Shelter	Random	Adults	Males only	107	Clinician assessment of presence of problem	22% had symptoms
Crystal and Goldstein, 1984	Shelter	Systematic	Adults	Both sexes	922	Clinician assessment of disorder and/or prior hospitalization	22% men 47% women had any psychiatric problem or history
Crystal et al., 1982	Shelter	Systematic	Adults	Males only	128	Clinician assessment of presence of problem	36% had symptoms
Arce et al., 1983	Shelter	Universe of admissions—two months	Adults	78% Male 22% Female	193	DSM-III criteria applied to psychiatric interview	84% met DSM-III criteria for psychiatric disorder
Lipton et al., 1983	Psychiatric E.R.	Systematic	Adults	75% Male 25% Female	90	Hospital record diagnosis	100% had psychiatric diagnosis; 72% schizophrenia
Bassuk et al., 1984	Shelter	All available 5 nights	Children Adults	83% Male 17% Female	78	DSM-III criteria applied to psychiatric interview data, BPRS, GAS[a]	90% met DSM-III criteria for psychiatric disorders

Table 4.2 (*continued*)

Investigators	Where sample chosen	Sample selection	Age group	Sex	Sample size	Method of assessment in psychiatric disorder	Prevalence of psychiatric disoraer
Shaffer and Caton, 1984	Shelter	Systematic	Minor youths	50% Male 50% Female	118	Self-report of major psychiatric symptoms	Psychiatric diagnosis not available, but 33% girls and 15% boys prior suicide attempt
Morse and Calsyn, 1986	Shelter	Random	Adults	50% Male 50% Female	248	Brief symptom inventory; Periodic Evaluation Record	46.9% scored above cutoff on global indicator
Crystal et al., 1986	Shelter	Systematic	Adults	Both sexes	8,061	Self-report of current mental problems or outpatient care, past hospitalizations	24.9% reported symptoms
Farr et al., 1986	Shelter Meal programs Day centers	Random	Adults	96% Male	379	Diagnostic Interview Schedule	28% met DSM-III criteria for psychiatric disorder
Roth and Bean, 1986	Shelter Street	Random	Adults	81% Male	979	Psychiatric Status Schedule	31% had symptoms

Study	Setting	Sampling	Age	Sex	N	Method	Findings
Fischer et al., 1986	Shelter	Random	Adults	94% Male	51	Diagnostic Interview Schedule	37% met DSM-III criteria for psychiatric disorder
Bassuk et al., 1986	Shelter	Systematic	Adults	100% Female	80	DSM-III criteria based on clinical interview	27% met DSM-III criteria for Axis I; 71% met DSM-III criteria for Axis II
Snow et al., 1986	Shelter Street	Random Convenience	Adults	95% Male	911	DSM-III criteria applied to agency record data (shelter)	15% had symptoms, not necessarily meeting DSM-III criteria
Rossi et al., 1986	Shelter Street	Random	Adults	76% Male	722	CES-D, for depression, PERI scales for psychosis[b]	50% had depression severe enough to require treatment; 15% symptoms of psychosis
Struening, 1986	Shelter	Random	Adults	75% Male	1,172	CES-D for depression, questions on psychotic beliefs	21% depressed most of the time in past week; psychotic beliefs 10%

[a]BPRS = Brief Psychiatric Rating Scale; GAS = Global Assessment Scale.
[b]PERI = Psychiatric Epidemiology Research Interview.

ample, some individuals may have symptoms such as depression or paranoia without having the full-blown syndromes of major depressive illness or schizophrenia. Hospital records have also been used to determine whether subjects can be classified as suffering from psychiatric disorder. Lipton et al. (1983) looked at hospital record diagnoses of the 90 emergency room subjects they studied and found that all subjects were given a psychiatric diagnosis.

Subjects' self-report of psychiatric symptoms was the method used by Shaffer and Caton (1984) and Crystal et al. (1986). The former study of homeless youth found that depression, antisocial behavior, and suicide attempts were common. No less than 33 percent of the girls and 15 percent of the boys had made at least one suicide attempt. In Crystal et al.'s study of over 8,000 homeless adults, nearly one-quarter reported that they had psychiatric symptoms. However, the presence of symptoms did not necessarily mean that they were suffering from a diagnosable mental illness.

Symptom rating scales have also been used in surveys of the homeless to determine the psychiatric status of study subjects. Morse and Calsyn (1986), in using the Brief Symptom Inventory and the Periodic Evaluation Record, found that 46.9 percent of their subjects scored above the cutoff on a global indicator of pathology. Roth and Bean's (1986) use of the Psychiatric Status Schedule in their study yielded the finding that 34 percent of subjects had psychiatric symptoms. Rossi et al. (1986) and Struening (1986) used the Center for Epidemiologic Studies Depression Scale (CES-D scale) to assess depression; while in the former study 50 percent of the subjects were found to be suffering from depression severe enough to require treatment, only 21 percent of Struening's subjects were depressed most of the time in the week prior to testing. Rossi et al. used the Psychiatric Epidemiology Research Interview scales to determine whether any subjects suffered from psychosis, finding that 15 percent did indeed suffer from its symptoms. When Struening questioned his subjects on psychotic beliefs he got similar results—10 percent had psychotic symptoms.

Studies that have applied DSM-III (the third edition of the Diagnostic and Statistical Manual of Mental Disorders of the American Psychiatric Association) criteria to classify subjects, relying on agency clinical records or psychiatric interview data, have produced widely varying findings. Arce et al. (1983) found that 84 percent of the sheltered adults they saw met DSM-III criteria for psychiatric disorder. Similarly, Bassuk et al. (1984) found the rate of diagnosable mental illness in a Boston shelter to be 90 percent. In sharp contrast, Snow et al. (1986) found that only 15 percent of their 911 shelter and street subjects had psychiatric symptoms, which did not necessarily meet DSM-III criteria for a mental disorder. Bassuk et al.'s (1986) study of homeless mothers revealed that 27 percent met DSM-III criteria for Axis I (or major clinical syndrome) disorder, a high figure in light of the fact that few of these women had histories of psychiatric hospitalizations. In the only attempt so far to evaluate Axis II (or personality) disorders, this study found that 71 percent of the homeless mothers met DSM-III criteria for personality disorders.

To date only two studies have employed research diagnostic interviews to evaluate the rate of diagnosable mental illness among the homeless. Fortunately, both studies have used the same instrument, the Diagnostic Interview Schedule. Farr et al.'s (1986) use of the Diagnostic Interview Schedule on a sample of sheltered homeless revealed that 37 percent met DSM-III criteria.

A major difficulty in distilling the findings from studies of psychiatric disorder among the homeless is that investigators have employed different research approaches. Indeed, the widely varying figures concerning the rate of diagnosable mental illness among the homeless, from 15 percent (Snow et al., 1986) to 90 percent (Bassuk et al., 1984), has aroused considerable controversey and debate among policymakers and investigators in the field (e.g., see Snow et al., 1986).

Types of Psychiatric Disorders

Six studies of diverse groups of homeless subjects have provided detailed information on their psychiatric diagnosis (see Table 4.3). Lipton et al.'s (1983) study revealed that 72 percent of undomiciled in a psychiatric emergency room were schizophrenic. A diagnosis of schizophrenia was also common in the studies of sheltered adults conducted by Arce et al. (1983) and Bassuk et al. (1984), finding 37 percent and 30 percent, respectively, diagnosable as such. In contrast, only 14 percent of skid row subjects in Farr et al.'s study were diagnosed as schizophrenic, but 30 percent were found to have affective disorder, the most common diagnosis in this study. To demonstrate the wide variety of findings, another study of homeless adults (Fischer et al., 1986) diagnosed only 2 percent as schizophrenic, while 20 percent were found to be suffering from anxiety disorders.

Personality disorders were also common. Two studies found approxi-

Table 4.3 Types of DSM-III disorder among the homeless

Investigators	Schizophrenia	Affective disorder	Anxiety disorder	Cognitive impairment	Substance abuse	Organic	Personality disorder	Other
Arce et al., 1983	37.4%	5.6%	—	—	24.6%	5.0%	6.7%	5.0%
Lipton et al., 1983	72.2%	6.7%	—	—	4.4%	—	12.2%	4.4%
Bassuk et al., 1984	30.3%	9.2%	—	—	28.9%	—	21.0%	1.3%
Farr et al., 1986	13.7%	29.5%	14.3%	5.4%	69.2% (lifetime)	—	26.8%	8.4%
Fischer et al., 1986	2.0%	2.0%	19.6%	7.8%	19.6%	—	9.8%	—
Bassuk et al., 1986	—	10.0%	—	—	9.0%	—	71.0%[a]	—

[a]*Types of Axis II Disorders*
Dependent 24%
Atypical 10%
Borderline 6%

mately 20 percent of homeless adults to be suffering primarily from personality disorders, usually antisocial personality (Bassuk et al., 1984; Farr et al., 1986). While Axis I disorder was not common in Bassuk et al.'s (1986) study of homeless mothers, they did find 71 percent to have personality disorders, most often dependent personality (24 percent) and atypical personality (10 percent).

Substance Abuse

As shown in Table 4.3, three studies of homeless adults found that from 20 to 30 percent of those surveyed had a primary psychiatric diagnosis of substance abuse (Arce et al., 1983; Bassuk et al., 1984; Fischer et al., 1986). Farr et al. (1986) assessed lifetime disorder and found that nearly 70 percent of the subjects had, at one time, diagnosable substance abuse.

Although these three studies focused on substance abuse, all but one of the contemporary surveys of the homeless discussed here have explored this issue. Each used different techniques to probe the presence of psychiatric problems, including substance abuse. Not unexpectedly, these differing approaches yielded varying results. For example, Morse and Calsyn (1986) used an alcoholism screening instrument, the S-MAST, and found that nearly 36 percent of subjects had serious problems in this area. Responses to the Psychiatric Status Schedule item in Roth and Bean's (1986) study, "Drinking some or a lot in the past month," were positive in 64 percent of cases. ("Some" is defined as more than five drinks per day.) An interviewer's judgment of need for help in Struening's (1986) investigation revealed that nearly one-quarter of those interviewed were felt to require help for drug problems and nearly one-third required help for alcohol problems. All surveys were uniform in revealing that substance abuse is a significant problem among the homeless, particularly the homeless mentally ill (Crystal et al., 1986; Morse and Calsyn, 1986). More information, using standardized assessment procedures, is needed in future studies of the homeless.

In summary, one-fourth to one-third of the homeless have a history of prior psychiatric hospitalization. At least 40 percent show evidence of a current major psychiatric disorder. Depression and personality disorders are common, and the majority have a substance abuse problem.

Indeed, exact numbers are perhaps less important than overall trends and patterns. Clearly, however, some differences are related to differences in the populations that are sampled. Street-bound homeless appear to be different from the sheltered homeless, while homeless families (usually women and their children) have different characteristics than single men and women. Arce et al. (1983) have profiled the chronically street-bound homeless as being over the age of 40, having a variety of health problems and a history of state hospitalization, and with a current diagnosis of schizophrenia, substance abuse, or both. They tend to be floridly psychotic, and unable to "stick" in a residential setting. This view is supported by other studies of street-bound homeless. The episodic (or shelter-bound) homeless tend to be under 40 years of age, black, without a history of state hospitalization, and are more frequently diagnosed as having a personality disorder, an affective disorder, or a substance abuse problem.

In the following section, we will discuss factors in the development of homelessness among the mentally ill.

Causes of Homelessness Among the Mentally Ill

In the 1950s, with the advent of antipsychotic medication and with a shift in philosophy toward social treatment of the mentally ill rather than confinement, the community mental health movement was born. Many believed that severely mentally ill patients could live in their communities with their families, receiving better care than in an institution. Civil rights and civil liberties advocates, supported by the values of society at the time, began a powerful activist legal campaign against the poor conditions and abuse of patients reported in some state institutions. They favored extending the rights of the mentally ill so that they could leave the institutions, and restricting the state's powers to hospitalize patients involuntarily. This process became known as "deinstitutionalization."

The deinstitutionalization forces were further fueled by frequent reports in the mass media and professional journals of the deteriorating effects that years of institutional isolation, neglect, abuse, and lack of social stimulation were having on the mentally ill. States' economic incentives to close mental institutions were furthered by the growth of federal welfare programs in the 1960s, which allowed financially constrained states to shift the costs for the mentally ill from the state-funded institutions to federally supported social programs in the community.

As a result, there was a massive and precipitous emptying of state mental institutions. Deinstitutionalization, especially the way in which it was implemented, is thought to be the major cause of homelessness among the mentally ill. Thousands of patients were discharged to unprepared and unreceptive urban communities before any support systems could be put into place. From 1955 to 1987, the patient population in public mental hospitals dropped from 560,000 to about 116,000. In New York state alone, from an inpatient census of 93,000 in 1955 the institutionalized population dropped to about 20,000 in 1987. At the same time, due to the coming of age of 64 million babies born between 1946 and 1961, the absolute number of people at risk for developing schizophrenia increased dramatically. Thus, the impact of these policies can be seen not only in the many patients that have been discharged from institutions without aftercare plans or support, but in the many mentally ill patients that are denied access to long-term care in hospitals because of strict policies of admission.

Unable to negotiate the complexities of the mental health and social welfare systems, and in the face of minimal resources of the communities, particularly supportive housing, thousands of mentally ill joined the ranks of the homeless. Further, it was not appreciated at the time how the state hospitals served as crucial supports for the chronically mentally ill. The state hospitals provided asylum from the pressures of the world and social stimulation, as well as medical care, a social network, and needed structure and support. Chronically mentally ill people are unable to cope with the ordinary demands of life, have strong dependency needs, require psychiatric services—many indefinitely—and are unable to live independently. Many mentally ill tend to be loners, having great difficulty in attaching themselves to people or places, and as a result, frequently move from place to place. In this way, they can deny their dependency, avoid conflict with their caretakers, and maintain an isolated existence. Thus, for them homelessness and periodic decompensations into an acute phase of their illnesses are the price they pay for the actualization of their conflicts over dependency. Extensive illicit drug use, especially among the "young chronics," also contributes to the potential for decompensation, violence, and homelessness.

Although some chronically mentally ill are able to live with family members, most continue to need structured supportive housing arrangements. Yet an acute shortage of such housing has existed over the past ten years. In addition, the dramatic shrinkage of low-income housing, especially single room occupancy (SRO) hotels which provide one-room apartments, where many ex-patients had gravitated, has exacerbated an already dire situation. For example, in New York City alone, between 1970 and 1982 more than 110,000 SRO units were lost (87 percent of the total supply), while in the same period nationwide 1,116,000 SRO units were lost (47 percent of the supply). The streets and shelters have become the only remaining options. The rapid growth of the shelter population over the last ten years could be linked to the loss of SRO housing over the same time period. Currently, only about 2,300 community residence beds are being operated in New York City, perhaps a mere 5 percent of the number needed. Indeed, the lack of specialized housing prevents effective coordination of services and implementation of rational and comprehensive planning.

The task of providing comprehensive community-based service systems for the chronically mentally ill is clearly a formidable undertaking. Not only are the mentally ill a diverse group with various functional levels and needs, but the diversity of services they require is so extensive that it is extremely difficult to provide them and coordinate all of the various agencies who participate in aftercare rehabilitation. This, combined with the fact that these people are often poorly compliant as patients, results in many ''falling between the cracks.'' In addition, due to the great costs of chronic care, the responsibility for its provision is constantly shifted from the state to the local community to the federal government and back to the state again, increasing the obstacles to obtaining care. Much organizational confusion and political ''passing the buck'' occurs; as a result, the buck does not stop anywhere. The treatment of patients with chronic mental illness is substantially a task of maintenance and rehabilitation, requiring long-term responsibility in order to maintain continuity of care. The community must now provide the multiple services formerly supplied by state mental hospitals, such as sanctuary, psychiatric and medical care, and social services.

Finally, there are important questions that still need to be answered. Why do some chronic mentally ill become homeless while others do not? To what extent does drug and alcohol abuse contribute to the homelessness problem? How can paranoid traits so common among the chronically mentally ill be dealt with in a way that does not drive patients to seek anonymity in the streets? Do commitment laws need to be changed to provide greater protection to the mentally ill from themselves? Will society be able and willing to pay the cost of comprehensive community mental health care?

The Homeless Mentally Ill and the Mental Health Service System

The homeless with psychiatric problems are among the most difficult people to manage using traditional mental health approaches. Studies have identified two main groups of hard-to-reach people: (1) those who have psychiatric symptoms but have never made contact with the service system; and (2) those who report that they have been treated in a psychiatric hospital but do not use psychiatric outpatient services, despite an obvious need for such care (Farr et al., 1986; Rossi et al., 1986; Roth and Bean, 1986; and others). Estimates of the size of these two groups vary considerably, as documented elsewhere in this chapter. Roth and Bean's statewide survey of the homeless in Ohio reveals that only about one in five of those with mental health problems receives mental health services. Rossi et al. (1986) have also noted that the homeless do not use the mental health service system to the extent warranted by their mental health status. Indeed, nearly two-thirds of respondents who had been discharged from psychiatric hospitals made no contact with outpatient programs for ongoing follow-up care (Rossi et al., 1986, p. 128). A recent study found only 8 percent of Los Angeles skid row subjects had professional outpatient mental health contact, even though more than one-third had histories of psychiatric hospitalizations (Farr et al., 1986, p. 163).

While little is known about the reasons why the homeless fail to use outpatient mental health care, Farr et al. (1986) and others point out that homelessness requires the expenditure of great effort just to survive. Each day, time must be devoted to finding a place to sleep, waiting in food lines, searching out places in which to rest or relieve oneself, and remaining alert to impending danger. Such activities may take precedence over both scheduled appointments and following through with prescribed treatment regimens. Moreover, geographic instability undermines service planning and continuity of care. Failure to follow through with treatment prescriptions is also due to the fact that many of the current generation of young adult chronic mental patients tend to deny their illnesses and the consequent need for treatment (Pepper, Kirshner, and Ryglewicz, 1981; Schwartz and Goldfinger, 1981; Bachrach, 1984). Practical matters, such as not having a watch or clean clothing, also hampers the homeless mentally ill from obtaining mental health care in traditional clinic settings.

Although there is not much information on effective methods of treating the homeless, policymakers and clinicians are beginning to identify some of the problems and issues in efforts to deliver services to this population (Levine, 1984; Jones, 1986). For example, in some cases the weak links to family, friends, church, and organized social life are also manifest in the way that the homeless relate to the mental health system. The limited capacity to establish relationships with helping professionals is shown in their lack of cooperation and compliance with treatment plans (Breakey, 1987). Some of the homeless report having had bad experiences with helping agencies and are wary of further involvement with service providers, an issue often compounded by reports that clinicians are often biased against the poor and undomiciled. Staff see the homeless as hopeless or capable of limited improvement at best. In addition, the homeless mentally ill are a group whose chronic psychiatric disorders are often complicated by medical problems and drug or alcohol abuse. As Breakey (1987) has stated, there are few simple, uncomplicated cases. The homeless mentally ill are, in general, a multiproblem group.

Clinical Approaches to the Homeless

Many traditional mental health interventions are based on the assumption that the patient has a stable support network and a permanent residence. Because the homeless are often unwilling or unable to make good use of clinic-based outpatient care, mental health services have been taken to them—in street and shelter locations. One of the first programs of this nature, New York City's Goddard-Riverside Project Reach Out (Barrow and Lovell, 1982), is targeted to people who wander the streets of Manhattan's Upper West Side. Professional social-service and support staff travel the neighborhood in a van, stopping to engage needy-looking people in casual conversation by offering them food or drink and probing their needs for a variety of health, mental health, and life-support services. Once trust is established, which often requires many contacts, referrals are made to appropriate service programs. The primary purpose of the mobile outreach team is to assess needs and direct the subjects to the appropriate service programs; it does not directly treat patients. Examples of the types of services the team provides include showering and delousing, clothing, food, assistance in obtaining entitlements, and transportation money.

However, direct treatment programs designed to serve the homeless mentally ill who are receptive to participating in psychiatric care have been established in many shelters for adults. Staff often adopt a nondirective approach to allow a trusting relationship to evolve before active psychopharmacologic or rehabilitative therapy is initiated. It often takes weeks or months before a person is ready to accept treatment, and some of the homeless mentally ill may deny the need for psychiatric care or actively resist a change from the homeless to a homed state.

Although outreach and on-site services are often necessary to engage the mentally ill homeless in treatment, it is generally held that community-based service systems already in place for the chronically mentally ill should be utilized as homeless people make the transition from crisis to permanent housing (Breakey, 1987). The needs of many people for assistance from multiple human service systems—mental health, general medical, substance abuse, and social welfare—underscore the merits of comprehensive case management. To better ensure that the homeless are able to sustain living in community-based housing and obtain the necessary treatment and support in that setting, case managers function as arrangers, expeditors, troubleshooters, and the connecting links to needed services. Effectiveness is increased when follow-up by the same case manager, with the authority to designate and implement a service plan, can be sustained for a long period of time (Lamb, 1984; Goldfinger and Chafetz, 1984; Lipton and Sabatini, 1984).

The development of new programs for the homeless mentally ill is of necessity rooted in the experience of caring for the seriously mentally ill in general. It is critically important that scientific principles be applied to weighing the strengths and weaknesses of innovative efforts in this area. The systematic identification of interventions that benefit certain types of patients ensures the overall quality of mental health care, contributes to the science of psychiatry, and provides a firm base for policy and program planning.

5 | Medical Problems of the Homeless

ARNOLD DRAPKIN, M.D.

In 1771 the Encyclopedia Britannica defined medicine "to be the art of preserving health when present, and of restoring it when lost"—a difficult feat under optimal circumstances and currently impossible in the homeless population.

The medical problems of homeless people are those of all humankind, intensified and complicated by their wretched lifestyle. They suffer from "all the ills to which flesh is heir, magnified by disordered living conditions, exposure to the extremes of heat and cold, lack of protection from rain and snow, bizarre sleeping accommodations, and overcrowding in shelters. These factors are exacerbated by stressors, psychiatric disorders and sociopathic behavior problems" (Brickner, 1985), which include abuse of alcohol (Bassuk, 1983; Brickner, 1985) and drugs (Brickner, 1985) and frequent physical trauma (Kelly, 1985), all compounded by malnutrition (Winick, 1985). Malnutrition together with other factors can compromise the immune system (Rubin, 1988) and increase susceptibility to infection and malignancies. Acquired immune deficiency syndrome has been found and is probably increasing in homeless sheltered men (Drapkin, personal observation, 1984; Kolata, 1988), and is probably related to intravenous drug abuse as well as homosexual activity, which could be enhanced by the shelter ambiance.

Adequate large-scale medical evaluations of the homeless population, including history, physical examinations, appropriate laboratory studies, and X-rays, have not been done; nor is there accurate data on the number of homeless people in this country, although the consensus is that this population is large and growing (Marwick, 1985). The medical data on the homeless is derived mostly from emergency room treatments (Marwick, 1985), interviews of homeless people in shelters (Brickner, 1985; Marwick, 1985), clinic visits (Brickner et al., 1972; Brickner and Kaufman, 1973; Brickner, 1985), and mortality statistics (Bogue, 1963; Alstrom, Lindelius, and Salum, 1975). These methods tend to lead to underestimations of the occurrences of various medical disorders, as primarily only those problems sufficiently troublesome to cause homeless people to seek medical assistance in emergency rooms and clinics or those problems homeless people describe to interviewers are determined. Less obvious or asymptomatic disorders such as early tuberculosis, hypertension, diabetes mellitus, acquired immune deficiency syndrome, cancer, anemia, malnutrition, hepatitis, venereal diseases, and others are unlikely to be described or detected early.

A comprehensive and systematic medical assessment of homeless people in shelters very likely would uncover many more medical problems of all varieties and severity than have been described so far. In reviewing the incidence of hypertension (10 percent), arthritis (5 percent), and diabetes mellitus (2 percent) among the homeless people evaluated in the Basic Shelter Project of Los Angeles (Marwick, 1985), a general practitioner noted that in his private practice the incidence of hypertension (30 percent), arthritis (25 percent), and diabetes mellitus (20 percent) was so much higher that perhaps his patients should "take to the road" (Wolf, 1985). A recent book on the health care of the homeless (Brickner et al., 1985) devoted as many pages to scabies and lice as it did to alcoholism, tuberculosis, thermoregulatory disorders (exposure), trauma, infections, nutritional deficiency, hypertension, peripheral vascular disease, or diabetes mellitus. Undoubtedly the itching, scratching, and subsequent complications of scabies and lice (cutaneous parasitic infestations) would be sufficiently troublesome to cause homeless people to seek medical assistance and sufficiently obvious and contagious to prompt health and shelter personnel to record the problem and provide treatment. Less symptomatic and less obvious disorders would be less likely to cause homeless people to seek medical assistance, less likely to be detected by health and shelter personnel (unless specifically searched for), and therefore more likely to be underestimated.

Treatment of acute disorders in homeless people such as trauma, acute infections, and seizures can correct or mitigate the immediate disorder, but follow-up treatment to prevent recurrences (as with seizures), to prevent complications (as from trauma), and to ensure cure (as with infection) is discouragingly difficult since these people often are not prone to follow instructions related to taking medication, diet, or follow-up appointments. Treatment of chronic disorders is similarly difficult. Some therapies require taking oral medication regularly (as with seizure disorders, hypertension, and tuberculosis), adhering to specific diets (as with hypertension and diabetes mellitus), and taking medication regularly by injection (as with insulin-dependent diabetes mellitus). All treatment is complicated by alcohol and drug abuse, poor clothing, poor shelter, and malnutrition.

During a personal visit by this writer to a large shelter in New York City, the shelter's nurse was observed as she compassionately and competently performed her duties. Within less than one hour three middle-aged men, who typify the difficulties in treating chronic disorders in this population, sought her help: the first was an insulin-dependent diabetic who had no insulin and had taken none in three days; the second had active pulmonary tuberculosis (probably contagious) who had no antibiotics and had taken none for over one week; the third had a seizure disorder and had taken no antiseizure medication for over one week. All were alcohol abusers and heavy cigarette smokers.

There is ample evidence of the deplorable medical status of the impoverished people of our society. This applies to overall mortality, infant mortality, number of hospitalizations, and disability due to chronic illness (Graham and Reeder, 1972; Alstrom et al., 1975; Asander, 1980). The incidence is high of virtually all medical disorders (Filardo, 1985), such as hypertension, arteriosclerotic cardiovascular disease, chronic lung disease, asthma, epilepsy (seizure disorder) and other neurologic diseases, physical trauma (Brickner, 1985), and tuberculosis (Leads from Morbidity and Mortality Weekly Report, 1987a, b), including drug-resistant tuberculosis (Leads from MMWR 1985, 1987c). Severe psychiatric disorders are more common in economically deprived people (Babigian, 1985), as are alcohol (Goodwin, 1985), and drug abuse (Jaffe, 1985). Since the homeless are the poorest of the poor, it is not surprising to find the incidence and severity of medical, mental, and substance abuse problems so disturbingly high in these unfortunate people.

Specific Medical Disorders of the Homeless

Trauma

Trauma is one of the major causes of morbidity and death among the homeless. Because of their lack of a safe refuge and often impaired over-all ability to function due to malnutrition, alcohol abuse, drug abuse, and medical, neurologic, and psychiatric disorders, they are particularly vulnerable to injuries, either self-induced or inflicted by others.

During the first six months of 1983, about 30 percent of all homeless patients seen (156 of 524) in San Francisco emergency rooms were treated for trauma (Kelly, 1985), mostly stab wounds and major fractures or dislocations (65 percent). Other trauma included lacerations, bruises or contusions, blunt trauma, minor post-traumatic cellulitis, head trauma, minor abrasions, minor bites, wound follow-up, multisystem trauma, minor burns, minor fractures, sprains, gunshot wounds, suicide attempts, major burns, major bites, major cellulitis, minor puncture wounds, suture removal, concussions, eye injuries, and arthritis or bursitis. From December 1983 through May 1984, 25 percent of 238 homeless persons surveyed in Los Angeles had suffered significant trauma over the preceding two months, including fractures and lacerations (14 percent), burns and falls (5 percent), and "other accidents" (6 percent) (Marwick, 1985). In New York City, 20 percent of the homeless people seen in a clinic serving a large welfare hotel were treated for accidents, assaults, and burns (Brickner et al., 1972). Among 6,032 homeless men studied in Stockholm, 327 deaths (about 20 percent of all deaths) were due to trauma (falls, accidents, poisoning, drowning, or murder), an incidence 12 times that of control subjects (Alstrom et al., 1975).

Sexual assault is particularly common among the homeless. In San Francisco, during the first nine months of 1983, 9 percent of all treated adult sexual assault victims were homeless people (Kelly, 1985). Since the homeless at that time made up only 0.4 percent of the San Francisco population, the frequency of sexual assaults among the homeless was 20 times greater than that of the rest of the population.

The problems of trauma in homeless people are compounded by their lifestyle and the inadequate medical care concomitant with that lifestyle. Thus, the superficial abrasion on a poorly shod foot, not properly treated, could lead to infection and then, if the arterial circulation is poor, gangrene, and ultimately amputation. The stab or puncture wound of the chest not properly treated and followed up could lead to major intrathoracic infection (empyema), which requires thoracic surgery and antibiotics for effective treatment. The stab or puncture wound of the abdomen, similarly, could lead to a major intra-abdominal infection (peritonitis), which requires antibiotics and perhaps surgery. Head trauma, so common among the homeless, could cause intracranial hemorrhage, such as sub-dural hematoma. If not properly assessed, followed up, and treated, in-tracranial hemorrhage could lead to altered mental status, seizures, and coma. This sequence of events, with reduced level of consciousness (or coma), could be complicated further due to impairment of the cough re-flex and resultant aspiration of mouth contents into the airway, causing asphyxiation or pneumonia.

Substance Abuse: Alcohol

Alcoholism is one of the country's major health problems, afflicting at least 10 million people (Alcoholism, 1984). Seventy percent of the adults in the United States drink on occasion and 12 percent are heavy drinkers (a person who drinks almost every day and becomes intoxicated several times a month). Twenty percent of the men who drink and 8 percent of the women who do are heavy drinkers. They account for most of the alcohol consumption in this country: 10 percent of the drinkers consume 50 percent of the alcohol; 30 percent of the drinkers consume 80 percent of the alcohol. The remaining 20 percent of the alcohol sold is consumed by the rest of the drinking population (70 percent) (Goodwin, 1985). Over 20,000 drinkers die each year from cirrhosis and other alcohol-related diseases. Each year alcohol is implicated in 20,000 traffic deaths, 15,000 murders or suicides, and about two and one half million arrests (Chafetz, 1975). Each year approximately 69,000 to 200,000 Americans die either directly or indirectly as a result of alcohol abuse, at an esti-mated cost to society of $60 to $90 billion annually (Alcoholism, 1984; Harwood et al., 1984; Harwood, Kristiansen, and Zachal, 1985). As im-pressive as these figures are, they are probably low, since alcohol abuse may be difficult to diagnose and therefore not ascribed in cases where it was a factor (Reich, 1988).

As many as 15 to 35 percent of the impoverished of our society, in-cluding the homeless, may be alcohol abusers (New York State Psychi-atric Institute, 1981–82, 1983). In earlier surveys of the homeless, the incidence was even higher (Solenberger, 1911; Anderson, 1923). Blacks in urban ghettos seem particularly prone to alcohol problems (Goodwin, 1985).

Long-term heavy alcohol use can affect every organ system of the body. Alcoholics in general have a 10 to 12 year decrease in life expectancy, and alcohol is a major factor in the four leading causes of death in men between the ages of 25 and 44: accidents, homicides, suicides, and alcoholic cirrhosis (Cassem, 1979; Alcoholism, 1984).

There are many serious medical consequences of heavy alcohol consumption. Intoxication can inhibit the cough reflex, which may lead to aspiration with asphyxiation or pneumonitis. In addition, intoxication can result in ataxia, increasing the likelihood of falls and injuries. Thermoregulatory mechanisms may be impaired by heavy alcohol consumption, leading to an increased risk of hypothermia and heat-related disorders and their consequences (Goldfrank, 1985). Intoxication can even cause coma and death by depressing the respiratory center (Goodwin, 1985).

Other complications of heavy alcohol consumption include gastritis, pancreatitis, diarrhea (Goodwin, 1985), and peptic ulceration of the esophagus, stomach, and duodenum (Gray, 1985), especially if alcoholic cirrhosis develops (Gregory, 1984). Gastritis and/or peptic ulceration can lead to gastrointestinal bleeding.

Alcohol has a direct toxic effect on the liver, which is probably enhanced by malnutrition. Chronic ingestion of large quantities of alcohol first leads to fatty infiltration of the liver (reversible if alcohol consumption ceases), and then to alcoholic cirrhosis and perhaps portal hypertension, with its complications of esophageal varices, ascites, and hemorrhoids, among others (Gregory, 1984). The liver may be so impaired by cirrhosis that it can no longer metabolize substances. In addition, when portal hypertension is present blood flow to the liver is impaired and additional circulation pathways open up to facilitate blood bypassing the liver. The combination of impaired liver function and blood bypassing the liver can result in toxic metabolites, normally metabolized by the liver, reaching the central nervous system and producing hepatic encephalopathy. This is characterized by obtundation, asterixis (irregular flexion of the hands when the upper extremities are extended horizontally and the hands extended upward at the wrist), and fetor hepaticus (an offensive feculent fruity odor of the breath). Many factors can contribute to hepatic encephalopathy, such as elevated concentrations of blood ammonia (resulting from excessive protein intake or gastrointestinal bleeding), alkalosis (which enhances penetration of ammonia into the brain), and elevated levels of short chain fatty acids, false neurotransmitters, and certain amino acids. Additional precipitating factors could be hypoxia (low arterial blood oxygen), hypercapnea (carbon dioxide retention), electrolyte imbalance, and other medications (Cutler, 1983; Gregory, 1984). If the factors contributing to hepatic encephalopathy cannot be treated effectively, hepatic coma could follow.

There are other serious nervous system disorders that occur in alcohol abusers. Peripheral neuropathy (numbness and/or weakness of an extremity) is the most common neurologic problem associated with alcohol abuse and seems to be due, at least in part, to vitamin B deficiencies. It is usually reversible with abstinence, adequate nutrition, and vitamin B supplements. Retrobulbar neuropathy is another complication of alcohol abuse and can lead to amblyopia (loss of vision). Once again, abstinence, adequate nutrition, and vitamin supplements can usually reverse this disorder (Goodwin, 1985). Wernicke's encephalopathy occurs in chronic alcoholics with inadequate diets and is characterized by confusion, disturbances of gaze, and ataxia. Vitamin B_1 (thiamine) usually reverses this disorder. If untreated, permanent brain damage and Korsakoff's psychosis could result. Korsakoff's psychosis is characterized by short-term memory loss, progressive amnesia, and confabulation; it is not reversible.

Approximately 50–70 percent of sober skid row former alcoholics have been found to have central nervous system impairment (Thompson, 1980). Long-term heavy alcohol abuse can lead to cerebral cortical atrophy and cerebellar degeneration (Cassem, 1979; Bergenan, Borg, and Hindmarsh, 1980; Carlen and Wilkenson, 1980). Computerized axial tomography (CAT) scans of the brain have made diagnosis and follow-up of these problems much easier. Some recovery from brain atrophy has been noted after months of abstinence from alcohol (Parson, 1975).

Chronic pancreatitis occurs in 5–10 percent of alcoholic patients and is the most common cause of pancreatic enzyme deficiency in the United States (Cerda and Brooks, 1967). All pancreatic function can be affected, including insulin production. Chronic pancreatitis typically is manifested by acute and chronic abdominal pain, voluminous foul-smelling stools containing increased fat (steatorrhea), abnormal glucose metabolism (diabetes mellitus), and calcification and perhaps pseudocysts of the pancreas. Because of the malabsorption of fat in chronic pancreatitis, absorption of the fat-soluble vitamins (A, D, E, K) may be impaired. Proper diet, pancreatic enzyme supplements, vitamins, analgesic drugs, and abstinence from alcohol may help, but the pain is often intractable.

Alcohol also has a direct toxic effect on the small intestine, which can interfere with the absorption of essential nutrients such as amino acids, vitamin B_{12}, folic acid, and other vitamins and can inhibit the production of intestinal disaccharidase (an enzyme important in the digestion of certain sugars) (Perlow, Baraona, and Lieber, 1977; Cassem, 1979).

Chronic heavy alcohol abuse can lead to dilated cardiomyopathy, perhaps enhanced by malnutrition. This disorder is characterized by cardiomegaly, congestive heart failure, tachyarrhythmia, and embolization (both systemic and pulmonary). The most common complication is congestive heart failure, which is the cause of death in 75 percent of patients with dilated cardiomyopathy (De Sanctis, 1987). Alcoholic cardiomyopathy may be reversed if alcohol consumption ceases early in its course and appropriate treatment instituted (Friedberg, 1966). The increased incidence of hypertension resulting from consuming 2½ ounces or more of pure alcohol per day further complicates cardiovascular problems (Klatsky, 1979).

Alcohol abuse may reduce production of blood platelets (thrombocytopenia) and white blood cells (leucopenia), increase the potency of some drugs (benzodiazepine, chloral hydrate, and antipsychotic drugs), decrease the potency of phenytoin (Dilantin) and tricyclic antidepressant drugs, and cause flushing and vomiting with sulfonylurea drugs (hypoglycemic drugs used in the treatment of diabetes mellitus) and metronidazole (Flagyl) (Cassem, 1979). In addition, the likelihood of gastrointestinal bleeding is increased when alcohol abuse is associated with the use of salicylates, nonsteroidal anti-inflammatory drugs (ibuprofen and others), and corticosteroids (Aronstein and Arnett, 1985).

Alcohol is a causative factor in cancer of the mouth, pharynx, larynx, and esophagus, particularly when associated with the use of tobacco (Li, 1986).

When heavy alcohol abusers stop drinking, the alcohol withdrawal syndrome can occur, with tremulousness being the most common manifestation. Tremulousness can happen within a few hours after imbibing ceases or during periods of reduced consumption. Transitory hallucinations may occur 12 to 24 hours after drinking stops. Delirium tremens, characterized by major memory disturbances, vivid hallucinations, agitation, and tremulousness, may begin two to three days after consumption ends and may persist for several days. Often there is a medical problem associated with delirium tremens, such as hepatic decompensation, pneumonitis, subdural hematoma, pancreatitis, or an injury as a result of falling (Goodwin, 1985).

Seizures (often called rum fits) can occur two to three days after drinking has stopped. Usually, alcohol abusers who experience seizures do not have a seizure disorder, at least as can be determined by their electroencephalograms; their seizures result only from withdrawal (Goodwin, 1985). Drinking alcohol after 48 or more hours without food can cause hypoglycemia, sometimes profound, which can result in altered consciousness and seizures (Drapkin and Reed, 1962; Cahill, 1986). In addition, the propensity of the heavy alcohol abuser to fall and sustain head trauma warrants considering subdural hematoma as a possible cause of seizures (Drapkin, personal observation, 1958).

Substance Abuse: Cigarette Smoking

Cigarette smoking is a major public health problem and is the most preventable cause of premature death in this country (The Health Consequences of Smoking, 1988). Smoking is widespread in our population. There are no precise statistics on the prevalence or degree of smoking in the homeless but it has been reported to be higher in the "lower social classes" (Graham and Reeder, 1972). More current data suggest that smoking cigarettes is "increasingly becoming a behavior primarily of the less educated and socioeconomically disadvantaged." (Pierce et al., 1989). Others feel that smoking, as well as alcohol and other substances, is particularly common in the homeless (Goldfrank, 1985). The morbidity and mortality from all diseases appears to be higher in the homeless population (Filardo, 1985), and many of the disorders are exacerbated and more prevalent due to cigarette smoking.

Cigarette smoking increases the frequency of such respiratory diseases as chronic bronchitis and emphysema (Fanta and Ingram, 1988). In addition, it is an important cause of lung, mouth, pharynx, larynx, esophagus, liver, pancreas, kidney, and bladder cancer (Li, 1986). Cigarette smoking causes peptic ulcers to heal more slowly. The combination of smoking and aspirin consumption is especially harmful in peptic ulcer disease (Gray, 1985).

Perhaps most important in terms of morbidity and mortality are the effects of cigarette smoking on the cardiovascular system. Complications from arteriosclerosis are the leading cause of permanent disability and death in the United States. They account for 50 percent of all deaths and 33 percent of deaths between ages 35 and 65. Arteriosclerotic heart disease (also called coronary or ischemic heart disease) is responsible for 75 percent of the deaths from arteriosclerosis. The highest risk group for arteriosclerosis is males over 35 years old. Within this group, cigarette smoking, hypertension, and elevated blood cholesterol are the major causes and probably account for about 66 percent of all major coronary artery events (myocardial infarction or heart attack) each year (Hancock, 1983).

Cerebrovascular accident or stroke is the third leading cause of adult deaths (after heart disease and cancer) in the United States. The major causes of cerebrovascular accidents are similar to those for arteriosclerosis, though hypertension plays a more important role than cigarette smoking (Cutler, 1986; Wolf et al., 1988).

Peripheral arterial vascular disease results from arteriosclerosis of the descending aorta and the arteries nourishing the lower extremities. The reduction of blood flow to the lower extremities can cause pain with exertion and, if the condition is more severe, even when at rest. It can lead to ischemic ulceration, poor healing of injuries or infection, greater susceptibility to frostbite, and, in the most severe cases, gangrene. Diabetes mellitus is a major factor in this disease as well as cigarette smoking (Hancock, 1983; Hancock, 1985; Cahill, Arky, and Perlman, 1986). The connection of smoking with this disease was observed more than 70 years ago by the great Canadian physician Sir William Osler, who noted the association of "syphillis, alcohol and tobacco" to peripheral arterial disease of the lower extremities (Osler, 1916a).

Substance Abuse: Drugs

The frequency of use of different drugs, either singly or in combination, is not known for homeless adults. Figures for drug abuse have been reported as low as 3 percent (Arce et al., 1983) and as high as 30.8 percent (Farr, Koegel, and Burnam, 1986). The toxicity of abused drugs can seriously complicate the medical and psychiatric status of the user.

The reasons people abuse drugs is not clear. Personality may play an important role, since polydrug abusers and sociopaths have much in common (Vaillant, 1978).

Information on the consequences of long-term drug abuse is meager. In addition to its deleterious effects on the psychosocial, occupational, and health aspects of the abuser's life, there is evidence that persistent psychopathology may result from certain types of drug abuse. A six-year study (McLellan, Woody, and O'Brien, 1979) of 51 male drug abusers divided them into three groups: stimulant users (amphetamines and related compounds), narcotics users (opioids, including morphine, heroin, methadone, codeine, and related compounds), and sedative-hypnotic users (including barbiturates, benzodiazepines, meprobamate, methaqualone, chloral hydrate, and glutethimide). The subjects were evaluated yearly.

Initially the drug abusers were comparable from a psychiatric point of view. However, at the end of six years, six (over half) of the stimulant users had a psychosis indistinguishable from schizophrenia; eight (over half) of the sedative-hypnotic users had serious depression, with five having attempted suicide; the narcotics users, interestingly, showed no significant change in psychopathology. Though there seems to be a surprising absence of long-term toxic effects from long-term opiate abuse, there are endocrine changes, which seem to be reversible, and there are behavior aberrations such as criminal activity, impulsive behavior, family disturbance, and employment problems (Kreck, 1973; O'Brien et al., 1981).

Periodic or chronic use of hallucinogens (including lysergic acid diethylamide [LSD]), mescaline, psilocybin, and phencyclidine (PCP or angel dust) may disrupt cerebral processes and impair thought and speech formulation and coherent communication (Renner, 1978). Cessation of hallucinogen abuse, particularly LSD, is often associated with occasionally disabling flashbacks (spontaneous transitory recurrence of the substance-induced experience), which can occur years later, commonly in association with marijuana *(Cannabis)* use (Renner, 1978; Grinspoon and Bakalar, 1985).

Chronic PCP (angel dust) abuse may lead to depression, thought disorders, dulled thinking and reflexes, loss of memory, impaired impulse control, lethargy, and inability to concentrate (Cohen, 1977; Grinspoon and Bakalar, 1985). Treating the neuropsychiatric toxicity of PCP may be particularly difficult because it can remain in the body tissues for months (Bernstein, 1983).

MARIJUANA

Marijuana *(Cannabis)* is derived from the hemp plant *Cannabis sativa*. Preparations of marijuana vary widely in potency and quality, depending on the type of plant and environmental factors. It is the plant resin that contains the active substances. The cheapest and least potent form of marijuana, called bhang, is obtained from the cut tips of uncultivated plants, which have a low resin content. Much of the marijuana smoked in this country is this variety. A high quality marijuana with greater quantity of resin is obtained from the flowering tops and leaves of cultivated plants and is called ganja. This grade is becoming more common in the United States. The highest quality is derived from the tops of mature plants and is called hashish (Grinspoon and Bakalar, 1985).

Marijuana has been known for thousands of years as a medicine and intoxicant and in the nineteenth century was used as an analgesic, anti-convulsant, and hypnotic. This drug has also been effective in treating glaucoma and the nausea of chemotherapy. One of marijuana's nonpsychoactive components has anticonvulsant properties (Grinspoon and Bakalar, 1985).

Almost 60 percent of the people in the United States have tried marijuana at least once and the number of regular users has been estimated between 6 million (Department of Health and Human Services, 1986) and 20 million (Jenicke, 1987). The frequency of marijuana abuse in the homeless population is not known, but its relatively low cost and availability make it a substance this group is likely to use.

The drug can be ingested or smoked. In the United States it is generally smoked. When smoked, 2,000 identifiable metabolites are produced, many of which remain in the fatty tissues of the body for weeks. A single marijuana cigarette ("joint") contains a 2 percent concentration of the active ingredient THC (delta-9-tetrahydrocannabinol), which has a half-life of 3–7 days and can take several weeks before all of it is eliminated from the body (Jenicke, 1987). Pure marijuana is not always smoked since occasionally it is adulterated with PCP, insect spray, shredded dried cow manure (which could contain *Salmonella bacteria*), and herbicide spray (Schwartz, 1983).

Generally marijuana inhalation initially causes anxiety, sometimes associated with paranoid thoughts, followed by euphoric relaxation, contentment, improved social interaction, and feelings of heightened self-awareness. The effects of smoking usually last 2–4 hours and when ingested may last 5–12 hours (Grinspoon and Bakalar, 1985; Jenicke, 1987). Marijuana may precipitate a relapse or worsen symptoms in patients with a history of schizophrenia or affective disorders. A rare effect of marijuana use, which can occur in susceptible individuals, is toxic psychosis (an acute brain syndrome or delirium), resulting from toxic substances that interfere with many cerebral functions. This syndrome may include altered consciousness, restlessness, confusion, bewilderment, disorientation, dreamlike thinking, fear (even panic), illusions, and hallucinations. A large dose of THC is necessary to produce a toxic psychosis, and the reaction is rare when marijuana is smoked. There is no adequately documented case of a death directly caused by the use of marijuana (Grinspoon and Bakalar, 1985).

Chronic heavy use of marijuana has been associated with an amotivational syndrome of laziness, apathy, depression, chronic anxiety, and personality disorder, but it is not clear if marijuana is the primary cause of this syndrome. So far there is no conclusive evidence that prolonged use of marijuana causes permanent changes in the central nervous system or behavior (Grinspoon and Bakalar, 1985; Jenicke, 1987).

The acute physical (nonpsychoactive) effects of marijuana smoking include conjunctivitis, dose-related increase in heart rate, and bronchodilation (Grinspoon and Bakalar, 1985; Jenicke, 1987).

Smoking a single marijuana cigarette, as compared to smoking a regular tobacco cigarette, results in a nearly fivefold greater increase in carboxyhemoglobin (which reflects the amount of carbon monoxide absorbed), approximately a threefold increase in the amount of tar inhaled, and one-third more of the inhaled tar retained in the respiratory tract. These differences probably reflect the greater puff volume, depth of inhalation, and longer breath-holding characteristics of marijuana smokers as well as the physical characteristics (shorter, unfiltered, loosely packed) of the marijuana cigarette (Wu et al., 1988). Long-term use of three to four marijuana cigarettes per day is associated with the same frequency of signs and symptoms of acute and chronic bronchitis (Tashkin et al., 1987) and the same type and extent of epithelial damage in the central airways as is seen in habitual smokers of at least 20 cigarettes per day (Gong et al., 1987). These changes justifiably raise concern regarding permanent pulmonary dysfunction and respiratory cancer with prolonged regular use of marijuana. If tobacco cigarettes are smoked simultaneously, the harmful consequences are likely to be cumulative.

COCAINE

Cocaine is an alkaloid derived from the shrub *Erythroxylon coca,* a plant indigenous to Bolivia and Peru. Peasants of these countries chew the leaves for their stimulating effect. Cocaine was isolated in 1860 and in 1884 became the first effective local anesthetic (Grinspoon and Bakalar, 1985). Since 1970 it has been regarded as the champagne of drugs, with its high price limiting its use. In recent years the price has fallen considerably, and its use has become progressively more common.

Street cocaine can vary considerably in purity, usually being mixed ("cut") with sugar, procaine, and other impurities. The primary methods of use has been snorting (snuffing), injection (intravenous or subcutaneous), and smoking (freebasing) (Grinspoon and Bakalar, 1985).

In 1986 a potent new form of cocaine, crack, became available, which could be smoked in cigarettes or glass water pipes and produce the same euphoric effect as intravenous use (Jenicke, 1987).

There is no data on the frequency of cocaine use in homeless people, but with the availability of this drug increasing and the cost falling, ever greater use seems likely. In a large New York City shelter where 850 homeless men sleep each night, it has been estimated that 66 to 85 percent of the men use cocaine (crack) (Barbanel, 1988).

Cocaine is highly addictive and causes euphoria, hallucinations, and feelings of enhanced mental and physical prowess. In addition, abusers may become depressed, hyperactive, paranoid, impulsive, psychotic, and suicidal. Toxicity is manifested by anxiety, seizures, hypertension, fever, cardiac tachyarrhythmia, cardiac or respiratory arrest (Grinspoon and Bakalar, 1985; Jenicke, 1987), intracranial hemorrhage (Wojak and Flamm, 1987), and acute myocardial infarction (Zimmerman, Gustafson, and Kemp, 1987).

Chronic snorting of cocaine can produce inflammation and atrophy of the nasal mucosa and occasional perforation of the nasal septum (Grinspoon and Bakalar, 1985; Jenicke, 1987). Chronic inhalation can cause lung damage (Jenicke, 1987). Deaths from cocaine and opiates taken together intravenously are more common than when cocaine is used alone (Grinspoon and Bakalar, 1985).

Binge cocaine use may be followed by severe depressive symptoms, irritability, and anxiety, which can persist for hours or seven days (Jenicke, 1987). During periods of abstinence, most heavy abusers of cocaine experience an anhedonic dysphoric state, during which time they are especially prone to resume using cocaine. Many abusers of cocaine suffer from an affective disorder and use this substance in an effort to relieve their depressed mood (Gawin and Kleber, 1986).

Acquired Immune Deficiency Syndrome (AIDS)

The Acquired Immune Deficiency Syndrome (AIDS) is caused by a newly recognized human retrovirus (discovered in 1984 by Robert C. Gallo and Luc Montagnier), now known as human immunodeficiency virus (HIV) but previously called lymphadenopathy associated virus (LAV), human T lymphocyte virus type III (HTLV-III), AIDS-associated virus, or immunodeficiency-associated virus. AIDS was first recognized in the United States in 1981. By 1986 more than 25,000 cases of AIDS had been reported to the Centers for Disease Control (Rubin, 1987). In July 1988 the number of cases was over 66,000 and more than half—over 37,000—had died, including over 80 percent of the patients diagnosed before 1985. The number of cases in the United States may reach 365,000 by 1992 (Heyward and Curran, 1988).

HIV is a transmissible blood-borne virus that can be spread by blood transfusion, infusion of blood products (such as platelets), injection with blood-contaminated needles, anal and vaginal sexual intercourse (especially anal intercourse) and by infected mothers to their new-born infants. The transmission of HIV to infants could be *in utero* or through breast feeding (Heyward and Curran, 1988). The virus can also be transmitted via organ transplant from an infected donor (Rubin, 1987). Prior to screening blood for HIV contamination, which started in mid-1985, the risk of acquiring HIV infection from a single blood transfusion had been about 0.1 percent (one donor in one thousand is HIV-positive) (Kuretsky, 1985). However, receiving a unit of HIV-contaminated blood is very likely to result in HIV infection (Heyward and Curran, 1988). Before a test was developed to screen blood, about 1.7 cases per 100,000 receiving transfusions appeared to develop AIDS; in hemophiliacs, who continually receive multiple transfusions of blood or blood products, the rate was 200 cases per 100,000 receiving transfusions. Fortunately, other treated blood products such as immunoglobulin preparations, hepatitis B vaccine, and albumin do not transmit HIV (Rubin, 1987). The risk of HIV infection through accidental needle puncture from a needle contaminated by blood from an HIV infected person is about 1 percent (Lifson et al., 1986) or less (Stricof and Morse, 1986). HIV infection can be acquired from infected persons who do not have AIDS, but is more readily transmitted when AIDS is present (Heyward and Curran, 1988).

HIV is present in the saliva and tears of infected individuals in low concentration, but no documented case of infection through exposure to saliva or tears has been reported (MMWR, 1985). There are no studies to indicate that HIV can be transmitted by insect vectors. In addition, there is no evidence to suggest transmission of HIV through casual or household contacts; in spite of tens of thousands of days of household exposure to infected individuals, except for sexual partners and new-born infants, not one of over 400 family members studied became infected. (Heyward and Curran, 1988). There are isolated cases of HIV being spread in health workers by exposure of mucous membrane (mouth) and skin (hands) to blood, other body fluids, and stool from patients with AIDS, but this is extremely rare and not likely to occur (MMWR, 1986; Leads from MMWR, 1987c; Barnes, 1988).

There are between 1 and 1.5 million Americans infected with HIV who do not yet have AIDS. Many will develop AIDS over the ensuing years, but what percentage is not known.

New York, Washington, D.C., and New Jersey were the areas in the United States with the highest cumulative reported cases of AIDS as of late March 1988 (more than 5 per 10,000 population) (Heyward and Curran, 1988). In 1987 the worldwide case rate per 100,000 was 56.2 for French Guiana, 33.9 for the Bahamas, 13.0 for Bermuda, 8.9 for the United States, and 5.0 for Haiti (Mann et al., 1988).

In the United States homosexual or bisexual men without a history of I.V. drug abuse account for 63 percent of the AIDS cases, and heterosexual men and women I.V. drug abusers 19 percent (Heyward and Curran, 1988). Haitians living in the United States (of whom at least 50 percent deny I.V. drug abuse or homosexual behavior) represent 4 percent of the cases (Rubin, 1987). Almost 3 percent of the cases are associated with transfusions of blood contaminated with HIV (Heyward and Curran, 1988). Others with AIDS in this country include hemophiliac men who are not homosexual or I.V. drug abusers, prisoners, heterosexual partners of someone with HIV infection, and children of high-risk mothers (Rubin, 1987). In the United States the incidence of AIDS is over three times as high among blacks and Hispanics as among whites. Most whites with AIDS are homosexual or bisexual or have been infected through receiving blood products; most blacks and Hispanics have a history of I.V. drug abuse, heterosexual contacts with high-risk people or are children (MMWR, 1986; Heyward and Curran 1988). The major source of HIV transmission in the United States in heterosexual men and women is I.V. drug abuse. The fastest growing group of AIDS patients are children of women who have been sexual partners of high-risk men, particularly I.V. drug abusers (Heyward and Curran, 1988).

With initial HIV infection, the virus replicates prolifically, and free virus appears in the cerebrospinal fluid and in the blood. A febrile illness with rash, flulike symptoms, and neurologic complaints is often associated with this early phase of HIV infection. Within a few weeks the level of HIV in the cerebrospinal fluid and blood drops, and all signs and symptoms disappear. The HIV is still present, but moves into cells of the body's immune or defense system—the T4 lymphocytes, macrophages, and monocytes (precursors of macrophages). Once in these cells, the virus can lie dormant in the T4 lymphocytes for many years, only to destroy them during a surge of replication of the virus when the T4 lymphocytes are stimulated to protect the body, as from an infection. In the macrophages and monocytes, the virus replicates slowly and continuously, probably altering the function of these cells but not destroying them (Haseltine and Wong-Staal, 1988). The decline in the T4-lymphocytes is the primary factor in the compromise of the immune system (immunodeficiency) and the subsequent infections and malignancies that occur (Redfield and Burke, 1988).

The most common manifestation of AIDS is an opportunistic infection such as *Pneumocystis carinii* pneumonia, which is the presenting disorder in about 50 percent of the cases. Other common opportunistic infections are mucosal candidiasis (called thrush when in the mouth), herpes simplex infection, disseminated cytomegalovirus infection, which causes pneumonia and encephalitis, dissmeninated atypical mycobacterial (tuberculosis) infection, toxoplasmosis (particularly of the central nervous system), *Cryptosporidium* or *Isospora bella* infection, causing persistent diarrhea, *Cryptococcus* causing meningitis and disseminated infection, and many others. More conventional infections, such as pneumonia from *Hemophilus influenzae* type B and *Streptococcus pneumoniae,* can occur and are generally very serious in the AIDS patient (Rubin, 1987). In addition there is an increased incidence of syphilis (Leads from MMWR, 1989) and the typical type of tuberculosis, usually disseminated, associated with AIDS (Braun et al., 1989). The risk of malignancy in the AIDS patient may be related to certain viral infections: Epstein-Barr virus infection is associated with lymphomas; cytomegalovirus has been linked with Kaposi's sarcoma; herpes simplex virus type 2 and papilloma virus with carcinoma of the rectum; and herpes simplex virus type 1 with squamous cell carcinoma of the tongue (Rubin, 1987).

The therapeutic approach to AIDS requires preventive, therapeutic, and supportive measures. Education has resulted in safer sexual practices in homosexual men, and the spread of HIV in this group has been reduced. Treating and preventing I.V. drug abuse is essential if HIV transmission is to be reduced in this population. Screening blood donors for HIV antibodies and a high-risk lifestyle has reduced the risk of HIV transmission in transfusion (Heyward and Curran, 1988). Treating the HIV virus directly with AZT (Zidovudine) and the secondary infections with a variety of antibiotics has prolonged the life of AIDS patients, but no cure has been found so far. Death is generally due to disseminated infection and cachexia. The economic, personal, and social costs are staggering and recommendations to ease these problems are being made (Health and Public Policy Committee, 1986; Ron and Rogers, 1988) and debated (Oryshkevich, 1989; Ron and Rogers, 1989).

The incidence of AIDS in the homeless population is not known, but it is likely to be high. It has been estimated in New York City to be present in as many as 10 percent of shelter residents, a percentage probably increasing as many shelter residents continue to use intravenous drugs with shared needles and have homosexual relationships (Kolata, 1988). Homeless people are generally found in areas afflicted with unemployment, welfare dependency, prostitution, crime, high school dropout rates, and teenage pregnancy, where intravenous drug abuse flourishes (Fineberg, 1988).

Once a homeless person acquires HIV infection, the development of AIDS is likely to be accelerated by malnutrition and the repeated infections he or she is prone to acquire, which lead to activation of the HIV-infected T4 lymphocyte, resulting in replication of the HIV virus, death of the cell, compromise of the immune system, and subsequent development of AIDS. The diagnosis of AIDS in homeless people is difficult to make because of their general reluctance to seek medical help voluntarily and perhaps their fear of discrimination against them in the shelters if the diagnosis was established (Kolata, 1988).

Tuberculosis

Tuberculosis is a disease caused by the tubercle bacillus *Mycobacterium tuberculosis*. It must have oxygen to survive and thrives best in those human tissues with a higher oxygen content, such as the apices of the lungs. It reproduces slowly, having a generation of time of 12–18 hours, resulting in infections that typically evolve in a subacute or chronic manner. Diagnosis can be confirmed by direct identification of the tubercle bacillus, which can be found in the sputum and elsewhere in infected people. Culturing the organism from body sources is the most definitive diagnostic procedure and takes three to eight weeks. Special staining techniques permit identification of the organism microscopically. A positive tuberculosis skin test (Purified Protein Derivative [PPD] Test or Tine Test) generally indicates prior exposure to or infection from tuberculosis but need not indicate an active or contagious form of the disease. The organism may lie dormant but viable in people with positive skin tests, perhaps activating in the future to cause clinical disease. In the United States tuberculosis is acquired primarily via transmission in the air of the bacillus from the coughing or breath of an infected person. The more crowded the living conditions, such as in shelters for the homeless, the greater the risk of spread. Once airborne, infected droplets, as from a cough, may remain aloft and contagious for hours. Adequate ventilation could reduce airborne spread of the disease. Infected droplets cannot cause illness if they land on clothing, furniture, or floors—they must be inhaled. Washing and cleaning could reduce the spread of the disease by simply eliminating any viable bacilli that may have landed on an object and still have the potential to be inhaled.

Pulmonary tuberculosis is the most common form in the United States; only 10 percent of the cases are extrapulmonary (Simon, 1984). Cough, fever, pleurisy, shortness of breath, and weight loss are common manifestations of pulmonary tuberculosis. When the disease is extrapulmonary, any organ of the body could be involved, and the signs and symptoms would depend on the area involved and degree of involvement.

The existence of tuberculosis has been noted through all recorded history, having been accurately described by ancient Greek and Roman physicians and physically detected in Egyptian mummies. In the early eighteenth century, it was estimated that one-seventh of all deaths in the world and one-ninth of all deaths in the United States were due to tuberculosis (Osler, 1916b). At the start of the twentieth century, tuberculosis was the most frequent cause of death in all countries of the temperate zone (whenever vital statistics were collected) and probably second only to malaria in tropical areas (Muschenheim, 1967).

Poor living conditions were always recognized as crucial factors in the occurrence, spread, and mortality rate of tuberculosis. The yearly mortality from tuberculosis in England fell from 219 per 100,000 people in 1871–80 to 117 per 100,000 in 1901–10 as a result of improved living conditions, including "less drunkenness, less overcrowding, better care and better food" along with "less spitting in public" and "segregation to protect the healthy from the sick" (Osler, 1916b). Comparable factors were operative in the United States; the yearly mortality from tuberculosis fell from 200 per 100,000 people in 1900 to 10 per 100,000 in 1954 (Muschenheim, 1967). The introduction of streptomycin in 1945, isoniazid in 1952, and other antibiotics helped change the character of tuberculosis from a widespread disease with a mortality of 50 percent in five years (Iseman, 1985) to a largely curable disease which has progressively decreased in frequency.

This decreasing trend was halted in 1979 with the influx of refugees from the Far East (MMWR, 1984), many of whom were carriers of tuberculosis. Since then, with the increase in homeless people, particularly in certain areas such as New York City, the increase in immigrants (particularly from Southeast Asia) who may have been infected abroad, the spread of acquired immune deficiency syndrome and its association with tuberculosis, and with the prevalence of alcohol and intravenous drug abuse in impoverished people, the incidence and mortality of tuberculosis has risen (Iseman, 1985; CDC, 1986; Sunderdam et al., 1986; Leads from the MMWR, 1987a; Lambert, 1988).

In 1985 the number of cases of tuberculosis declined by only 54 (0.2

percent) from 1984, and in 1986 there was an increase of 374 cases (1.7 percent) over the 22,201 cases reported in 1985. The increase in tuberculosis in 1986 was the first one since national reporting of the disease was started in 1953 (Leads from the MMWR, 1987a).

As with other medical problems, the homeless suffer to a disproportionate degree from tuberculosis. Assessment of selected homeless populations have revealed that 1.6–6.8 percent have clinically active tuberculosis (Slutkin, 1986), which is 150–300 times higher than the national rate (Leads from the MMWR, 1987b). The incidence of asymptomatic tuberculosis infection among the homeless has been reported as high as 22–51 percent (McAdam et al., 1985; Barry et al., 1986; Slutkin, 1986), indicating the existence of a large reservoir of potentially active tuberculosis. As with other contagious diseases, the lifestyle of the homeless, including the crowded and poor hygienic conditions of the shelters, may play an important role in the spread of tuberculosis.

Prior to the use of chest X-rays, which reveal the old tuberculous foci in the lungs, and when the probability of tuberculosis was greater than it is now, infection from the outside (exogenous infection) was considered to be the most important factor in the occurrence of tuberculosis in adults (Rich, 1951). Subsequently, epidemiologic evidence suggested that the main cause of tuberculosis in the United States was reactivation of existing foci rather than exogenous infection (Stead, 1967). Reanalysis of the data leading to this conclusion once again established the importance of exogenous infection in adult tuberculosis, particularly in situations of high exposure, as with the homeless (Romeyn, 1970). The overall declining incidence of tuberculosis in developed countries and the generally better health of their inhabitants has reduced the likelihood of exogenous infection as a source of tuberculosis. In underdeveloped countries, with large segments of their populations poor, living in crowded inadequate environments, and suffering from malnutrition and multiple diseases, adequate immunity is not likely to develop from prior tuberculosis exposure or infection, so that exogenous infection is an important factor in the prevalence of tuberculosis (Stead and Bates, 1980; ten Dam and Pio, 1982).

The living conditions of the homeless are similar in many ways to those of the majority of people in poor underdeveloped countries, and the incidence of tuberculosis, particularly that due to exogenous infection, is high. Alcoholism, physical and emotional stress, malnutrition, low body weight, and drug abuse all contribute to impaired immune response and susceptibility to tuberculosis and other infections in these people (Kissen,

1957; Hunngren and Reizenstein, 1969; Edwards et al., 1971; Reichman, Felton, and Edsall, 1979; McAdam et al., 1985; Nardell et al., 1986).

In addition to the already high incidence of tuberculosis among the highly susceptible homeless population, strains of the disease resistant to antituberculous drugs are emerging and spreading in shelters for the homeless (Leads from the MMWR, 1985; Nardell et al., 1986; Daley, 1987). Sheltering the homeless is essential, but the occurrence and ease of transmission of tuberculosis among shelter denizens emphasizes the plight of these people and the ineffectiveness of measures devised to help them.

Screening for tuberculosis and follow-up sustained treatment of infected individuals is difficult with transient, homeless people, generally poorly compliant as well, but it must be done if effective treatment and containment of this disease is to be accomplished. One possible method would be to have medical personnel or trained shelter staff screen homeless people as they enter the shelters. Workers could identify those with a persistent cough, fever, and/or emaciated condition and then promptly refer them for medical evaluation. For the rest of the shelter population, skin testing them for tuberculosis (PPD test or Tine Test), obtaining chest X-rays in those with positive skin tests, would be helpful in identifying shelter inhabitants who have had prior tuberculosis exposure or infection and those with current infections.

Effectively treating tuberculosis in homeless people is probably more difficult than finding it because of their lifestyle and generally poor compliance. Perhaps the best way to treat tuberculosis in this population would be direct observation of therapy (administration of medication such as isoniazid, ethambutol, and rifampin) on a daily or twice weekly basis, which would minimize treatment failures, spread of infection to others, and emergence of drug-resistant strains (which are likely to develop if medication is not taken regularly or for the necessary period of time). A federal review of tuberculosis in New York City led to a proposal for residential centers or even court-ordered quarantine to ensure proper treatment for those unlikely to comply (Lambert, 1988).

The increase in shelter-related tuberculosis infection has been noted in staff members as well as in shelter inhabitants (Nardell et al., 1986). It would be helpful for staff members to receive a tuberculosis skin test (such as a PPD test) and a chest X-ray, if the skin test is positive, at the start of employment. Those with negative skin tests should be retested every six to twelve months. If a skin test goes from negative to positive, chest X-rays and appropriate therapy or preventive therapy according to current guidelines should be administered (American Thoracic Society/ Centers for Disease Control, 1983; Leads from the MMWR, 1985).

Hypertension

Hypertension is the nation's most common chronic disorder, with about 60 million people afflicted (National Committee on Detection, Evaluation, and Treatment of High Blood Pressure, 1984). It is a major contributor to cardiovascular disease, which is the country's leading cause of death (National Center for Health Statistics, 1984), the major risk factor for strokes, and has a major impact on kidney failure (Haber and Slater, 1979; Cutler, 1986).

While better detection and early treatment of patients with hypertension have reduced the incidence of cerebrovascular, cardiac, and renal complications from this disorder on a national basis (Veteran's Administration, 1967, 1970; Hypertension Detection and Followup Program, 1979), perhaps as much as 20 percent of the population (Kaplan, 1982), including the homeless, are outside the realm of sustained health care and have not benefited. The homeless population is relatively inaccessible to health surveys and care, so the true incidence of health problems in this group, including hypertension and its complications, is not known.

Some informal studies indicate that hypertension and cardiovascular disease are very common in homeless people. Using blood pressure readings of over 140 mmHg systolic and 90 mmHg diastolic as indicative of hypertension, a survey of 683 persons in New York City shelters and SRO (single room occupancy) hotels revealed a 28 percent incidence of hypertension in the shelter population and a 60 percent incidence in the older SRO hotel population (Kellogg et al., 1985). In a Washington, D.C. clinic, hypertension was found in 28 percent of homeless people (Bargmann, 1985). Medical examinations of 250 homeless people in a New York City shelter revealed over 14 percent to have hypertension (Human Resources Administration, 1980). The physical and psychological stresses of homelessness, including alcohol abuse, very likely contribute to the high incidence of hypertension in these people (Celantano, Martinez, and McQueen, 1981).

Hypertension is a disorder that generally displays no signs or symptoms until a major complication such as cerebrovascular accident (stroke), heart failure, or kidney failure occurs. These complications can be irreversibly disabling or fatal. In view of this, early detection and treatment of hypertension is necessary if health is to be preserved. This is especially difficult with homeless people since treatment may require special diets as well as taking antihypertensive medication on a regular basis, which is most unlikely to be achieved in this population.

While it has not been determined to what extent hypertension contributes to the increased mortality of homeless people, the death rate from heart disease in skid row males has been estimated to be 233 times that of other males (Bogue, 1963).

Diabetes Mellitus

Diabetes mellitus is a genetic-based, chronic disorder of carbohydrate, protein, and fat metabolism, with the most notable feature being disturbed carbohydrate metabolism resulting in hyperglycemia.

The actual incidence of diabetes mellitus in the United States is not known, but it is estimated that more than 5 percent of the population (more than 12 million people) suffer from it (Cahill et al., 1986). Probably the real incidence is considerably higher. Homeless people most likely have a higher rate of diabetes mellitus than the general population since occurrence of this disorder is enhanced by physical and psychological stress, both of which are endemic among the homeless.

The basic problem of diabetes mellitus is insufficient production of the hormone insulin by the beta cells of the pancreas. Insulin increases the transport of blood glucose (sugar) and amino acids into the body's cells, where they are converted to energy or stored as glycogen and fat. Insulin is produced in response to elevation of blood glucose and/or amino acids, as occurs with eating. Diagnosis of this disease is established by finding elevated blood glucose either after fasting or postprandially. A glucose tolerance test is the most precise way to diagnose diabetes if its existence is suspected. Screening urine for glucose (glucosuria) without monitoring blood glucose is inadequate for determining if a patient has diabetes mellitus since considerable hyperglycemia is necessary before glucosuria occurs.

Generally diabetes mellitus is divided into two subgroups: insulin-dependent diabetes mellitus (IDDM), which often begins in childhood or adolescence and requires insulin to maintain control of carbohydrate metabolism and to prevent the most serious immediate diabetic complication, diabetes ketoacidosis; and noninsulin-dependent diabetes mellitus (NIDDM), which usually appears later in life, can be controlled with diet, oral hypoglycemic agents, and by achieving and maintaining a reasonable weight (patients with NIDDM are often obese), and is not prone to diabetic ketoacidosis. Patients with NIDDM have sufficient insulin to prevent diabetic ketoacidosis but not enough to achieve normal carbohydrate metabolism. NIDDM is far more common than IDDM, occurring in 90–95 percent of patients with diabetes mellitus (Cahill et al., 1986).

With IDDM the beta cells of the pancreas, which are the source of insulin, become deficient in insulin-producing ability, due at least in part to an autoimmune response to the beta cells (Cahill et al., 1986). First degree relatives of persons with IDDM may have beta cell antibodies, abnormal glucose tolerance tests, and autoimmune disorders such as hypothyroidism, Graves' disease (a form of hyperthyroidism), Addison's disease (adrenocortical insufficiency), myasthenia gravis, and pernicious anemia (Powers and Eisenbarth, 1985; Srikanta et al., 1985). IDDM commonly becomes manifest as a result of marked hyperglycemia, which causes glucosuria, the "spilling" of excess blood glucose into the urine along with plentiful water. This water loss could be excessive and lead to voluminous urination (polyuria), which in turn could result in dehydration, and marked thirst and water drinking (polydypsia) in an effort to correct the dehydration. The loss of glucose and water in the urine and the inability of the body to metabolize glucose for energy (because of the insulin deficiency) leads to weight loss, often despite excessive eating (polyphagia), which is the body's attempt to provide adequate sources of much-needed energy. Confusion and ataxia could occur from the dehydration and subsequent hypotension of uncontrolled diabetes mellitus. The insulin deficiency and subsequent inadequate body fuel or energy results in mobilization of fat (lipolysis), glycogen (glycogenolysis) from the liver and muscle, and amino acids from muscle in an effort by the body to provide alternate sources of energy. The glycogenolysis produces more glucose and even greater hyperglycemia and glucosuria, and the lipolysis releases fatty acids which, along with the amino acids, are metabolized in the liver to produce still more blood glucose (gluconeogenesis). So the body's efforts to make up for the insufficient insulin and energy compound the problem by further raising the blood glucose, increasing the glucosuria, and worsening the dehydration. If the insulin deficiency continues untreated, products of lipolysis called ketoacids (acetoacetic acid and beta hydroxybutyric acid) are released into the blood (ketonemia) and then into the urine (ketonuria). When the blood level of these ketoacids becomes sufficiently elevated, the acidity of the blood increases and diabetic ketoacidosis evolves, which may lead ultimately to vascular collapse (hypotension with poor perfusion of blood to brain, kidneys, and other organs), coma, and death. Because diabetic ketoacidosis can be fatal, especially if treatment is delayed, prompt treatment of this condition with insulin and intravenous fluids is essential.

The initial appearance of IDDM (perhaps as diabetic ketoacidosis) could be precipitated by an acute stress such as injury or infection (increasing insulin requirements), which would have to be treated effectively if satisfactory control of diabetes mellitus is to be accomplished. Alcohol or drug intoxication, head trauma, perhaps with subdural hematoma, and hypoglycemia (perhaps from insulin therapy without adequate food intake, or alcohol consumption without eating for a prolonged period of time) must be considered in the evaluation of altered consciousness or coma. Blood and urine tests should help clarify the diagnosis quickly.

NIDDM is characterized by impairment of beta cell function, with resultant insufficient insulin production and diminished tissue sensitivity to insulin (DeFronzo, Ferrannini, and Koivisto, 1983), particularly in the liver and muscles. The diagnosis of NIDDM is commonly made in the course of a routine check-up, perhaps in response to some other problem such as an injury, infection, or myocardial infarction. Often patients with NIDDM do not show the symptoms of diabetes mellitus; they may present polyuria, polydypsia, polyphagia, and weight loss, but less so than patients with IDDM. An acute illness in a patient with NIDDM could necessitate insulin therapy at least until the acute process clears. In elderly debilitated patients with NIDDM and a serious illness superimposed, carbohydrate metabolism can progressively deteriorate and, if adequate water is not consumed, progress to mounting hyperglycemia, hyperosmolar dehydration, renal insufficiency, coma, and death. Treatment of this disorder with appropriate fluids and small doses of insulin (since they are not as insulin-deficient as patients with IDDM) is necessary. The prognosis is often poor, however, due to the superimposed problem (stroke, myocardial infarction, pneumonia, etc.) and the advanced age of the patient (Drapkin and Matz, 1967).

The goal of treatment in diabetes mellitus is to keep the blood sugar at or near normal levels most of the time by diet and perhaps oral hypoglycemic drugs in NIDDM and by diet and insulin in IDDM. Care must be exercised not to keep the blood sugar too low since hypoglycemia could occur, especially with insulin therapy in patients who do not eat regularly. Hypoglycemia could cause confusion, seizures, coma, and, especially in elderly patients, brain damage.

Obviously, reasonable control of homeless diabetic patients is likely to be very difficult in view of their lifestyle and propensity for noncompliance. There are no studies to indicate the impact of diabetes mellitus on homeless people but given the metabolic characteristics of IDDM, home-less people with this disorder are likely to have frequent hospitalizations and significantly increased mortality.

The major long-term consequences of diabetes mellitus involve the larger arteries (arteriosclerosis), microscopic blood vessels (microangiopathy), and the nervous system.

Arteriosclerosis is accelerated in diabetes mellitus. Myocardial infarc-tion is 2–10 times more frequent, peripheral arterial disease 5–10 times more frequent (along with the potential for gangrene and amputation), and strokes are twice as frequent in diabetic patients when compared to nondiabetics. Diabetic patients who survive myocardial infarction have a mortality rate three times that of nondiabetics who survive (Smith, Mar-cus, and Serokman, 1984; Cahill et al., 1986). In the general population as many as 50 percent of amputations in diabetic patients might have been preventable with timely medical treatment (American Diabetes As-sociation, 1984). The percentage of preventable amputations might be even higher in homeless people given their exposure to cold, poorly fit-ting shoes, and penchant for not seeking early treatment for injuries and infections.

Microangiopathy (microvascular disease) resulting from diabetes mel-litus is characterized by changes in the arterioles, capillaries, and venules of every organ and tissue of the body. These changes may correlate more closely to the severity and duration of hyperglycemia than other compli-cations of diabetes (Cahill et al., 1986). Significant microangiopathy of the retina (diabetic retinopathy), often with impaired vision, is present in 75 percent of patients who have had IDDM for at least 20 years. About 5 percent of all patients with IDDM will become blind. Diabetic retino-pathy occurs in 1 of 15 patients with NIDDM and about half of them will become blind. The incidence of cataracts and glaucoma is also substan-tially increased in diabetes. Diabetics are 25 times more prone to blind-ness than nondiabetics (Cahill et al., 1986). Microangiopathy of the renal glomerulus can be observed within two years of the diagnosis of IDDM and about 40 percent of these patients will develop renal failure 20–30 years after its onset. Persistent protein in the urine (proteinuria) is com-monly observed in these patients (Viberti et al., 1982; Anderson et al., 1983). When the microangiopathy involves the skin, it can be a factor in cutaneous infections, poor healing of ulcers or injuries, and gangrene.

Patients with diabetes mellitus often manifest neurologic complications after several years of the disease. Occasionally a neurologic complication such as urinary retention, double vision (diplopia), or burning of the feet can be the initial symptom of diabetes mellitus. About 10 percent of diabetics develop significant neurologic symptoms. The most apparent anatomic change in peripheral nerves is segmental demyelinization (Cahill et al., 1986). Major nerve fibers could be damaged due to occlusion of a nutrient artery from arteriosclerosis or microangiopathy. Cranial nerves, peripheral nerves, the autonomic nervous system (sympathetic and parasympathetic nervous system), and the spinal cord can all be involved in the pathologic metabolic processes of diabetes mellitus.

Involvement of peripheral nerves (diabetic peripheral neuropathy) and the spinal cord (diabetic myelopathy) could cause altered sensation in the lower extremities, including pain, burning, and paresthesia. Often the sensory discomfort of diabetic neuropathy and myelopathy occurs mostly at night. When the autonomic nervous system is affected by diabetic autonomic neuropathy, urinary retention (perhaps with hydroureter, hydronephrosis, and infection), postural hypotension (with increased tendency to fall when arising from a sitting or supine position), gastric atony with dilatation, diarrhea, fecal incontinence, and impotence can occur. Cranial nerve involvement can cause diplopia (double vision). These neurologic complications are disabling in about half the patients who have them. Optimal control of blood glucose may improve nerve conduction (Cahill et al., 1986), commonly impaired in diabetic patients, and prevent or delay long-term neurologic complications.

In homeless people with diabetes mellitus, reduced sensation, particularly in the feet, could increase susceptibility to injury and infection, which could be especially serious when compounded by vascular changes and their unhealthy lifestyle. Diabetes mellitus appears to increase the incidence of many infections including *Staphylococcus* pneumonia and *Klebsella* pneumonia (Edsall, Collins, and Gray, 1970; Khurana, Younger, and Ryan, 1973). Urinary tract infections may be more common in diabetics because of autonomic neuropathy with resultant urinary retention, and the infections are more likely to progress to pyelonephritis, perinephric abscess, papillary necrosis, and bacteremia than in nondiabetics. The reasons for the increased susceptibility of diabetics to serious infections may be related to hyperglycemia, microangiopathy, and impaired immune response, but this has not been clarified.

Diabetes mellitus is yet another disorder that can add substantially to the problems and mortality of homeless people. It is sufficiently common (over 5 percent of the population) to warrant blood glucose tests as part of the routine evaluation of homeless people whenever they receive any type of medical assessment or treatment.

Peripheral Vascular Disease

PERIPHERAL ARTERIAL DISEASE

Peripheral arterial disease causes reduced blood flow to the lower extremities, which could result in ischemic muscle pain with exertion (claudication) and compromise of the vitality of the skin of the feet and toes with impaired healing of injuries and reduced capacity to fight infections. When ischemia of the lower limbs is extreme, pain could occur even at rest. Cigarette smoking and diabetes mellitus are both causes and exacerbating factors in peripheral arterial disease (Hancock, 1983; Cahill et al., 1986). The problems of peripheral arterial disease are compounded in the homeless by their lifestyle, which could include exposure to a subfreezing environment, poorly fitting or badly worn shoes, poor hygiene (including poor nail care), and delay in seeking medical assistance should injury or frostbite occur. Peripheral arterial disease with an injury or infection augmented by the lifestyle of homeless people could lead to gangrene and amputation. The incidence of peripheral arterial disease in homeless people is not known but probably correlates with cigarette smoking, diabetes mellitus, and age, though such complications as gangrene and amputation may be higher with them than in the general population.

The diagnosis can be made by noting reduced or absent arterial pulses in the lower extremities, particularly in people who have lower extremity muscle pain with exertion (claudication) or pain at rest, and in those with frostbite, cyanosis, ulceration, infection, or gangrene of a foot. The Doppler ultrasound techniques for assessing blood flow could be used for confirmation.

Prevention, of course, would be better than treatment, but this is most difficult among the homeless. Any prophylactic measures would involve cessation of smoking, optimal treatment of diabetes mellitus, and keeping the feet warm, dry, clean, and properly shod. Early treatment of injuries, infection, and frostbite would be important in preventing gangrene and amputation. If major occlusive vascular disease is present with ischemic complications in the feet (such as cyanosis, pain when at rest, ulcerations or infections that do not heal), surgical intervention to relieve or bypass the occlusion could prevent gangrene and amputation.

PERIPHERAL VENOUS DISEASE

Venous disease of the lower extremities seems to be more common than arterial disease, or at least it has been better documented. It has been estimated in New York City that 10 percent of homeless people suffer from venous insufficiency (McBride and Mulcare, 1985). This disorder is manifested by the inability of the veins to carry blood out of the lower extremities due to incompetent venous valves and dilatation of veins (varicose veins), which leads to edema (swelling), stasis of blood in the legs, dermatitis secondary to stasis (stasis dermatitis), and then fissures, ulcerations, and perhaps infection of the skin (cellulitis). The congestion and edema of the skin increases its fragility and compromises the skin's viability, which in turn increases susceptibility to infection and poor healing of fissures and ulcers. Inflammation of the veins, thrombophlebitis or venous thrombosis, occurs secondary to venous dilatation and stasis, aggravating the condition by further impeding venous blood flow and adding to the edema and stasis of blood.

Generally the problems of peripheral venous disease arise primarily from chronic insufficiency of the long saphenous vein, which has its origin near the medial malleolus (inner aspect of the ankle), the site of most venous or stasis ulcers. From the medial malleolus the long saphenous vein ascends the medial aspect of the leg and thigh, finally emptying into the femoral vein in the upper anteromedial thigh. When the long saphenous vein is compromised, insufficiency of the deeper venous system (short saphenous vein of the posterior calf, which becomes the popliteal and then femoral vein as it ascends into the thigh) or the communicating veins between the long saphenous and deeper veins could hasten the complications of venous insufficiency, as could congestive heart failure with edema.

The proclivity of street people to sit with their legs dependent on park benches or steps further increases the venous pressure and stasis of blood in the lower extremities. Inadequate housing and clothing are likely to increase exposure to cold and trauma and accelerate devitalization of the skin of the lower extremities, which in turn will enhance the complications of venous insufficiency.

Treatment of venous insufficiency with stasis dermatitis requires reduction of venous pressure, edema, and stasis. The earlier treatment is instituted the less likely ulceration and infection will occur. Compression stockings and avoiding sitting with lower extremities dependent are effective therapeutic measures. Standing should also be avoided because of the associated increase in venous pressure and stasis in the lower extremities. Since walking facilitates driving the blood out of the lower extremities by the contractions of muscles, it should be encouraged. When compression stockings are used, attention must be paid to the arterial circulation since if peripheral arterial disease is present, including the microangiopathy of diabetes mellitus, compression stockings could further reduce the arterial blood supply to the feet and precipitate ischemic complications, including gangrene. If ulceration or infection has occurred, homeless people should be treated in the hospital to ensure optimal treatment. Acute thrombosis (thrombophlebitis) of the long saphenous vein should be treated with bed rest, heat, and elevation for a few days and perhaps a nonsteroidal anti-inflammatory drug (ibuprofen and others) or anticoagulant therapy. Occasionally, if long saphenous vein thrombophlebitis is persistent or recurrent, surgical removal (stripping) of this vein might be necessary. Thrombosis of the deeper veins (short saphenous, popliteal, and femoral) would require a few days of bed rest in a hospital and a few weeks of anticoagulant therapy (parenterally administered heparin initially and then an oral anticoagulant drug), which should be started while the patient is in the hospital. Failure to treat short saphenous-popliteal-femoral vein thrombophlebitis with anticoagulant therapy could lead to pulmonary embolism, which is much less likely to occur with long saphenous vein thrombophlebitis. Outpatient therapy with anticoagulant drugs requires compliance in taking the medication and reliability in reporting for blood tests to monitor the effect of the anticoagulant medication, circumstances unlikely to prevail in the homeless. Hazardous side effects of anticoagulants include hemorrhagic complications such as gastrointestinal and intracranial bleeding, which would be enhanced by falls, other trauma, and alcohol and drug abuse—all common among the homeless.

Parasitic Skin Infestations: Pediculosis and Scabies

Because of the major discomfort such as itching or pain associated with common skin disorders, it is likely that homeless will often seek treatment for these problems. Also, poor hygiene, poor nutrition, and crowded living conditions in the shelters increases the frequency of skin parasites and enhances their spread from one person to another. The two most common diagnoses in the emergency room of a large San Francisco hospital in 1983 were pediculosis (lice) and scabies (Green, 1985).

PEDICULOSIS

Pediculosis can involve the head *(Pediculus humanus capitis),* the body *(Pediculus humanus corporis),* and the pubic area *(Phthirus pubis).* Lice are small wingless flat insects with six legs ending in claws. Unfortunately, humans are the only hosts of these parasites, whose entire life cycle is completed on the host and whose food comes entirely from the frequent sucking of blood from their hapless victim. Head and body lice travel easily by swinging from hair or clothing fibers, which makes them quite mobile and adept at moving from one host to another. Body lice are frequently seen along the seams of clothing removed from infested people. Pubic or crab lice (they look like crabs under the microscope) generally are on or in the skin of the pubic area and inhabit hair only to lay their eggs (nits). Pubic lice are less mobile and require close contact to go from host to host. Cutaneous lesions, associated with itching, lead to scratching, sometimes resulting in excoriations that can become infected. Identification of the offending louse or its eggs (which are in nits on hair) is relatively easy, as is treatment with a topical medication, gamma benzene hexachloride. Proper treatment also requires laundering of the patient's clothes and bed linen; otherwise reinfestation is almost certain to occur. In addition, the patient's close associates may be infested and must be similarly treated if reinfestation is to be prevented. Unfortunately, in shelters for the homeless there could be many people infested, making eradication and control of this parasite extremely difficult.

SCABIES

Scabies is caused by a highly contagious host-specific cutaneous parasitic mite, *Sarcoptes scabe var hominus*. This mite is translucent, eyeless, oval, has eight short legs, and brown spines and bristles. The male mite is 1.2 mm in length and the more common female is 0.3 mm. The female lays 10–25 eggs in burrows dug in the most superficial layer of skin. The resultant skin reaction is a cell-mediated hypersensitivity response (Burkhart, 1983), which may take weeks to develop after the initial infestation but appears more quickly on reinfestation. A rash, minute blisters, and small linear crusts (burrows) associated with intense pruritis are characteristic manifestations. The typical areas involved are the webs of fingers, flexor aspects of wrists, the buttocks, lower back, and scrotum, and the breasts and nipples of women. Occasionally pruritis occurs with very little in the way of skin lesions. Intense scratching can lead to excoriations and skin infection. Other complications from secondary infection, particularly if diabetes mellitus is present, include internal abscesses, pneumonia, septicemia, and secondary impetigo with acute glomerulonephritis (Green, 1985). Immunocompromised hosts could be infested with millions of parasites in crusted, generally nonpruritic lesions which are highly contagious (Farber and Abel, 1979). The mite is spread by close contact with an infected person or the clothes of such a person. The parasite can survive only two to three days in clothes without human contact. The diagnosis can be made with certainty only by direct identification of the mite. Treatment with topical gamma benzene hexachloride is effective so long as clothes and bed linen used within the last three days are laundered and close associates of the infected person simultaneously treated, which is again quite difficult to achieve in the homeless population.

Pregnancy and Infancy

American families are becoming homeless at a progressively increasing rate. It has been estimated that in 1984 homeless families made up 21 percent of the homeless population (U.S. Department of Housing and Urban Development, 1984). Homeless mothers and their offspring are an understudied group, but it seems clear that homeless pregnant women in general receive less prenatal care and deliver lower birthweight babies than women who are not homeless. In addition, newborn infants of homeless mothers are more likely to die within the first year of their lives than those born to women with homes (Vermund, Belmar, and Drucker, 1987).

Homeless families, generally one-parent and female-headed, live in hotels or shelters (Slavinsky and Cousins, 1982; Sebastian, 1985). Approximately 16 percent of the homeless families in New York City include pregnant women who commonly are not able to utilize prenatal care because of the stressful conditions of their living arrangements (Chavkin et al., 1987).

A recent survey of women in New York City who delivered live singleton babies between January, 1982, and June, 1984, compared homeless women living in hotels (401) with poor women living in low-income housing projects (13,247) and all other New York City women residents (241,558) (Chavkin et al., 1987). The homeless and project women were younger and a greater percentage were black and Hispanic than the citywide group. The highest proportion of unmarried women was in the homeless group. About 40 percent of the homeless women received no prenatal care compared with 15 percent of the project women and 9 percent of the women citywide. Sixteen percent of the homeless women delivered babies with birthweights less than 2,500 grams as compared to 11 percent and 7 percent of the project and citywide women, respectively. The lower the birthweight, the higher the infant mortality, which was about 25/1,000 live births for the homeless and 17/1,000 and 12/1,000 for the project and citywide women, respectively.

From this and other investigations one can infer some of the reasons why homeless women living in hotels receive little or no prenatal care. One reason may be that the disruption of their lives due to eviction from their homes or to a fire which forces them to live in a hotel far from their prior residence cuts off their support systems (friends, relatives, income source, food stamp source, and health care facilities) (Fennelly et al., 1979; Cousins, 1983).

The lifestyle of homeless pregnant women and their newborn infants is filled with health hazards. Low birthweight infants have a high enough mortality on their own, but it is worsened by the condition of homelessness. The living arrangements among the homeless are usually crowded due to other children, and often there is no refrigeration for preserving infants' milk formulae and other foods, necessitating time-consuming daily shopping. Mothers harasssed by too many chores may inadequately feed their infants.

By not providing pregnant women and their offspring with adequate health care, housing, and other social support, we burden these unfortunate people needlessly, contribute to high infant mortality, and deprive everyone of potential contributions to society by these young women and their children.

Conclusions and Recommendations

Homelessness is a state which can create and perpetuate poor health for a multitude of reasons, discussed in this chapter. The medical problems of the homeless cannot be treated and resolved effectively until the genesis of homelessness is better understood and appropriate preventive and early intervention measures are utilized.

In the meantime, if the medical plight of the homeless is to be eased, medical evaluation and treatment will have to be made available wherever the homeless congregate, such as in shelters. A medical evaluation of all those in shelters could include a medical history, physical examination, tuberculosis skin test (PPD or Tine), chest X-rays (at least in those who test positive on the tuberculosis skin tests or show respiratory signs or symptoms), electrocardiogram (at least for older people or those with cardiovascular signs or symptoms), and appropriate blood, urine, and stool tests. In this way hypertension, diabetes mellitus, peripheral vascular disease, tuberculosis, pneumonia, veneral disease, parasitic infestation, AIDS, and other diseases could be detected and appropriate treatment utilized or additional diagnostic studies undertaken. Early detection and treatment of most disorders would reduce morbidity and hospitalizations and increase longevity. Furthermore, by identifying those with contagious diseases and by promptly initiating appropriate therapeutic measures, the spread of these diseases could be minimized.

This type of medical assessment and treatment is costly, but not doing it is even more so. Consider the cost of a day, a week, a month, or longer in the hospital compared to the cost of outpatient treatment. Consider the cost to society of untreated or inadequately treated tuberculosis, perhaps drug-resistant, and other contagious diseases that could spread to workers caring for the homeless, their families, and the general population.

The medical and psychosocial problems of the homeless are the problems of all of us, not just the homeless. The moral and physical health of our society can best be measured by the manner in which we deal with the disenfranchised, the poorest of the poor—*our homeless.*

6 | Crisis Shelter and Housing Programs

CAROL L. M. CATON

The homeless have sought shelter in a myriad of settings. Some have taken refuge under bridges, in church doorways, in subway tunnels, or on the heating grates of modern office buildings. Others have gone to low-cost hotels, hospitals, police stations, missions, and shelters. The increased demand for shelter services throughout the 1980s has given rise to new crisis shelters, offering the homeless an alternative to makeshift accommodations and living in streets and byways.

Crisis shelters, targeted to subgroups within the homeless population such as single adult males, single adult females, families, and children and youth, provide a respite from the ravages of homelessness. But they do not solve their housing needs on a long-term basis. More permanent remedies to the homeless problem fall into two general categories: social welfare policy effecting the procurement of low-cost housing and special housing programs for the disabled.

Crisis Shelters

The cornerstone of the provision of housing services to the homeless is the crisis shelter, an institution bearing striking resemblance to the almshouse (see Chapter 1). Although crisis shelters vary considerably in the types of accommodations and services provided, the common denominator is a place to sleep.

With the exception of New York City, which operates 25 shelters for single homeless adults, few local governments (only 6 percent nationwide) operate shelters. Instead, public funds are channeled to private agencies to operate them. Indeed, most shelters in the United States are privately run by voluntary (54 percent) or religious (40 percent) organizations (U.S. Department of Housing and Urban Development, 1984, p. 43). Thus the funding of crisis shelters is largely private; 63 percent of the 1983 operating budgets for all shelters (or $138 million) came from private individual or corporate donations, with the remainder coming from city, county, state, or federal sources. Shelters also receive substantial in-kind donations in the form of voluntary services, food, and clothing (USHUD, 1984, p. 43).

The average cost for a night of lodging in a crisis shelter including all services, is $19 (USHUD, 1984, p. 42). Costs are slightly lower, $14 per night, in those with a bed capacity of 51 or more, and slightly higher, $22 per night, in smaller shelters (bed capacity of 50 or less) (USHUD, 1984, p. 42).

The U.S. Department of Housing and Urban Development (1984) has estimated that on any given night, 111,000 persons can be housed in emergency shelters nationwide. Included in this figure are approximately 12,000 beds for runaway youth and 8,000 beds for battered or abused women. The majority of beds, however, serve single men, single women, and parents with children (USHUD, 1984, p. 34). Nearly half of the shelters in existence today are new, having been founded in the 1980s in response to the increased need for them. Moreover, new expansion efforts are currently underway in many metropolitan areas (USHUD, 1984, p. 34). The policy of housing the homeless in crisis shelters has been sharply criticized by advocacy groups who contend that the $600 or more per person cost each month could be spent on more adequate, permanent housing (Baxter and Hopper, 1981).

Nearly all shelters are open year-round, even though four out of five experience their heaviest use during the winter months (USHUD, 1984, p. 34). The average shelter is of medium size, able to accommodate 53 people per night. However, one in four shelters is large enough to provide lodging for 100 or more persons each night (USHUD, 1984, p. 37).

The majority (75 percent) of crisis shelters restrict admission to certain types of homeless persons, such as single adult women, women and children, and single adult men, primarily because most shelters provide communal sleeping and bath accommodations, and do not have adequate staff to monitor a two-sex situation. Most shelters screen out medical and psychiatric emergencies, referring such persons directly to a hospital. Others refuse admission to those who are serious abusers of drugs or alcohol, or who are violent.

Many shelters impose a limit on length of stay, the average maximum being about two weeks. However, there is considerable variation from one locale to another. New York City municipal shelters do not impose any limit on length of stay by order of a consent decree resulting from a class action lawsuit brought against the City on behalf of the homeless (USHUD, 1984, p. 37). This decree requires that shelter be provided to whomever requests it for as long as needed. Other municipalities have set very strict limits. For example, a privately operated shelter for single men in Miami, Florida, has a maximum stay of seven nights a year so that as many men as possible can be served by the program.

Three out of five shelters allow their guests to remain on the premises all day, but in other cases able-bodied guests are required to leave the premises for an 8- to 10-hour period. Thus, many homeless have no place to go other than transportation depots, parks, abandoned buildings, or the street. Daytime programs for homeless people are not common.

In addition to lodging, most shelters offer food (95 percent of shelters in the 1984 USHUD study), showers or baths (96 percent; USHUD, 1984), laundry facilities (86 percent; USHUD, 1984), clothing (83 percent; USHUD, 1984), and television (86 percent; USHUD, 1984). Psychiatric counseling or referral, most often carried out informally and not necessarily by trained counselors, is available in more than three-fourths of all shelters nationwide. Counseling is *required* in more than one-half of shelters, particularly in the Northeast (USHUD, 1984).

More than two out of three shelters require guests to carry out chores (USHUD, 1984). In some cases guests assist in the operation of a facility by serving as cooks, janitors, or maintenance workers. New York City has piloted a ''work experience'' program in which all employable shelter residents work in the shelter 20 hours per week for an allowance of $12.50 in addition to free food and lodging. Some shelters have employment training services, and nearly two-thirds of all shelters make referrals for housing and jobs.

Utilization Patterns

Despite the steady increase in homelessness in recent years, substantial underutilization of crisis shelter services has been reported (USHUD, 1984;

Rossi, Fisher, and Willis, 1986). During January 1984, shelters across the nation were only 70 percent occupied (USHUD, 1984, p. 39). Even in large Eastern cities, the shelter bed vacancy rate was close to 20 percent. Thus, during the winter months when occupancy should have been at a peak, crisis shelter beds remained unfilled.

What are some of the reasons shelter beds go unused when the homeless problem is on the increase? Rossi et al. (1986) studied attitudes toward shelters among the Chicago homeless. The researchers found that while both frequent and infrequent shelter users viewed shelters as dangerous places, the homeless who spent more time on the streets had markedly more negative attitudes toward shelters. Another significant factor in underutilization is the fact that shelters have rules and regulations, such as not using or possessing drugs or alcohol, not smoking, not assaulting or abusing staff or other shelter residents, and not carrying weapons. Some shelters require advance notice of intention to use their services or have set a specified time for check-in. Once registered, guests must remain in the shelter without leaving and re-entering for the duration of the night. In other cases guests are required to shower or delouse themselves or perform bedmaking or other housekeeping chores. For a portion of the homeless population, such as those who abuse drugs or alcohol or who have a fiercely independent lifestyle, the "structure" of shelters makes them unattractive.

Sometimes guests are refused admission because of previous violations of the rules. According to the national shelter survey, 84 percent of shelters will evict and/or refuse to re-admit persons who possess alcohol or drugs while in the shelter (USHUD, 1984, p. 41). Some shelters, particularly those run by volunteers or church groups, typically ask no questions of those seeking admission and allow guests to return as often as desired without having to explain themselves or agreeing to seek help from counseling or social rehabilitation programs.

The national shelter survey found that the provision of services by shelters, such as job and housing referrals, appear to attract guests. As evidenced in Table 6.1, those shelters having job referrals for their guests had an average occupancy of 75 percent; those without such a service were 60 percent occupied. Similarly, shelters which provided housing referrals were 75 percent occupied compared to a 63 percent occupancy rate for those which did not.

Other reasons why shelters are not always fully occupied include the fact that some people prefer to exist out in the open in parks or beaches in good weather, findings such settings more appealing than shelters. Moreover, another reason for non-use is the fees some shelters charge.

Table 6.1   Average monthly percentage of occupancy in January 1984, for shelters with and without selected requirements and services[a]

	Without	With
Requirements		
Chores	64	69
Must leave during day	70	64
Meeting with caseworker when necessary	65	70
Attendance at religious services	71	67
Services available		
Psychiatric counseling (or referrals)	66	71
Job referrals	60	75
Housing referrals	63	75

[a]The data for this table are from the national shelter survey. Differences are statistically significant at the .05 level.

Source: USHUD, 1984, p. 41.

The USHUD (1984) national shelter survey reports that in Houston, Texas, which has about 2,000 shelter beds for the homeless, the no-fee shelters are most often filled, while the shelter with a $5.00 fee is not utilized to capacity.

The Department of Housing and Urban Development has also noted, in their national shelter survey, that shelters may turn away guests even though they have vacancies (USHUD, 1984, p. 40). The authors of this report suggest that this phenomenon may indicate a highly fluctuating number of people seeking housing each night or a problem of matching homeless people to appropriate shelters.

What Are Shelters Like?

The conditions in present-day shelters, particularly in urban centers, have been described as overcrowded, oppressive (Lipton and Sabatini, 1984; p. 161), dangerous (Hopper, Baxter, and Cox, 1982), unhealthy (Baxter and Hopper, 1981, p. 15), and similar to nineteenth-century almshouses and the worst of public mental institutions (Lipton and Sabatini, 1984). A journalistic account of life at a municipal shelter for men in New York City reported that use of ''crack'' was pervasive and associated with both fighting and theft (Barbanel, Feb. 18, 1988).

Yet, in fact, accommodations provided by crisis shelters vary considerably. Temporary shelters hastily created from armories, church basements, and school gymnasiums often lack privacy because sleeping areas are open and communal. Tens or hundreds may sleep in a single large area, requiring both light and security throughout the nighttime hours. Lavatory facilities are usually inadequate to handle large crowds, and often shelter guests must leave the premises for meals. More permanent shelters, such as those converted from defunct hospitals or other institutions, generally have more adequate sleeping, lavatory, and cooking facilities.

Some established shelters have a communal activities room for table games, music, or television watching. Often smaller shelters are quite homelike, being somewhat similar to group homes or foster family settings. An example is an 18-bed shelter for homeless women in New York City operated by an order of Roman Catholic nuns. Its location is a renovated townhouse, within walking distance of Manhattan's central transportation depots. Staff assist with obtaining entitlements, expediting medical and mental health care, and arranging for more permanent housing at a nearby welfare hotel. Guests sleep in bedrooms shared by two or more persons and take their meals, served family style, in a communal dining room.

Nonshelter Emergency Housing Assistance

In some cases the government pays full price for people to reside in hotels or apartments through the mechanism of temporary vouchers, an alternative to crisis shelters. The Federal Emergency Management Agency, and other federal, state, and local agencies employing block grant funds from the Department of Health and Human Services (USHUD, 1984, p. 36), provide lodging through vouchers to an unknown, but presumably substantial, number of persons. For example, on an average day in January 1984, more than 2,600 families were housed by the City of New York in hotels and apartments until permanent housing was found. Figures are also high for other metropolitan areas (USHUD, 1984, p. 36). The hotels and apartments where homeless persons are placed are profit-making business enterprises that serve nonhomeless as well. Because of their more pressing needs for privacy and access to lavatory and cooking facilities, homeless families are often provided shelter through the voucher system.

In some cases, adequate housing is too costly to be purchased with the modest amount of money available through the voucher system. Consequently, families are placed in run-down welfare hotels to exist in deplorable circumstances. Following is a journalistic account of a New York City welfare hotel.

At the Latham, in the light of bare bulbs and short white strands of neon lights, rats crawl across the floors, and paint peels on the walls. Roaches, water bugs and ants crowd the sinks. Toilets frequently do not work, and repairs are slow. Halls and stairwells reek of mildew, urine and marijuana.

With nothing to fill their days, children scream up and down the littered hallways. Many of their parents say the children are not properly fed. In some cases, four or more people sleep in a room 12-feet square, sharing two twin-size beds.

Sleeping is often impossible. With too many people in too few beds in a small room without air-conditioning or fans, the heat and smell can be stifling. Insects scamper across the bed sheets.

And the walls are thin. Children are awake at all hours. Many wear thongs, which bat against the stairs, making a noise like gunfire. (Shenon, The *New York Times,* August 31, 1983, p. B1)

In some instances homeless families have been placed in expensive hotels when no alternative lodgings have been available. Public outcry at the expenditure of tax monies in this way has surfaced when such incidents have been reported in the mass media. Reaction to a New York City municipal caseworker placing a homeless welfare family in the Waldorf-Astoria in the early 1970s led to the development of an innovative alternative housing program.

Instead of being placed in a welfare hotel, a select number of single homeless mothers—110—were placed in a public housing project (Phillips et al., 1981). An average mother was between the age of 25 and 30, with three or four children. Each family was given access to a live-in social casework team who taught parenting and home management skills to the mothers and assisted with the children's school problems. At the end of six months, mothers sought housing in the open market with their public assistance entitlements. Unfortunately, this project has not been evaluated experimentally to determine its efficacy in reducing recidivism in homelessness. Its cost in public dollars in 1984 was modest; $14 per day for adults, with $9 per day added for each family member.

It has been suggested that public entitlements for welfare mothers should increase rent allowances to keep pace with inflation in the housing market

(The *New York Times,* Sept. 9, 1983). But such a policy is meaningful only when there is available housing for the poor.

Another type of emergency housing assistance is direct payment of rent to prevent evictions and possible homelessness. For example, in Houston, Texas, an association of churches uses donations to make back rent payments for some families. A Portland, Oregon, program offers a $1,000-loan to assist in meeting expenses associated with the move to permanent housing, such as security deposits and move-in fees. Unfortunately, statistics on the number of people served by such programs are not available. It is clear, however, that emergency housing assistance extends well beyond the crisis shelters (USHUD, 1984).

Long-Term Housing for the Homeless

For some, homelessness is a temporary condition that is alleviated by the first paycheck from a new job or by relocation after the destruction of a home through a natural disaster. For others, chronic homelessness has become a way of life. A recent study of New York City shelters revealed that the adult clients interviewed had been staying in shelters for an average of almost one year, and in the current shelter for an average of five months (Crystal and Goldstein, 1984).

There is a pressing need for long-term solutions to the homeless problem geared to the specific needs of individuals to either live independently or in some type of supportive communal setting. The vast majority of the able-bodied employable young men, women, and mothers with children can be "mainstreamed" into open, competitive housing. Government policies which might expedite this goal are those designed to increase the amount of low-cost housing units or enhance the purchasing power of persons on limited income (see Peter Marcuse, Chapter 7).

Types of Community Residence Programs for the Mentally Ill Homeless

The housing problems of the mentally ill homeless cannot be solved merely by increasing public entitlements or creating new housing for the poor. Disabled by the chronic mental disorders from which they suffer, the homeless mentally ill need housing that frequently includes supervision and support. Although community residence programs have increased in the 1980s as a result of initiatives on behalf of the chronically mentally ill (Budson, 1978; President's Commission on Mental Health, 1978; Turner and Tenhoor, 1978; Cournos, 1987), there is still a shortage of appropriate long-term housing for this constituency (Baxter and Hopper, 1981; Sheffer, 1980; USHUD, 1984).

The most rapidly expanding segment of community residential care is the large, multibed, proprietary adult home, a clear-cut business enterprise requiring substantial capital investment and concern for costs and profits (Emerson, Rochford, and Shaw, 1981). Segal and Aviram (1978) report that in California 72 percent of community residences fall into this category, serving 82 percent of the sheltered care population in that state. Many such facilities are staffed by untrained persons without a therapeutic orientation. Reports of inadequate care and supervision and even exploitation of patients has not been uncommon (Van Putten and Spar, 1979).

The needs of the chronically mentally ill for housing, both transitional and long term, are increasingly coming under the purview of mental health care. A 1975 amendment to the Community Mental Health Centers Act (Title III, Public Law 94-63) included the community residence as one of the essential services of a community mental health center. As mental health professionals enter this new area of service responsibility it is useful to review what is known about community residence programs both from an operational perspective and in terms of their effect on patients.

Segal and Aviram (1978) have termed a residential setting that provides supervised living as "sheltered care" and have included in it foster family care, halfway houses, and board and care homes.

Foster Family Care

In *foster family care* a patient lives in a family residence, although there are no kin ties, in a manner similar to family membership. The household head serves as a "sponsor" for one or more patients, who occupy a bedroom that is an integral part of the family dwelling. Privacy can be sought at will in the bedroom, but the patient shares meals and the common rooms with the family. Frequently, the patient is asked to participate in social and leisure activities with the family. In some cases, the patient participates in the family's domestic chores and gets a job to supplement direct payments to sponsors from public or private agencies (Srole, 1977).

Placement of the mentally ill in families other than their own is one of the oldest forms of community care. The tradition of foster families can be traced to Geel, Belgium, the site of a medieval religious shrine dedicated to St. Dymphna, an insane princess. The mentally ill from various parts of Europe traveled to Geel seeking a cure, boarding with families of the colony while attending ceremonies at the shrine. Organized informally until the mid-1800s, foster family care eventually became an important local enterprise and was brought under government regulation.

As the idea of foster family care spread from Geel to other European countries, the number of patients per home grew larger. Linn (1981) reports that placement of one to four patients with a family was typical. However, in Germany, some large villas were converted into family care homes that housed as many as 30 patients.

The concept of family care was introduced to the United States by social reformer Dorothea Dix after a visit to Scotland in 1809. However, the first systematic program of American family care, in Massachusetts, was not established until 1885. Family care programs remained small, despite a resurgence of interest in the 1930s. In 1935, Dr. Horatio M. Pollock touted the advantages of a foster family care system along the lines of Geel for "custodial" cases over long-term state hospital treatment (Pollock, 1936). Foster family care has not, however, achieved widespread acceptance as an alternative community placement for state hospital patients. The largest American program of foster family care, initiated in 1951, is sponsored by the Veterans' Administration and has reached approximately 60,000 veterans.

The foster family care system of Geel survives to the present day and was studied extensively by Srole (1977). In 1971, when Srole was in the midst of his study of the Geel colony, there were 1,200 patients in foster care in this 30,000-member community. No more than two patients are placed in a single home, thus preventing foster care from becoming a major source of a family's income. Geel foster homes are places of residence, not of treatment. A back-up inpatient facility provides crisis intervention when necessary, and staff of the hospital monitor medication. Visits to the foster home by medical personnel are not uncommon, but there is little direct psychiatric treatment rendered to the patient in the foster family.

Srole (1977) investigated 64 patients transferred from a Belgian mental hospital to Geel families from as short a period as six months to as long as seven years post-placement. The majority of patients were middle-aged females, diagnosed as chronic schizophrenics or as mentally retarded. Follow-up, based on information from the clinical staff of the mental health service network serving Geel residents, revealed that only five required rehospitalization due to a deteriorated psychiatric condition. The vast majority (49 cases) of patients were considered relatively well integrated into foster family life. Five-sevenths of the patients who remained in foster care had a positive relationship with their foster mother, undoubtedly a critical factor in the success of the program.

In another work on the Geel system, Pierloot and Demarsin (1981) studied 78 patients in foster family care. They found that most were unmarried and ranged in age from 40 to 60 years. Twenty-eight were mentally retarded, while 41 carried a diagnosis of chronic schizophrenia. Only 58 percent had any contact with their natural families.

Foster family care has not been compared to other types of community living arrangements. Studies to date contrast foster care with long-term hospitalization. Murphy, Englesmann, and Tcheng-Laroche (1976) studied 106 primarily single, middle-aged male chronic schizophrenics in 58 different foster homes in three Canadian provinces. The foster homes were quite varied, ranging in size from less than 5 to 30 patients, and in most cases were operated by nonprofessionals. An 18-month follow-up compared the foster home patients with 28 control patients who remained in the hospital for administrative reasons. Both foster home and hospitalized patients experienced a substantial decline in symptoms, but neither group displayed any differences in social functioning.

Another comparison of foster family care with continued hospitalization was reported by Linn et al. (1977), who studied 572 psychiatric inpatients, 71 percent of whom were diagnosed as schizophrenic, at five Veterans' Administration hospitals. Before discharge, the 210 patients randomly assigned to foster care were prepared for placement with an average of 44 days of individual casework or a combination of casework and group therapy. Following baseline assessments, patients were evaluated again at placement and at four months and one year after discharge to a foster home. At four months, two-thirds of those placed were still in foster care and foster home patients had improved social functioning. At the end of one year, 88 percent of foster home patients were still living in the community. Patients diagnosed as suffering from chronic brain syndrome had the highest failure rate in foster care. Once placed, schizophrenics did as well as nonschizophrenics.

Keskiner and Zalcman (1974) developed a foster community model patterned after the Geel colony in two small Missouri towns, Troy and New Haven. The researchers encouraged local participation by educating the citizens about mental illness. Patient participants in the program, selected from a state hospital, were prepared for the community program by learning social and daily living skills while still in the hospital. Although the program was initially designed solely for foster family care, a component in which two or three patients were housed in an apartment under the supervision of community volunteers was added due to low community participation and the inability of some patients to tolerate the intimacy of family living. So far a controlled study of the program devised by Keskiner and Zalcman has not been done.

Advocates of foster family placement assert that it facilitates social adaptation as compared to when patients live with their natural kin. This is hard to prove because patients typically seek foster family placement only after natural family supports have been lost. Dynamic aspects of foster family environments, such as the level of interpersonal stress or degree of isolation of the patient, deserve as much attention in studies of foster care as they receive when the patient is residing with kin. Moreover, inclusion of foster family members in the patient's treatment might benefit the patient's adjustment in that setting.

Halfway Houses

Halfway houses are transitional living settings located off the grounds of a mental hospital. Their goal is to smooth the transition from the protected environment of the mental hospital to the demands of community life (Reik, 1953; Raush and Raush, 1968; Glasscote, Gudeman, and Elpers, 1971). In contrast to other types of community residences, halfway houses have closer ties to mental health professionals and a more therapeutic orientation (Landy and Greenblatt, 1965; Rothwell and Doninger, 1966; Raush and Raush, 1968; Glasscote et al., 1971). The most successful halfway houses are small enough (not more than 30 residents) for people to get to know one another and so provide mutual support. Supervision is provided by live-in houseparents who often attempt to create a familylike atmosphere (Budson, 1978). Halfway houses are open settings, but they usually have rules governing curfews, use of alcohol and drugs, and sexual behavior. Psychiatric and other medical and support services are obtained from outside programs. Residents typically work outside of the home during the day; however, they share meals and household chores.

The first halfway houses were founded as private, nonprofit corporations, but now sponsorship by public agencies is common. In most cases, residents' fees make up only part of the funding of halfway houses.

American halfway houses, which have their roots in British hostels of the nineteenth century, are a post-World War II phenomenon. Prior to

1954, the three halfway houses that existed were all in rural settings and were guided by the philosophy that a return to a simpler, more natural life was preferable. Rutland Corner House in Boston, which grew out of a shelter for distressed women set up in the 1870s, was the first of the modern, urban halfway houses. Since its establishment in 1954, halfway houses for the mentally ill have mushroomed across the country. Raush and Raush (1968) located 40 in the mid-1960s, and by 1970 there were 128 halfway houses in 90 cities (Glasscote et al., 1971). A National Institute of Mental Health survey in 1973 (Ozarin and Witkin, 1975) uncovered 209 halfway houses. There are undoubtedly countless others which have arisen since the 1975 amendment to the Community Mental Health Centers Act (Title III, Public Law 94-63) mandated transitional halfway house programs.

The first halfway houses were free-standing, and many had no close ties to mental hospitals and psychiatric outpatient programs. Since then, Raush and Raush (1968) found that although two-thirds of halfway houses are supervised on a day-to-day basis by nonprofessionals, a mental health professional was involved in the administration of most residences. A minority (19 percent) of halfway houses provide shelter only, 37 percent provide vocational services and 23 percent give counseling or guidance (Glasscote et al., 1971), reflecting their more therapeutic orientation. The profile of halfway houses emerging from the Glasscote study was that they were relatively small (an average of 22 residents, although the range was from 4 to 200) and had a duration of stay of four to six months. A little less than half (47 percent) limited their clientele to the mentally ill. The majority served the mentally ill along with alcoholics (27 percent), mental defectives (25 percent), drug addicts (11 percent), former convicts (11 percent), and the physically handicapped (8 percent).

Patients in halfway houses have widely varying clinical and social characteristics. However, halfway houses, more than other types of community residential programs, serve a younger, less chronically disturbed population. Segal and Aviram (1978) rated patients on level of distress and symptomatology in halfway houses, foster family care, and board and care homes. They found that halfway houses accept patients who were more verbal and had greater insight into their problems than those admitted to foster family care and board and care homes.

Although halfway houses have existed in the United States for over a quarter century, studies comparing their efficacy with other types of community residential programs are lacking. Moreover, comparisons of halfway houses which have different programs or treatment philosophies have not been done. Rog and Raush (1975) studied former residents of 36 halfway houses and found that 55.2 percent were employed or in school, 58.2 percent were living independently in the community, and only 20.5 percent were rehospitalized.

Other uncontrolled studies of patients admitted to specific halfway houses (Landy and Greenblatt, 1965; Grob and Singer, 1974) indicate that patients selected for admission are able to move on to more independent living arrangements. Studies have been skewed, however, to facilities serving middle- and upper-class patients. For example, in Grob and Singer's study of 75 ex-residents of Berkeley House (former McLean Hospital patients), 90 percent were between the ages of 17 and 24 and were from the middle or upper classes.

Although initially conceived as transitional living settings, some (Glasscote et al., 1971; Budson, 1978) have advocated expanding the function of the psychiatric halfway house to include long-term sheltered care or even to act as a permanent substitute for hospitalization.

The Community Lodge

Community lodges are similar to halfway houses, but they tend to be long-term rather than temporary. One novel community residence program was that initiated by Fairweather et al. (1969) in Palo Alto, California. A group of 33 patients with histories of multiple psychiatric hospitalizations were trained to live and work together as a "small society" in a community setting without staff in residence. They set up their living arrangements to be economically self-sustaining and free of intervention by mental health professionals. Selected for the lodge program during a hospitalization episode, they were prepared for community living and group relation issues through therapy during the inpatient phase. The importance of group decision-making, employment, money management, and peer social support were emphasized in the creation of a social environment in which members would take mutual responsibility for each other's welfare.

Staff assisted the patients in finding a suitable house and upon discharge helped them learn to maintain it independently. An experienced psychologist became the lodge coordinator. This role, which has been described by Fairweather as like a "teacher," was to "push, cajole, shape, and urge the group of ex-patients towards ultimate autonomy" (Fairweather, 1980, p. 19). The coordinator visited the lodge on a daily basis to supervise medication, provide job counseling, and deal with problems in interpersonal relationships. Lodge members established a janitorial and gardening business that eventually enabled the patient group to be self-supporting. A community-based physician was contracted to provide for lodge members' medical needs. He treated them in his private office, consistent with efforts to make relationships with the community at large as natural as possible. The level of involvement of the lodge coordinator was reduced as the group became more self-sufficient. After four years, the role of lodge coordinator was turned over to a layperson. Thus, the lodge society gradually became independent of the mental health service system.

Treatment of patients in the lodge program was compared to routine outpatient care and treatment in residence programs such as halfway houses. All patients completed the same small-group hospital treatments program before random assignment to treatment and control groups. The lodge program was effective in reducing recidivism, as evidenced by the fact that lodge residents spent about 98 percent of their time in the community during the first year in contrast to less than 30 percent for controls. During the second year, median percent time in the community was about 95 percent for lodge members and 30 percent for controls. Moreover, lodge members spent significantly more of their time in gainful employment than controls. During the first year, the median percent time in gainful employment was more than 50 percent for lodge members in contrast to minimal employment in the control group.

Lodge programs have been established in many other settings, albeit with many adaptations (Fairweather, 1980). An Alaskan group set up a house-cleaning business (Daggett, 1971) and in Williamsburg, a group of women who live together have formed a corporation in which they work at different jobs rather than conduct a single business. The inpatient phase has been dropped from most new lodge programs, and some, such as Cleveland's Panta Rhei, include group living in apartments.

Satellite Housing

Satellite housing, or "supervised apartments," is the term used to describe the sponsorship of independent community housing, such as apartments, duplexes, or small single-family dwellings, by treatment or rehabilitative agencies on behalf of the discharged patient. Housing is leased by the sponsoring agency or jointly with the patient. Patients occupy the apartments, usually in small groups of two to five, without live-in staff. Supervision is available from the sponsoring agency. Lamb (1981) has pointed out that satellite housing comes closest to a genuine natural community living arrangement.

The need for permanent housing in the period after release from halfway houses has stimulated the development of satellite housing. Fountain House, a social rehabilitation center in New York City, is credited with the innovation of using apartments for patient housing. In a typical satellite housing program, the sponsoring organization finds an apartment for the patient and may at first pay the full cost of rent and utilities. Apartment leases are eventually taken over by patients, who remain as long as they are willing and able to meet their contractual obligation. In the satellite housing program developed by the El Camino halfway house in San Mateo, California, from two to four residents who lived together in the halfway house are placed together in a shared apartment (Richmond, 1969). Similar satellite housing programs developed from Washington, D.C.'s Woodley House (Kresky, Maeda, and Rothwell, 1976) and Brooklyn's Boerum Hill. In some programs, patients are referred directly from the hospital or an outpatient clinic to an apartment in the community (Sandhall, Hawley, and Gordon, 1975), bypassing halfway houses. Another modification of the satellite housing concept is Goldmeier et al.'s (1978) program providing for temporary (Type A) and long-term (Type B) housing. In the first instance, the agency holds the lease, and in the latter case leases are held by residents. A program in Topeka, Kansas (Bowen and Fry, 1971), rents houses, into which patients move directly after discharge from hospital.

Board and Care Homes

Board and care homes are distinguished by their large size (typically 50 beds or more, but some running into the hundreds), entrepreneurial auspice, and nonaffiliation with a mental health facility. This type of open community residence provides a shared room, three meals a day, housekeeping services, and supervision of medications by a physician under contract to the operator (Lamb, 1981). A typical fee of $20 per day (in New York State) is charged. Staff are usually nonprofessional and care is custodial rather than actively therapeutic.

Board and care homes have rapidly taken over the custodial function of the state hospital. Lamb and Goertzel (1977) report that in California, 50 percent of long-term patients with a psychotic diagnosis and under age 65 live in such settings.

As with halfway houses, the mentally ill live with other disabled groups, such as the mentally retarded or frail elderly. However, unlike halfway houses, board and care homes are not therapeutically oriented. Segal and Aviram (1978) found that although the homes had some organized activities, they were usually voluntary. Approximately 50 percent of the California board and care homes which they studied had a curfew, and 82 percent had a system for dispersal of medication. Even when there were no curfews or bedchecks, meal hours were fixed and no drinking was allowed. Operators of such homes typically play a "parental" role; in half of the board and care homes studied by Segal and Aviram (1978) the operator controlled the patient's spending money. Similarly, Lamb (1981) found that a patient's personal funds were managed by staff in the California board and care home he studied.

The typical sheltered care resident in Segal and Aviram's (1978) study was between 50 and 65 years of age, white, Protestant, unemployed, and on Supplemental Security Income (SSI). Most were leading a fairly settled life in a facility not far from his or her home town.

In Lamb's (1981) study of one California board and care home, the median age of residents was 39 years. There were twice as many men as women. Most (86 percent) were on SSI and had a median of 18 months of prior hospitalization. Although duration of residence in the home ranged from four days to nearly 15 years, a median length of stay in the home was 32 months. Forty-two percent lived in the home for at least five years. Most (92 percent) residents were prescribed major tranquilizers, but 63 percent had no contact with a mental health professional other than the psychiatrist who visited the facility for medication management.

In a clinical interview, Lamb (1981) determined that 32 percent of residents of one home had experienced a hospitalization episode within the past year. About 90 percent either never tried to live alone (27 percent) or failed in their attempt to live independently (62 percent). Although 55 percent had some contact with family in the previous three months, 45 percent were isolated from kin.

Alternative Community Residences

The homeless crisis of the 1980s has produced other innovative housing programs for the chronically mentally ill. One such program is New York City's St. Francis Residence. Founded in 1980 by two Franciscan priests, the Residence occupies an old single room occupancy hotel, purchased with funds raised through voluntary contributions, private foundation support, and federal loans. After the hotel was renovated, its 101 rooms were rented out to the homeless mentally ill, who pay the average rent of $170 per month with public entitlements such as Supplemental Security Income. Revenues from rent are adequate to support the day-to-day operation of the Residence.

Residents have their own bedrooms but share communal lavatories. Breakfast and dinner are provided Monday through Friday. The Residence has a close collaborative alliance with local hospitals for the provision of medical and psychiatric care. There is an on-site mental health screening and counseling service funded by the city government that operates daily during the week. The program seeks out adults with a primary psychiatric diagnosis but no active homicidal or suicidal behavior who are socially adapted enough to benefit from the services provided through the Residence.

In a preliminary evaluation of the Residence, 49 homeless chronically mentally ill subjects were randomly assigned at hospital discharge to either this facility or the usual postdischarge care. Subjects were followed at four-month intervals for one year. Although the sample size was small and attrition from the study was high, subjects in the residential program had more nights of adequate shelter, spent fewer nights in the hospital or homeless, and were more satisfied with and committed to their living arrangements (Lipton, Nutt, and Sabatini, 1988).

Issues in Community Residential Care

Facility Size

Size is an important determinant of the location of a facility in the community. In some states, such as California and Wisconsin, small facilities (those from one to six beds) can qualify as single family units under state zoning laws. In Segal and Aviram's (1978) study of sheltered care in California, more than half of the small facilities were found in residential areas. Although regulations vary from state to state, intermediate-sized facilities (more than 6 but under 50) are considered group living, enabling their establishment in residential areas. Large facilities (more than 50 beds) are more definitely considered business operations and are in commercial districts.

Segal and Aviram (1978) reported that larger homes were associated with the entry of entrepreneurs into the sheltered care industry. About 9 percent of the sheltered care facilities in their study (the larger ones) served about one-fifth of the population. They also noted that community residences operated as businesses evoked a more negative reaction from patients than facilities run under other auspices. Thirty-seven percent of facilities run as businesses were viewed favorably by residents in contrast to 62 percent of other facilities.

It is often asserted that larger facilities are more institutionlike, and there is limited evidence that size alone has a critical impact on a patient's well-being. In one of the only studies of the relationship or characteristics of community residences to patient outcome, Linn, Klett, and Caffey (1980) found that patients in larger homes (more institutionlike) showed a decline in social functioning. Although this investigative group has advocated the "wisdom of Geel" by limiting the size of family care homes to no more than two patients per home, the issue of optimal size of community residences deserves further study and evaluation.

Operator Characteristics

The relative independence of sheltered care from the formal mental health delivery system has produced a cadre of facility operators with little or no professional training. Although it has been suggested that foster families be screened for psychopathology and alcoholism (Milosak and Basic, 1981), Baxter (1980) reports that in Geel, Belgium, a family's psychiatric history is not a consideration in the selection of foster homes. The tradition of foster families is transmitted from generation to generation, as evidenced by the fact that 75 percent of the foster families in Srole's (1977) study had relatives who took in "boarders." Families are given no formal training. Instead, they are expected to rely on intuitive understanding and skill acquired through their own life experiences and observations of friends and relatives who have taken on "boarders" in the past.

The economic motive is strong for shelter operators, as Srole (1977) noted in his study of Geel foster families. Segal and Aviram (1978) found that many sheltered care operators had backgrounds as hospital attendants or vocational nurses, and used the board and care home business as a vehicle for upward mobility. Seventy-five percent of the facilities were owned and operated by the same person, who experienced upward mobility in contrast to a previous occupation. Fifty-eight percent of the operators derived only part of their income from this activity. Most board and care home operators were women, over age 50, and married, and half of them were black.

In Beatty and Seeley's (1980) study of operators of 39 foster homes, the typical operator was a woman who had gained caretaking skills as a result of raising a family. Such women had had little formal education and no previous work experience. The skill of typical sheltered care staff in forming relationships which are beneficial to patients is an area in need of research and assessment.

Therapeutic Orientation

Many community residences provide shelter only. A patient is expected to make independent arrangements for psychiatric treatment. The exception is the larger board and care home in which medication maintenance is provided. In contrast, social therapy is built into Fairweather's lodge program and some halfway houses. A patient's daily activities are highly structured and there is every expectation that the patient will engage in competitive employment, sheltered work, or otherwise make productive use of his or her time.

Edelson (1976) has noted that a key factor in residential treatment is the extent to which the resident is "enveloped" by a housing facility, meaning the extent to which the facility limits the number of life choices the resident is free to make. *High envelopment* facilities, exemplified by hospitals and nursing homes, are often locked and have intensive round-the-clock supervision for severely disabled patients who present problems in management. *Midrange envelopment* facilities include open residences with some programmed social activities. Those settings most like natural living arrangements are termed *low envelopment* environments.

Community residences have also been classified by the activities of typical residents. *High expectation* environments encourage participation in activities involving society-at-large to the greatest possible extent. Budson (1978) defines "high expectation" as a situation in which residents are required to be attending school or working. An *intermediate expectation* environment is when residents are actively engaged in a day hospital program, an ex-patient social club, or a sheltered workshop. A *low expectation* environment leaves a patient to his or her own devices for meaningful use of time. There is virtually no attempt to involve the patient in work and social activities, or even such leisure activities as reading, art, theater, or crafts. Because no alternative for social and cultural stimulation is offered, television is often the primary link with the outside world in low expectation settings.

There have been few studies of the impact of environmental characteristics of sheltered care facilities on a patient's well-being. Linn et al. (1980) studied foster families and found that the presence of young children in the home was associated with improved adjustment in patients. Noting that there is an air of normality when there are children at play, this investigative team speculated that the spontaneity of children in social relations may have benefitted patients.

Linn et al. (1980) also found that a greater amount of sponsor-initiated activity in the home was associated with improvements for all but those carrying a diagnosis of schizophrenia. For schizophrenics, a highly stimulating environment was associated with deterioration in functioning. More intense supervision produced the same results—deterioration in schizophrenics but improvement in nonschizophrenics. Other studies have shown hyperarousal to be associated with deterioration in chronic schizophrenic patients (Venables and Wing, 1962). Brown, Birley, and Wing (1972) have warned that overly active efforts to rehabilitate long-term schizophrenics may lead to sudden relapse. Likewise, May (1976) has concluded that high stimulus input and role diffusion are disastrous to people who have deficiencies in perception, attention, and information processing. Clearly, the degree of stimulation and arousal provided in different types of living settings needs to be carefully assessed (Cournos, 1987).

A number of research approaches to assessing aspects of the social environment have been devised, such as the Community Oriented Programs Environment Scale (COPES) (Moos and Otto, 1972), and could be useful in studies in this area (Segal and Aviram, 1978; Coulton, Fitch, and Holland, 1985). Lamb and Goertzel (1972) studied a high expectation community program, which included a day treatment center and vocational rehabilitation services as well as a halfway house. The patient's level of social and vocational functioning was improved although the high expectation setting was no more effective than a low pressure setting in keeping patients out of the hospital.

Resident Characteristics

Budson (1978) maintains that there are two kinds of clients likely to benefit from halfway house programs. One is the chronic long-term patient who has been in the hospital so long that contact has been lost with family and friends. The second type is the young isolated adult who has suffered from a chronic psychotic illness for a number of years and has experienced severe social isolation during the critical developmental phase of late adolescence and young adulthood. After a brief period of hospitalization the patient either cannot return home due to parental rejection or because the atmosphere at home places the patient in a situation in which he is likely to regress to a dependent, nonfunctioning condition.

Glasscote et al. (1971) and White (1981) have pointed out that in the selection of patients for community residences, behavior is more relevant than diagnosis. Patients who display behavior that is dangerous or disturbing to themselves or others are greater risks in a community setting, particularly if the residence staff is unskilled or unprepared to deal with such problems. Violent patients are excluded from some community residence programs (Keskiner and Zalcman, 1974). Moreover, when residents display behavior that is intolerable to the community-at-large, the very existence of the residence program can be threatened. Alcoholism, drug addiction, violence, and deviant sexual behavior are the most common characteristics for exclusion from halfway houses (Raush and Raush, 1968; Glasscote et al., 1971), particularly if they are current.

Among those gaining acceptance into community residences, there are patients with specific clinical characteristics whose management is particularly problematic. White (1981) lists seven types of difficult patients: the paranoid patient, the medication-refusing patient, the "entitled" (demanding) patient, the assaultive patient, the medically ill patient, the patient over- or underinvolved with his or her family, the suicidal patient, and the community provocateur.

Although staff are not always professionally trained, they need to know how to handle psychiatric emergencies, such as what to do in case of overdose and how to control an assaultive patient. Staff should be aware of regulations and procedures governing restraint and emergency use of medication. A strong therapeutic alliance between residents and staff can ameliorate or forestall many difficult clinical situations. For example, patients are less likely to assault staff members with whom they have a positive and trusting relationship. Moreover, a strong therapeutic alliance with a patient refusing medication may result in improved compliance.

Patients who are frequently assaultive can be a management problem if they are placed in a community residence that lacks sufficient staff and a seclusion room. In fact, admission of violent patients is probably contraindicated. Management of infrequently assaultive patients is made easier when the circumstances associated with previous episodes of assault are known so that more accurate predictions of future violence can be made. A firm, calm, businesslike approach to the problem can preserve the patient's sense of dignity and self-respect by giving the patient a choice in the treatment plan, such as going to the hospital or taking additional medication. Early intervention and early recognition of symptoms of decompensation, before the onset of psychosis, is important in patients with a history of violence.

Segal and Aviram (1978) found that complaints from the "outside" world, more likely for patients rehospitalized in the past year, condition facility operators to seek services. Operators who use services more frequently have a treatment orientation and a larger, more "professional" facility. The Segal and Aviram study found that social workers were selected 42 percent of the time to deal with problems in a residence, general practitioners 20 percent, and psychiatrists 15 percent. Seventy-five percent of operators sought help for suicide attempts, refusal to take medications, sexual acting out, or disorganization in the patient. In smaller familylike homes, operators were more likely to seek help if the patient did not pay rent or misbehaved sexually.

Resident Mix

Unlike mental institutions, patients in community residences have an opportunity to live with nonpatients. A 1979 study of adult home residents in New York State revealed that only 29 percent of residents of such settings were former mental patients, sharing their fate with a variety of disability groups such as the frail elderly, the mentally retarded, and the mildly medically ill. According to some, the deliberate mixing of patients with those having no known history of psychiatric problems provides role models for patients to follow in social and work adjustment (Doninger, Rothwell, and Cohen, 1963; Bennett, 1964; Gumruku, 1968). Nonpatient residents have lived with the mentally ill at San Francisco's Conrad House (Gumruku, 1968). In addition, Harvard and Radcliffe undergraduates have lived with the mentally ill at Welmet, a halfway house in Cambridge, Massachusetts (Kantor and Greenblatt, 1962). At halfway houses in a YMCA (Baganz et al., 1971) and in a mid-Manhattan hotel, former patients have lived with residents who have no known psychiatric history. Doninger, Rothwell, and Cohen (1963) concluded from their experience at Woodley House that halfway houses should board two or three healthy people.

It is unfortunately not known how the mixing of the mentally ill with nonpatients influences their social adjustment, or whether a mixed resident group is more willing and able to interact with the world outside the residence than a facility made up only of the mentally ill. Future research on community residences should explore the effect of resident mix on patient adjustment and relationships inside and outside the home.

Community Reaction

From their inception in the United States, community residences have been vulnerable to the rejection of the community. In Raush and Raush's (1968) study of halfway houses, 17 of 40 experienced some kind of trouble in relation to the community at the beginning of the project. As these authors point out, "People may favor the idea of a halfway house, but like a fire department, no one wants it next door" (Raush and Raush, 1968, p. 52).

Segal and Aviram (1978) have noted that community reaction to residences seems to be based on a stereotyped fear response to the mentally ill, an actual threat to the community posed by the former patient group in terms of norm-violating behavior (such as loitering, odd, or bizarre behavior), and a concern that the value of property will decline in those areas of the community where the mentally ill reside in large numbers.

The fear expressed by community members toward the mentally ill is largely the result of the stereotyped notion that mental disorder is characterized by unpredictable and irrational behavior (Starr, 1955; Cumming and Cumming, 1957). Although studies in California and New York report high arrest and conviction rates among discharged patients for murder (California State Dept. of Health, 1973; Sosowsky, 1974; Zitrin et al., 1976), even the highest crime rate reported indicates that only 31 of 10,000 former patients represent a real threat to others (California State Dept. of Health, 1973). There is weak evidence to suggest that the average mental patient is an unusually and predominantly dangerous person. However, the crime rate is higher for younger than older former patients (Sosowsky, 1974).

Evidence regarding the actual impact of sheltered care facilities on property values is scarce, but indicates little, if any, effect occurs (Dear, 1977). Neighborhoods likely to attract a heavy concentration of sheltered care homes are often on the decline. The homes may, in fact, serve to revitalize the economic situation in the area. Using data from a county assessor's office, Garr (1973) found a steady increase over a five-year period in property values in an area with many sheltered care facilities.

Hazelton, Mandell, and Stern (1975) conducted a survey in Santa Clara County, California, and found that the social distance between the mentally ill and the general public is smaller than imagined. Eighty-three percent of neighborhood residents claimed to be willing to have a formerly hospitalized patient live in a supervised facility on their block, and 78 percent were willing to have the ex-patient as a next door neighbor. However, the community was unfamiliar with the treatment of mental illness and uninformed about the location and nature of treatment facilities.

In a study of public reaction to treatment facilities in Toronto, Dear and Taylor (1979) again found a low level of public awareness of existing mental health facilities. Only slightly more than one-third (36 percent) of respondents who lived within one-fourth mile of a mental health facility were aware of its existence. Only 13 percent of the 1,091 respondents in this study were outright opposed to having a mental health facility near them, although 12 percent rated a location within 7 to 12 blocks as undesirable to some degree, 22 percent revealed that a location within 2 to 6 blocks was undesirable, and 37 percent would find a facility within one block undesirable. However, survey questions posed hypothetical situations about the presence of shelters in one's neighborhood or section of a city, and did not relate to shelters that actually existed.

Exploring the issue of public reaction to mental health facilities further, Rabkin, Muhlin, and Cohen, (1984) conducted a telephone survey in three New York City boroughs in order to assess the impact of proximity to psychiatric facilities on attitudes toward the mentally ill. Ninety subjects who lived within one block of a designated psychiatric facility (a small residential facility, an outpatient clinic, or an SRO hotel) were queried along with a control group of 90 respondents not residing close to such an establishment. Respondents in this study were middle-aged, white collar, and well educated, and had lived at the same address for an average of nine years. It was found that attitudes toward mental illness and about the dangerousness of mental illness were not related to proximity to such facilities. A key finding was that three-fourths of those living within one block of selected facilities were unaware of their presence. Findings indicate that community psychiatric programs or shelters do not necessarily constitute a personal or community burden as far as neighbors are concerned. Ninety percent of respondents were unprepared to oppose the establishment of a mental health facility on their block. Indeed, the majority were not concerned about the effect of mental patients on their personal safety, property values, or neighborhood reputation.

Location of Community Residences

Community reaction toward residences for the mentally ill can be accounted for in part by the high concentration of facilities in a given geographic area, resulting in high visibility of ex-patients in the streets. For example, Sheffer (1980) cites that a 44-block area (72nd to 116th Street) in Manhattan's Upper West Side has had approximately 7,000 to 10,000 former mental patients. On one block (West 94th Street), there were five hotels housing ex-patients. Many former patients have lived in run-down and physically inadequate single room occupancy hotels.

Overconcentration of the mentally ill has prompted the city of Long Beach, New York, to pass an explicit exclusionary ordinance preventing persons requiring continuous psychiatric or medical services from registering in local hotels. In addition to this, there are innumerable ways in which board and care homes have been discouraged, both informally and legally.

Raush and Raush (1968) state that a community residence cannot avoid public confrontation in a small town or in a well-established, stable residential community. Indeed, locating a community residence in such a setting requires that confrontation be planned for. Quite different, however, are highly urbanized, somewhat transitional neighborhoods in large cities. Woodley House, in Washington, D.C., is in a "busy, mind your own business" neighborhood (Rothwell and Doninger, 1966) in which apartments, hotels, boarding houses, stores, and private homes are mixed in a middle-class section of the city. Facilities in such settings do not depend on the immediate local neighborhood for work or social opportunities. Because such neighborhoods are anonymous, the house can more easily maintain its own anonymity and protection from too many social pressures. Meenach (1964) recommends that psychiatric facilities be placed in neighborhoods zoned for business in or near a residential area, within walking distance to shops and churches, near public transportation, with well-lighted streets and police patrols, and near food markets. Hull and Thompson (1981) concur that a central location is optimal. Rural homes are more apt to be self-contained in terms of both work and social activities.

Segal and Aviram (1978) have confirmed that the closer a facility is to community resources and medical and social services, the greater the level of social integration of its residents. Middle-class neighborhoods composed of single-family homes may have a negative impact on the external integration (relationships of patients with the community) of residents because of such neighborhoods' distance from shopping areas, parks, libraries, theaters, and community centers. Psychiatric facilities in downtown areas are more likely to be closer to community resources and medical and social services and therefore tend to enhance the residents' social integration, as the facilities will tend to rely on programs already existing outside them than to develop their own internally oriented programs. In addition to the distance factor, middle-class areas tend to be characterized by more stable family networks. Socialization among these networks and disaffiliated individuals is difficult.

In terms of the procedure of setting up community residences, there are different philosophies. For example, Rothwell and Doninger (1966), when setting up Woodley House in Washington, D.C., moved in quietly, without informing the neighborhood of what they were doing, believing that the trouble with asking permission of too many people is that you might not get it. An opposing view, expressed by Levy (1980), contends that it's absurd to keep a low profile and assume that sneaking a facility past the neighborhood will work. Stickney (1980) advocates deliberate, cooperative planning at all levels of government and among various human service systems in order to avoid overconcentration of community residences in certain areas. Assessment of community attitudes, early involvement of local leaders and public officials, public education with the assistance of the mass media, organizing support in local mental health groups and political and civil organizations, and establishing a community advisory board can help to ensure the success of a new program.

There is no agreement on optimal patient density, yet policies concerning zoning of community residences are designed to prevent overconcentration. The patient density at Geel is 40 per 1,000 resident population (Srole, 1977). A program of community residential care with this level of density is feasible if instituted slowly and with thorough community preparation and participation. Greater patient density in foster family care, however, is more cost-efficient in delivery of professional and paraprofessional services for families and patients in the system.

Some states, such as Wisconsin (Cupaiuolo, 1980), grant community residences with up to eight persons with social, physical, or mental disabilities permission to locate in a single family use zone without the need for a zoning variance. Larger facilities (up to 46 residents) can be set up in other zones without applying for a variance. Overconcentration is controlled by granting municipalities the right to prohibit community residences from being established within 1,500 feet of each other. Density is monitored by allowing a municipality to prohibit additional community residences once the number of persons served already exceeds 100, or 1 percent of the population. Policies on zoning can facilitate the social integration of patients into their local communities if they are thoughtfully implemented.

7 | Homelessness and Housing Policy

PETER MARCUSE

Is Homelessness a Housing Problem?

Is homelessness a housing problem? An odd question, on the face of it—of course lack of housing is a housing problem. What's meant by the question, though, runs deeper. If the homeless are homeless because they have deep-seated personal problems, then merely providing housing may not be of much help. What would be needed are social services, medical care, group support perhaps, education and training, psychiatric care, or moral or social rehabilitation, going beyond "mere" housing.

In any discussion of what homelessness means, "shelter," "home," and "housing" must be distinguished from each other:

- *Shelter* means the basic physical structure that provides protection against the elements, minimally including four walls and a roof[1];
- *Home* is shelter that provides not only physical adequacy as shelter but also privacy, personal safety, security of occupancy, comfort, space for essential residential activities (varying both historically and with the individual, but typically including in the United States today cooking, eating, sleeping, child raising, tending to personal affairs, and social interaction both within the household and with outsiders), control of the immediate environment, and accessibility, all within a neighborhood that permits the home to fulfill its functions. It involves a set of relationships between a person and his or her housing that supports a

deeply felt personal (and socially conditioned) feeling of identity, belonging, security[2];

- *Housing* is the comprehensive term covering any living accommodation (including its neighborhood) from a minimal shelter to an ideal home. Good housing provides homes; bad housing provides only shelter. A housing problem is one that arises from the system of providing housing or that can be remedied by changes in that system.

The aim of this essay is to determine whether homelessness, using these concepts, is a housing problem or whether it is caused by something else. Understanding the causes of homelessness is critical for clarifying the goals of a policy designed to address it.

This chapter makes three general arguments on the relationship of homelessness to housing:

1. Homelessness is not just a shelter problem, but a problem of housing in its fullest sense. Homelessness is a degree of the general housing problem, not a different kind of problem.
2. The magnitude of the problem of homelessness is directly related to the magnitude of the general housing problem. But:
3. Homelessness is not *only* a housing problem, in the sense that housing problems are not only problems of housing. Housing problems, including homelessness, generally are the result of other social processes, economic conditions, political relationships, and changes in the spatial order of cities.[3]

From these three points, it follows that any solution to the problem of homelessness must include a solution to the housing problem generally.

The Definition of Homelessness

Being homeless is often taken to mean simply being without shelter. But that is hardly an adequate definition in a civilized society in which a decent life means more than mere physical survival. Considerations of security of occupancy, of personal safety, of physical adequacy, must play a role also.

A more useful definition for policy purposes[4] would be: *Homeless* means being without a home (as defined earlier), not having housing, or not being in a neighborhood that is minimally adequate in terms of shelter, privacy, personal safety, security of occupancy, comfort, space for essential residential activities, control of the immediate environment, and accessibility.

"Minimally adequate" is a historical construct, and will vary according to time and place (Hulchanski, 1987, p. 10). "Homeless" in a Third World country may mean something far different from "homeless" in a Western European country, and "homeless" today means something far different from what it meant 100 years ago. While the standard is thus relative, it is a social, not an individual, standard. To define homelessness as "any state where present accommodation is inadequate for reasons which seemed good to the applicant" (Watson and Austerberry, 1986) is too broad to be useful, although it highlights the fact that "home" properly means different things for different people.[5]

How long "security of occupancy" must last so that a person may be considered housed adequately is one of the few aspects of the definition for which precise figures have been proposed. British legislation uses 30 days; the state of Ohio 45.[6] The rationale for choosing any particular period is necessarily arbitrary. Whatever the choice, its main function should be to establish priorities among different households facing homelessness at some point in the foreseeable future. Any household whose occupancy will not last as long as that household desires, given a continuance of the initial circumstances of occupancy, does not have security of occupancy.

Some definitions of homelessness add "involuntarily" as a condition of being "truly homeless."[7] President Reagan, for instance, when he says—

> What we have found in this country, and we're more aware of it now, is one problem that we've had, even in the best of times, and this is the people who are sleeping on the grates, the homeless who are homeless, you might say, by choice.[8]

intends his comment to justify treating such persons as other than "homeless," but that adds a whole constellation of moral judgments to the decision that have nothing to do with the state of being homeless itself. It is hard to conceive of a person who, all other things being equal, *prefers* to be homeless.

Within the general definition of homelessness, given earlier, there is a range of categories important for analytic and planning purposes. Other taxonomies are of course possible.[9] However, I believe the following definitions help quantify "need" for policy purposes and correspond to intuitive reactions to what homelessness is.

- *Shelterless:* Living on the street or in any space not intended or normally used for nighttime accommodations or not providing safe protection from the elements.
- *Homeless in shelters:* Having as a primary nighttime residence a public or private shelter, emergency lodging, or a welfare hotel, such accommodations providing protection from the elements, but lacking most of all of the other characteristics of a home and/or intended for only a temporary stay.[10]

The categories of shelterless and homeless in shelters, taken together are what Watchman and Robson (1983, p. 7) called *"visible homelessness."*[11]

The following two categories taken together are frequently referred to as *"hidden homelessness."*[12]

- *Housed but imminently shelterless:* Those only temporarily lodged, living under makeshift and temporary arrangements that provide current accommodation of a transitional nature only. This includes doubling up with friends or relatives, illegally squatting, in grossly substandard housing, or facing eviction without alternative accommodations. The route to loss of shelter may be through the intermediate step of temporary accommodations, then none at all. This category adds a temporal dimension to the definition of homeless: Those who are currently housed but are in danger of being shelterless in the foreseeable future fall under the category of what Watchman and Robson (1983, p. 4) call "insecure accommodation."
- *Housed but not in homes:* Those living only in grossly inadequate accommodations. This category refers to those living under circumstances which may be temporarily stable but which are below acceptable standards of housing, as doubled up, in physically substandard accommodations, in an abandoned or beleaguered neighborhood, or in a housing unit not meeting other socially established norms for minimally decent housing. The route to loss of shelter may be through the intermediate step of grossly inadequate accommodations, then none at all. This category adds to the definition of homeless those whose shelter falls below minimally acceptable standards of quality. Watchman and Robson (1983, p. 6) call this category "intolerable housing conditions."

The preceding categories take a household's current housing (or lack of it) as the defining criteria for homelessness. In addition, for policy purposes the situation of those families who, without outside intervention, will likely become homeless in the future must be considered. So one final category:

• *At risk of homelessness:* Likely to become homeless, although currently in adequate and secure housing. Too high a rent burden, economic difficulties, or health difficulties without the economic means to deal with them are the most widespread form of such risk. Even where the risk is initially created by nonhousing factors, high costs and/or shortages of housing may compound the risk or push the household at risk over the threshold into homelessness.[13]

These terms have been abstractly defined: figures can make them more concrete, and show their relevance for shaping policy. The numbers cannot be cumulated, but an order of magnitude can be established from Table 7.1.

The relation of housing to homelessness can be viewed through these definitions. The shelterless do not have even basic shelter. Those in shelters and the hidden homeless (imminently shelterless or not in homes) differ from the shelterless only in the extremity of their situation on the spectrum of time or of quality. Those at risk of homelessness differ from those already homeless only in the immediacy of their future housing problems. In all cases, the connection between housing and homelessness is obvious and direct.

When we look at the flow rather than at one point in time, the patterns become more complex. Changes in the level of homelessness arise either from decreases in the supply or increases in the demand for housing of the relevant type. Both are housing-related changes; the source of decreases in available supply lies within the housing system,[14] the source of increases in demand for certain types of housing may lie either in the housing system (increases in rents in presently occupied units, eviction from SRO units, etc.) or outside the housing system (loss of income, increase in discharges from residential institutions, etc.).

In many cases, homelessness may begin with nonhousing changes. However, these changes lead to homelessness because the housing system as presently constituted does not provide for them. For example, when an elderly person loses a spouse or relative she or he often needs a support network or social institution to which to turn for assistance. The loss

Table 7.1 Homelessness in New York City[a]

Shelterless	
Living on the streets (estimated):	
adults	22,350
youth	17,000
Homeless in shelters	
Single individuals in shelters	13,114
Family members in temporary accommodations[b]	17,053
Housed but imminently shelterless	
Overcrowded, in private housing[c]	132,000
Evicted, annually[d]	69,660
Displaced by abandonment, annual[e]	25,000
Displaced by gentrification, annual[f]	75,000
Institutional discharges[g]	?
Projected loss of SROs, annual[h]	
(Less: Additions to available housing, annual)[i]	−4,000

[a] Figures, unless otherwise noted, are from Marcuse (1986), Stegman (1987), or Partnership (1989). Studies by the New York City Human Resources Administration (1986) show that, while the average *daily* caseload of families was about 4,000 during the six months studied, the *total* unduplicated count was 7,100 (see also Kirchheimer, 1987, p. 6). The annual count shown is conservatively estimated by using the six months ratio, unless otherwise indicated.

[b] Includes welfare hotels, emergency shelters, and transitional housing.

[c] Households in units with more than 1 person per room (Stegman, 1987, p. 138). Based on estimates by the New York City Housing Authority, there are at least 35,000 families doubled up in public housing.

[d] The figure would be 931,540 individuals if all 361,356 residential nonpayment and eviction proceedings filed in Housing Court in 1984 were included. The figure given represents 27,000 warrants of eviction that were actually executed during that year, with an average household size of 2.58, the 1984 average for the city (Stegman, 1985, p. 10). The number of "voluntary" moves under threat of eviction is not known (Marcuse, 1986, p. 81). The Coalition for a Moratorium on Evictions calculates that 368,864 households (about 1,500,000 persons) were evicted by a marshall between 1969 and 1985. The figure rose from 15,597

households in 1975 to 30,740 in 1982. See Brent Sharman (1986, p. 12).

[e] For derivation of the base figure, see Marcuse (1985, pp. 208–12), which estimates 77,500 persons per year displaced annually, based on 1978–81 figures. The rate of abandonment has however been declining, and the figure given assumes less than one-third the rate for the earlier period.

[f] For derivation of estimates, see Marcuse (1985, pp. 212–17).

[g] No attempt has thus far been made to establish this figure, although such a study would be entirely feasible.

[h] The annual rate of loss over the past 15 years has been about 6,800 units. The number of remaining units is now less than half of that 15 years ago, and limited protections are now in place; therefore a nominal figure of 10 percent of the rate of preceding years is used here.

[i] Only three sources exist for increases in the supply of units available to the poor: (1) more expensive units becoming cheaper ("filtering down"), an unlikely source in New York City today given the combination of gentrification ("upward-filtering,") inadequate incomes, and "milking" leading to abandonment; (2) additional federally funded units, nonexistent under the present federal budget except for a handful still in the pipeline; and (3) rehabilitation of formerly abandoned buildings. Figures based on Stegman (1987, p. 204).

(continued)

Table 7.1 *(continued)*

Housed but not in homes

In dilapidated housing	37,000
In housing with 3 or more deficiencies[j]	230,416
In inadequate neighborhood:	
on block with abandoned buildings	469,480
Formerly in SROs now lost[k]	109,000

At risk of homelessness

With high rent burden[l]	894,900
Below the poverty level[m]	455,928
Unemployed or intermittently employed[n]	242,000

Summary[o]

Shelterless	39,350
Homeless in shelters	30,167
Total visible homeless	69,517
Housed but imminently shelterless[p]	132,000
(potential increase, annual)[p,q]	96,700
Housed but not in homes[p]	550,000
Total hidden homeless	650,000
At risk of homelessness[p,r]	700,000

[j]Deficiencies include inadequate heat, peeling paint or broken plaster, rodent infestation, cracks in ceilings or walls, and holes in the floor. More than half a million households reported rodent infestation in New York City in 1984. The figures Stegman provides is calculated only on those reporting all five deficiencies (Stegman, 1987, p. 127) and does not include deficiencies in vacant units. The appropriate figure is more likely over 280,000.

[k]*Village Voice,* April 1, 1986. SROs are taken as the best available proxy for the different kinds of housing needed by particular subgroups, such as those discharged from mental institutions. Since some of those formerly in SROs are now in other categories, such as those in dilapidated housing or doubled up, there is likely to be overlap with other figures provided here.

[l]47.5% of all renter households, calculated at those paying over 30% of income for rent. At 40% of income, the figure becomes 593,500; at 50%, it becomes 433,000. There is overlap between those in danger of displacement because of high rents and those in danger because of gentrification.

[m]Calculated from Stegman (1987).

[n]U.S. Department of Labor, Bureau of Labor Statistics, February 1987.

[o]Because of the impossibility of accounting for overlapping, figures here should be taken as orders of magnitude only. Estimates are conservative.

[p]Conservatively allowing for substantial overlap of the categories.

[q]Evicted or displaced annually, net of units becoming available.

[r]Reduced to take into account that some with high-rental income ratios have adequate incomes to meet their payments.

is a personal problem, but a well-planned housing policy for the elderly could compensate for the housing effects of the loss by providing alternative living arrangements. Another case: A principal wage-earner in a working-class household struggling to make ends meet loses his or her job and is no longer able to afford the rent. Homelessness is imminent. The initial problem is unemployment, but a rent based on income would prevent homelessness as its result. Or take the case of a black family, victimized by inadequate education, discriminated against in the job market, living in a segregated neighborhood that suddenly becomes desirable. The family finds itself unable to meet the increased rent. Its problems include discrimination, educational failures, and inadequate income, but antidisplacement housing legislation would prevent homelessness as their consequence. Or consider a family on welfare, receiving less in their welfare housing allowance than their housing costs. A welfare policy problem, certainly, but also a housing problem. Similarly, for a retarded or mentally ill person, a supportive community residence can be supplied as either part of a housing or of a social services program; separating the two only makes sense in bureaucratic terms.

Housing is a problem in each of these cases, and providing it could eliminate the risk of homelessness in each. Although the increased risk of loss of housing emanates from outside the housing system in many of these cases, changes in the housing system could compensate for these outside problems; the failure to adapt to such problems is a failure of the housing system.

Parallel Changes in Homelessness and Housing

Although correlation does not mean causation, the striking parallels between the growth of homelessness and the escalating housing problem suggests a close relationship.

A caution is necessary here. Whether homelessness is a single concept that applies as well to the nineteenth century (or the feudal period) as it does today is debatable. Many equate homelessness historically with vagrancy and link the treatment of the poor through almshouses, workhouses, and other institutions with the current treatment of the homeless. The hobos of the 1930s indeed seemed to echo the situation of itinerant workers of the 1800s, for example. But there are fundamental distinctions between rural and urban settings, between a prevalent system of indentured or agricultural work and one of wage work, between an acceptance of street living as normal and an expectation of housing for all, between a laissez-faire state and one in which laissez-faire is an ideology with no correspondence to reality. For analytic purposes, to treat homelessness as if it were the same phenomenon throughout history, varying only in scale or characteristics, obscures critical examination (Marcuse, 1988a).

Homelessness is escalating exponentially today, much more rapidly than at any other time in the postwar years. Reliable statistics are hard to come by, in part precisely because of assumptions about housing. The Census Bureau does its tally by counting people in their homes; the basic census unit for counting population is a "household," those who "hold a house." Everyone is defined, in this sense, by their housing; those without disappear from the count.[15] Previous census efforts to count the homeless have been acknowledged as inadequate[16]; for the 1990 census a new effort will be made to count this population.

The increased use of emergency accommodations is one indicator of the extent to which the extreme forms of homelessness have increased, even though less than half of the shelterless are likely to be thus housed on any given night. The New York City use of emergency facilities (public only) has gone up from 3,752 single individuals and 1,008 families in 1982 to 9,343 individuals and 4,067 families in 1986.[17] Mayor Koch, in his December 12, 1986, testimony before Congress, gave a figure of 4,560 households, with 16,640 persons, for the number of homeless in family accommodations. Using that figure and calculating 3.65 persons per family,[18] the total number of homeless in New York City's emergency shelter system went from about 7,725 in 1982 to over 26,644 in 1986, an increase of 365 percent in four years. In the last two years alone, shelter usage in New York City increased 42 percent (NYCCIS, 1984, 1986).

These estimates understate the problem. A substantial number of homeless do not go to shelters, sometimes because there is no room for them, but more often because they do not wish to go, given the conditions in most shelters. The closest estimates are that the number of shelterless not "sheltered" is at least equal to the number in emergency accommodations. Thus the figure for the total number of shelterless or sheltered but homeless in New York City is more likely between 50,000 and 70,000 persons.

Further, a rapidly increasing number of households are among the hidden homeless. Figures since 1980 are more readily available for New York City than for any other urban center in the United States. In New York, for the first time in the postwar period, severe overcrowding (more than 1.5 persons per room) went up instead of down from 1981 to 1984;

it increased by almost 50 percent, going from 31,000 to 45,000 households. The increase was far greater for blacks and Puerto Ricans than for whites.[19] About 87,500 households share apartments with a nonrelative, or 4.6 percent of all households. While some of the sharing may be accounted for by higher income singles living with each other in two-person households, 5.1 percent of all six-person households have a nonrelative present, as do 6.6 percent of seven- or more person households (Stegman, 1985, p. 175). It is estimated that between one-third and one-half of all public housing units are now occupied by more than one family (*New York Times,* Nov. 17, 1986).[20]

Reports from other cities show that the pattern of increased homelessness is nationwide. In January 1981, 50 homeless were buried in Chicago's Potter's Field after freezing to death at night; 25,000 were estimated homeless in that city the next year. Detroit reported 27,000 homeless; Tulsa 1,000 (with 200–300 living under city bridges). Seattle turned away 4,000 families who applied for shelters in the winter of 1983; Hartford, 3,500 individuals in 12 months. In Flagstaff, Arizona, the National Forest campground has become a refuge for the homeless. Whether the region is frostbelt or sunbelt, East or West, manufacturing or service economy makes no difference. The National Coalition for the Homeless has estimated 20,000 homeless in Baltimore, 15,000 in Philadelphia (five times the number two years earlier) (Erickson and Wilhelm, 1986), 25,000 in Houston, 14,000 in Dallas, 4,000–5,000 in Phoenix, 10,000 in San Francisco, and 50,000 in Los Angeles.[21] The Coalition estimates the number of the homeless today at over 3 million.[22]

The housing shortage is also escalating, affecting the poorest most severely.[23] The New York City figures again are illustrative. The vacancy rate is 2.46 percent; 5 percent is considered the minimum for a healthy housing market with normal opportunities to move. Low-rent housing is in the shortest supply; there the vacancy rate is .96 percent (Stegman, 1987, p. xii). For a mother with one child dependent on the welfare rent allowance to pay for housing, the effective vacancy rate is 0.54 percent (Kirchheimer, 1987, p. 11). Median income of renters in the Bronx, the lowest income of the boroughs, went up only 10 percent between 1983 and 1986, but median rents went up by 23.4 percent (Stegman, 1987, p. xiv, xvi). The Consumer Price Index went up only 5.8 percent in the same period. The share of income required to pay rent went up from 21 percent in 1968 to 29.3 percent in 1984. With vacancies at 2 percent or lower, overcrowding increased for the first time since the aftermath of World War II (Stegman, 1985).

The figures nationally are similar. In an illuminating study, Wright and

Lam (1987) found that in 12 typical major cities, the number of those living under the poverty level increased by 36 percent over roughly 6 years, and the number of housing units they could afford decreased by 30 percent. Lam and Wright's figures are conservative, as they calculate that 40 percent of income goes to rent, and they do not adjust for family size. Most of the newly homeless had previously lived in poorer sections of central cities (New York Human Resources Administration, 1986), which are the areas subject to the highest abandonment (30,000 units a year at its peak in New York) and the worst quality of housing.

The rent-to-income ratio is the best single indicator of the affordability of housing. Until recently, one-fourth of one's income has been considered the most an average household should pay for housing. But for those earning under $5,000 in the United States in 1980, 50 percent of income for rent was the median actually being paid, and for those earning between $5,000 and $10,000 it was 35.5 percent. Seven[24] million households paid over 50 percent of their income for rent; among the very poor (earning under $3,000 a year), half were paying over 70 percent of their income for rent, and the situation is worsening steadily (Dolbeare, 1983; Bratt, Hartman, and Meyerson, 1986, p. xiv). Median rent–income ratios have increased in New York City from 18.9 percent in 1950 to 29.0 percent in 1987. The national median in 1983 was 29 percent (Bratt et al., 1986, p. xiv). The proportion of renters paying over 30 percent of their income to rent has gone from 25 percent to 48.2 percent in New York City in the same period (Marcuse, 1986, pp. 21, 30).

The curtailment of what limited commmitment there was by the federal government to low-income housing plays no small part in the creation of this housing shortage (Sanjek, 1986). Appropriations for new public housing—the housing of last resort for many of the poor—was virtually eliminated under the Reagan administration.[25] The New York City Housing Authority has a waiting list of 200,000 households for 190,000 occupied units, and the average length of time a nonpriority household would have to wait to get in would be over 35 years.[26] Baltimore has 13,000 on a waiting list for 17,000 units; Chicago has 44,000 waiting for 49,000 units. With turnover rates of 1 percent a year, and the absolute number of public housing units in the country actually declining because of demolitions, closings, and units rendered unusable (at the rate of about 70,000 a year), public housing will offer an alternative to homelessness for fewer and fewer families (Riordan, 1987, p. 27).

Other governmental programs show similar shortfalls. Nearly two-thirds of those on welfare in New York City now have rents over the maximum amount allotted to them for rent under existing law.[27] In Illinois, Peter

Rossi and his colleagues (1987) describe the general assistance payment as "simply not enough to enter the private housing market at any level." In Cincinnati, $67 a month is budgeted for two rooms for a single person on Poor Relief (Hope and Young, 1986, p. 9).[28] Housing vouchers and certificates, attempts to improve the housing of the poor without intervening directly in the housing market, are inadequate. In Boston, only 38 percent of all those assigned housing certificates actually found housing for which they could use them, and in New York City about half of those with certificates had to pay more than the theoretical maximum of 30 percent of income for their units (Riordan, 1987). The reaction of the federal government to the increasing pressure of rents on income in the private market was characteristic; it raised the minimum tenants were expected to pay from 25 percent to 30 percent of their incomes.

No wonder so many are homeless, with housing this hard to find. One might almost rephrase the question: "Why are some of the poor homeless?" (see Rossi et al., 1987, p. 13) to "How do so many of the poor manage to avoid being homeless?"

The Housing/Homelessness Link: The Gentrification/Abandonment Pattern

In both homelessness and housing a threshold has been crossed (Hopper and Hamburg, 1984). The existence of a new housing "crisis" is widely acknowledged. During the Depression, homeless families ultimately expected to get some type of permanent housing for themselves when times got better. Today, the housing market offers no such hope; even when times get better, the cost of housing rises and its availability to the poor declines. Historically, single individuals down on their luck had a range of alternatives for housing; today, they have virtually none.

The situation is qualitatively different from what it was 20, or 50, or 100 years ago. The new situation results from a conjunction of economic and political factors. The pattern has been described as the "retreat from the welfare state," or "post-Fordism" (Marcuse, 1988b), or deindustrialization (Bluestone and Harrison, 1982; Hopper et al., 1986).[29] Unemployment is on the increase. It went from 5.6 percent in 1972 to 7.2 percent in 1985 for all workers, from 4.5 percent to 6.1 percent for white males, 5.9 percent to 6.4 percent for white females, 9.3 percent to 15.3 percent for black males, 11.5 percent to 14.9 percent for black females—and from 35.4 percent to 40.2 percent for black teenagers. For those who are employed, real wages are shrinking; average gross weekly earnings declined in constant 1977 dollars from $187 in 1970 to $170 in 1985 (Statistical Abstracts of the U.S., 1985, pp. 378, 390, 401). As the ranks of the permanently unemployed and the marginally employed grow, so the ranks of the homeless may be expected to grow. Further documentation of the pattern of increasing unemployment and marginalization is hardly necessary.

The major link that connects homelessness to these fundamental socio-economic changes can be labeled ''the gentrification/abandonment pattern.''

During the Great Depression, real incomes plummeted. But the expectation was that they would rise again and that unemployment would not be permanent. Thus, although apartments and homes were vacated because their former residents could no longer afford them, those apartments or homes were not abandoned. They were retained by owners in the expectation that one day they would again return a profit. Most of their former residents doubled up with family or friends. When thousands ended up homeless at the same time, living on the streets, in Hoovervilles, or in temporary shelters, no one had any doubts as to why they were homeless, so there was no isolation, no concealment, no mystery, no blame attached to their homeless condition. Problems obviously pervaded the economic system, and solutions clearly had to cover a wider spectrum than housing. It was assumed that when things got better for some, they would get better for all. That outlook no longer holds. Now, while things appear to be good or getting better for some, they are getting worse for others, and there is no change in sight.

Abandonment in the late 1960s, 1970s, and into the 1980s displaced more people than gentrification (Marcuse, 1985). Shelterlessness was not the immediate consequence of abandonment, however; many people, homeless in the true sense, continued to be sheltered in buildings without heat, hot water, often without windows, with no security, and no protection. The homeless lived in abandoned buildings mostly far away from the central business district and out of sight of the affluent. In New York City, when the sight of the broken windows of abandoned buildings began to jar commuters driving into town from the suburbs on the Cross Bronx Expressway, the city pasted decals with pictures of shutters and flower boxes on the boarded-up windows. It was with gentrification, resulting in the presence of highly visible homeless in newly desirable neighborhoods, that homelessness began to hit the headlines and the TV news.

Homelessness today is thus essentially different from that of the Depression. The gentrification/abandonment syndrome is the result of the particular economic restructuring of cities that has taken place over the last 40 years, much of it with government support. Today, the poor and the homeless are neither understood and accepted, as in the Great Depression, nor hidden and out of the way, as 20 years ago. Where gentrification is dominant, the poor and the homeless are in the way of progress. They are visible in the wrong place. Poor people living at the margin of subsistence in the past used to live in flophouses, in single room occupancy hotels, in the cheapest of cheap apartments, and, during periods of abandonment, in abandoned buildings. But many such accommodations are now in the path of urban "progress."[30] Skid row after skid row is demolished as downtowns expand. Yerba Buena and South of Market in San Francisco (Hartman, 1984; Wright and Lam, 1987), Presidential Towers in Chicago, and the 42nd Street redevelopment project in New York City directly replace housing for the poor with housing for the rich (Moberg, 1987). Single room occupancy hotels are converted to condominiums; New York City alone has lost 109,000 SRO units since 1971 (*Village Voice,* 1986) to "upgrading."[31] The lowest priced rentals are abandoned, demolished, or converted and gentrified. The pressure on those at the bottom of the housing ladder is enormous, whether directly from eviction, as in the case of SROs being converted, or indirectly, through unaffordable rent increases. In either event, the most vulnerable of the poor are driven out into the streets.

But fundamental economic and spatial changes do not automatically lead to the disappearance of available housing for the poor, nor does poverty automatically mean homelessness. In a civilized and wealthy society there should be no poverty; but even if there is, the poor might be guaranteed minimum levels of food, clothing, and shelter. The specific character of our housing system, not some iron law of economic development, dictates that increasing poverty in a rich society results in increasing homelessness.

One certain way to break the link between poverty and homelessness in the United States would be to break the link between profit and housing. Housing is provided by private industry so as to produce the greatest profit.[32] Thus, new housing is built for those, and only for those, who can afford to pay for new construction; existing housing is allocated to those from whom housing providers can make the most money. That is how the private market system works. Where there is profit to be made, housing will be provided; where there is not, it will not. Therefore some never get housing, because no one would profit by providing it. They are the homeless.

Homelessness must be expected in any society that relies overwhelmingly on the private market to provide housing. And the long-term trend will be that the number of homeless will rise as both the number of the poor and housing costs rise. That is indeed the current situation in the United States.[33]

Denying the Housing Link: Isolating the Homeless

The preceding argument is almost self-evident, yet the link between private housing supply and homelessness is constantly ignored or directly denied. For instance, Reagan's Secretary for HUD asserted, ''The problems of the homeless rarely relate to lack of available shelter.'' If they do, he suggested, they ought to be solved by ''local initiative and private enterprise.''[34]

Other explanations for homelessness also disregard its origins in housing, but do so under a more sophisticated veneer. The HUD report on homelessness, for instance, asks, ''Why are people homeless?'' and gives three answers: ''chronic disabilities, personal crises, or economic conditions.'' Do ''economic conditions'' have anything to do with the housing market? No; they only involve unemployment and individual ''lack of resources'' (USHUD, 1984, pp. 23–27).

Research that focuses on the characteristics of the homeless, making the assumption that the problem lies in the victim, not in that which victimizes, also runs the danger of denying the housing roots of homelessness. Calling homelessness a ''personality disorder'' is perhaps understandable in those who deal professionally with the mental illnesses of the homeless; it is less understandable when presented as an explanation for their condition. One such formulation is:

> Homelessness is a condition of detachment from society characterized by the absence or attenuation of the affiliative bonds that link settled persons to a network of interconnected social structures.[35]

It almost perversely omits any reference to lack of housing.

Most of the mentally ill are in fact housed, and most of the homeless are not mentally ill. The reason some of the mentally ill are no longer housed today has to do with the shortage of housing, not with some long-term increase in mental illness, nor even with the short-term consequences of deinstitutionalization.[36] The same is true of the drug dependent, of alcoholics, of the elderly, of the mentally retarded. They are all, indeed, because of their particular characteristics, more *vulnerable* to homelessness than most. But their characteristics are not the cause of their being without homes. They would not be homeless were it not for the changes in the housing market produced by wider-reaching economic and political changes.

These simple observations are so often obscured because they raise unsettling questions. The private market, the myth goes, is the best supplier of housing for all. But will the private market supply housing for the homeless? Are not the homeless without homes precisely because they cannot contribute to any landlord's profits, to any builder's sales, to any realtor's commissions? Does not the private market in fact cause much of the recent growth in homelessness, through abandonment in one place and gentrification in others, and the conversion to other uses of the former homes of the presently homeless?

Isolating the homeless is the best defense of the status quo against the unsettling implications of these questions. Whether the homeless are hidden physically or are labeled as "different," enabling the rest of the population to emotionally distance itself, the result is the same; the established practices that create homelessness are not threatened. Isolating the homeless by labeling them as different is the single biggest intellectual obstacle to the design of sound policies and programs for dealing with the issue of homelessness.

Policy Implications

Two policy conclusions flow from this analysis:

1. The homeless must be provided with homes as an integral part of a system that provides housing generally for those in need of it, not as a special group and not in isolation from other housing policies.
2. Housing for the homeless must be provided with their particular needs in mind, just as all housing should be provided with the particular needs of its occupants in mind, so that such housing will provide homes, not just shelters.

The first of these conclusions would hardly require restatement were it not so often ignored. Roisman and her colleagues (undated, p. 20) formulate the point succinctly: "The single most effective thing Congress could do to combat homelessness would be to increase substantially the stock of decent, affordable, low-rent housing." The three major problems of the homeless, says Robert Hayes of the Coalition for the Homeless in New York, are "housing, housing, and housing."[37]

Nor are the problems of housing the homeless accidental blips in an otherwise smoothly functioning system. In Chester Hartman's words: "Homelessness is an extreme manifestation of the structural defects in the country's housing system . . . Central . . . [to a solution] are changes in [that] housing system" (1986, pp. 71, 78). Among other elements of a comprehensive housing program,[38] the specific programs he then recommends includes massively increasing the housing units available to lower income households; reducing federally required rent–income ratios from 30 percent to a level realistically manageable by poor households; preserving and modernizing existing, and expanding future, public housing; and implementing eviction protection and establishing nationally a right to shelter.[39] These recommendations parallel the proposals put forward by the National Coalition for the Homeless in the Homeless Persons' Survival Act of 1986,[40] which has as one of its three titles "Increased Low Income Housing," calling for increased funding for the present Section 8 program and expansion of public housing. Significant portions of the bill were in fact adopted by Congress in 1987. However, as might have been expected given the isolation approach that is the primary obstacle to effective solutions of the homelessness problem, those provisions of the bill dealing with housing generally were not passed; those most narrowly addressing the issue were the most easily adopted, and actual funding has been far below need.

"Public/private" partnerships are much in vogue these days, and to the extent that "private" means "nonprofit," they have much to commend them. Public/nonprofit partnerships can provide flexibility, a human scale, individuality of treatment—all often difficult for government to achieve. But if the private aspect of the partnership is profit-motivated, it will not work in the same way. After all, homelessness exists today not because something is wrong in the private housing market, but precisely because that market is working well. A public/private-for-profit partnership for the homeless means the public sector is trying to induce the private sector to serve a public priority. Perhaps the private sector can be regulated, threatened, or cajoled into cooperating, and certainly many in the private-for-profit sector individually are committed to the cause of good housing for the poor. The point is simply that the economic logic of private enterprise, the basic driving force of the private-for-profit housing industry, will not lead it in this direction. Profit-maximizing in the housing industry and providing decent housing for all are different and often conflicting goals. But acknowledging this openly has political implications. That is why, at the level of public statements, the necessary public responsibility for dealing with housing problems remains a matter of studious avoidance or outright denial.

Public provision of permanent, decent, substantial housing, housing with all the characteristics that make good homes, must be the cornerstone of any policy designed to provide solutions rather than Band-Aids for the problem of homelessness. That does not necessarily mean large, bureaucratic, impersonal institutions running massive, faceless "housing projects." It can mean publicly supported, limited-equity cooperatives, mutual housing associations, public ownership with nonprofit management, small projects or suburban apartments, congregate quarters, or single-family houses, as well as well-run public housing. It should mean housing with public services, community institutions, accessibility, and support services appropriate to its residents—just as all good housing must have these in adequate form and quantity for a decent residential life.

The homeless differ from those that are not homeless in that they have no homes, but they are like all others in that they have a diversity of needs and desires—for housing, neighborhood, community, for security, support, and protection. Like many others, only more so, the homeless have problems in satisfying those needs in the private housing market. To quote Hartman (1986, p. 83) again, "Homelessness is not a discrete housing phenomenon. It is one end of a spectrum of general housing problems." To provide those without shelter only emergency shelter, or "transitional" housing, without dealing with what kind of housing the transition is to, invites a recurrence of the problem. To truncate one end of the problem—the basic shelter end—and "solve" it separately, meets only one part of the need and makes the satisfaction of the rest even more difficult, because it creates the veneer of a solution while the problem remains concealed beneath.

This issue of the "special" characteristics of the homeless— "specialism"[41]—is potential quicksand for policy design. On the other hand, a call to integrate the homeless into the society of their neighbors should not be taken as a call to ignore their special needs. This is the problem of "generalism," the flip side of "specialism" (Marcuse, 1989). Pretending that the homeless only need some homogeneous form of shelter to solve all their problems is as misleading as considering the homeless a separate "sick" population whose housing needs must be considered differently from the needs of everyone else.[42] The resolution of the dilemma lies in the appropriate definition of what housing really is, or ought to be, for all people, and acting on that definition.

Adequate housing means homes—not just shelters—for the homeless, as for everyone else. We need a housing system that will guarantee the right to a home for all.

Notes

1. There are nine different "attributes" of tenure that may be separated out in a legal definition of the relationship between an individual and his or her shelter; they are discussed in detail in Marcuse (1972).
2. I discuss this sense of home as the opposite of "alienation" in Marcuse (1975).
3. See Marcuse (1988a, 1988b) for a fuller discussion.
4. On the politics of defining homelessness, see Marcuse 1988a, and Hulchanski (1987).
5. The working definition used by the National Institutes of Mental Health is likewise too vague, and in addition makes homelessness a personality characteristic. A homeless person is defined as "anyone who lacks adequate shelter, resources, and community ties." Quoted in GAO (1985, p. 4).
6. D. Roth et al., *Homeless in Ohio: A Study of People in Need,* Columbus: Ohio Department of Mental Health, 1985, cited in Marjorie Hope and James Young, *The Faces of Homelessness,* Lexington, Lexington Books, 1986, p. 19.
7. The British Minister of State for Health and Social Security, for instance, required a person to have applied to the welfare department of a local authority for assistance before the government would recognize that person as "truly homeless" (Watchman and Robson, 1983, p. 3).
8. As quoted by Hartman and Robbins, *Village Voice,* April 1, 1986, p. 32.
9. Other taxonomies besides that suggested here are of course possible. The U.S. General Accounting Office, for instance, differentiates among "population in shelters," "population on the streets," and "population at risk" (see Blau, 1987, p. 22).
10. Six months has become a *de facto* dividing line between temporary and permanent in the United States.
11. The definition used by the U.S. Department of Housing and Urban Development also includes both these categories: "A person is counted as homeless if his/her nighttime residence is: (a) in public or private emergency shelters which take a variety of forms—armories, schools, church basements, government buildings, former firehouses and, where temporary vouchers are provided by private or public agencies, even hotels, apartments, or boarding homes; or (b) in the streets, parks, subways, bus terminals, railroad stations, airports, under bridges or aqueducts, abandoned buildings without utilities, cars, trucks, or any other public or private space that is not designed for

shelter'' (HUD, 1984, p. 7). The two categories are also congruent with the definition suggested by the National Coalition for the Homeless in its fact sheet; see *Safety Network,* May 1987, p. 2. New York City's official definition is much more restrictive and essentially includes only those in publicly supported shelters. ''The City government's definition thus excludes all persons whose housing needs are in some fashion accommodated in the private sector, and homelessness occurs by definition only at the point that a person requests and sleeps in a bed in an organized shelter that is publicly financed and regulated'' (Kirchheimer, 1987, p. 6). In Britain some distinguish between ''rooflessness,'' which is equivalent to ''shelterless'' as defined here, and ''houselessness,'' which includes those in shelters and other types of nonpermanent accommodations (Watchman and Robson, 1983, p. 2).

12. HUD is explicit in rejecting a hidden component as any part of the definition. '' 'Homelessness' refers to people in the 'streets' who, in seeking shelter, have no alternative but to obtain it from a private or public agency. Homeless people are distinguished from those who have permanent shelter even though that shelter may be physically inadequate. They are also distinguished from those living in overcrowded conditions'' (HUD, 1984, p. 7).

13. The McKinney Act defines as homeless essentially the visibly homeless, but uses the concept ''at risk of homelessness'' to cover the ''hidden homeless,'' as here defined.

14. In a few cases, losses of housing units may occur for reasons outside the housing system: condemnation for highway construction or other public works, destruction from floods or hurricanes, etc. Numerically, such losses are far less than those caused by changes within the housing system: abandonment, demolition for replacement by newer housing, price increases bringing units out of the range of affordability.

15. Substituting the term ''undomiciled'' for ''homeless'' is a curious reflection of the attempt to make the problem fit into a conventional bureaucratic mold (Rossi et al., 1987).

16. For the Census count, see Rossi et al. (1987). For a summary of some of the varying estimates, see Schwab (1986). In desperation for a proper way to account for the 150 persons who called the railroad's Pennsylvania Station in New York their ''home,'' the Census Bureau listed the station as ''group quarters''! (Hopper, Susser, and Conover, 1986, p. 31).

17. *Village Voice,* April 1, 1986, citing the New York City Human Resources Administration figures.

18. The figure for average number per family is higher than the 2.58 persons per household, since the household average includes single persons and the family average does not.

19. The percentage of households with over 1.5 persons per room went from 1.3 percent to 1.4 percent for white households, 1.9 percent to 2.5 percent for black, and 1.6 percent to 2.3 percent for Puerto Rican. The situation is worst

for large families; of households with six or more persons living together, 14.4 percent had more than 1.5 persons per room in 1981, 22.8 percent in 1984 (Stegman, 1985, pp. 170, 172, 174).

20. The Partnership for the Homeless estimates the total doubled up in the City much higher, at 230,000 (*New York Times,* Jan. 12, 1986, 14).

21. *Newsweek,* Jan. 2, 1984, quoted in Erickson and Wilhelm (1986, p. 3); Fabricant and Kelly, 1986. National Coalition estimates are for July 1986. The estimates are of the same order of magnitude as in HUD's survey that gave 20,000 for Chicago, 7,500 for Detroit, and 32,500 for Los Angeles.

22. Other estimates, not derived in the same manner as the Coalition's, placed the figure at 2,000,000 in 1983 (Physicians' Task Force on Hunger in America, 1985). The U.S. Department of Housing and Urban Development in 1984 estimated the figure at 250,000–350,000 (USHUD, 1984). That estimate has been sharply criticized by advocates for the homeless and researchers on the grounds of flawed methodology (see, for instance, Appelbaum, 1984).

23. For an excellent general discussion, see Hartman (1983, 1986). For other valuable discussion, see Wright and Lam (1987, pp. 48–53).

24. For figures on U.S. central cities and the six largest cities separately, see Marcuse, 1986, p. 86.

25. Total federal authorizations fell from $30.2 billion in 1981 to $7.4 billion in 1987; new construction of public housing went from 30,000 a year to 2,200 a year average. (CLPHA, 1988, p. 7).

26. The situation is similar elsewhere. Robert Rigby of the Jersey City Housing Authority says the city has a "10-year-plus" waiting list and is currently "115% occupied" (Daniel Wisenschal, president of the Council of Large Public Housing Authorities, and Rigby, as quoted in Riordan, 1987, pp. 2, 27).

27. The maximum welfare allowance was not increased in New York between 1975 and 1983; even today, the maximum of $202 for rent for a family of four is less than half the federally established fair market rent, $436, for equivalent apartments established under Section 8 (Spagnolo, 1987, pp. 5, 10).

28. "Poor Relief" is the official statutory derogation in Ohio.

29. This is not an ideal term, since industrialization continues, if often overseas, albeit with changes in the manner of production and the jobs needed.

30. Hopper and Hamberg (1984, p. 34) provide a figure of 1,116,000 single room units disappearing from the housing inventory between 1970 and 1982, nearly half of the total stock.

31. Cincinnati lost 79 percent of its SROs between 1970 and 1980 (Schwab, 1986, p. 25). Nashville was down to only one SRO hotel by December 1985 (Wright and Lamb, 1987, p. 11). In other cities, rooming houses play the role that SROs play: Montreal lost 50 percent of its rooming housing stock

in the last decade; Vancouver and Toronto report similar patterns (Peddie, 1987, p. 8).

32. The government directly provides less than 3 percent of all housing units in the United States, and to the extent it subsidizes other units, does so largely to facilitate the market (Achtenberg and Marcuse, 1986).

33. It is the situation in most private market industrialized countries today. The reason homelessness is so vastly greater a problem in the United States than elsewhere is that the role of government in directing the housing market and itself supplying housing is so much less here than elsewhere. The situation in England may be fast approaching that in the United States, but the reserve of social housing there remains far greater than it has ever been here (Harloe, 1984).

34. HUD News Release No. 85-163, Nov. 7, 1985, quoted in Roisman, p. 6.

35. Caplow, T., 1968.

36. As Hopper, Susser, and Conover write, "So long as affordable housing was in ready supply, the severely disabled managed for the most part to avoid the streets and shelters" (1986, p. 25). For a more detailed treatment of the "deinstitutionalization explains homelessness" argument, see Marcuse (1987).

37. Quoted in Riordan (1987, p. 31). Compare with the three causes of homelessness cited in the HUD report quoted previously.

38. A more detailed formulation of what a comprehensive housing program might look like has been prepared by a group assembled through the Institute for Policy Studies in Washington, D.C., and edited by Richard Appelbaum; this author participated in the work. Copies are available from Chester Hartman, at the Institute, 1601 Connecticut Avenue, N.W., Washington, D.C. 20009.

39. Calling it "the right to a home" might be preferable, but it is the content, not the word, that counts.

40. Introduced as S. 2608, 99th Congress, 2nd Session.

41. I have discussed the issue at some length in Marcuse, 1989.

42. The "specialism" approach to homelessness criticized here is perhaps best exemplified by Thomas Main, the leading conservative writer on the subject, who heads his policy prescription: "Separate Policies for Separate Sub-Populations."

Advocacy for the Homeless in the 1980s

KIM HOPPER

I get worried about a society which consumes with such avidity the display of charity that it forgets to ask itself questions about its consequences, its uses and its limits.

Roland Barthes, "The Iconography of Abbé Pierre," 1957

In a striking departure from the journalistic commonplace, *New York Times* columnist Anna Quindlen asked how it was that the problems of people are so easily converted into "issues," and our neighbors abstracted into mere tokens of larger forces and failings. Could it be, she wondered, that in this way custom enables us to "take people's pain and lessen our own participation in it"? Adjectives become nouns—"the homeless, not Ann or the man who lives in the box, or the woman who sleeps on the subway grate"—in the service of making remote and "other" that which we would otherwise shudder to behold. Lines of kinship, or at least of a common humanity, are muted. The wrenching spectacle of people with faces, families, and—somewhere in their pasts—homes of their own, who find their food, places of rest, solace, and company in the streets because something has gone terribly wrong with the elemental supports of their lives, that spectacle has been lifted from the everyday and referred to the proper bureau. Reclassified as a "problem," even a "crisis," it ceases to exist as an insistent intrusion upon our everyday attention. The sight no longer demands a response. By a trick of grammar, the shock is grounded and we are spared the jolt ("Life in the 30s," *New York Times*, January 7, 1987).

Rarely had so honest an effort been made to wrest a middle-class sensibility from the received categories to which urban homelessness has been consigned. That same week, in an estimable publication found in the clutter of supermarket checkout counters everywhere *(The Sun),* the following headline appeared: "Bag Lady Peddles Wino Bodies to Dog Food Factory."

From the literate to the tabloid: when a subject can span that distance, culturally, it seems safe to say, it has come of age.

This chapter will attempt a kind of stocktaking of advocacy efforts on behalf of the homeless poor as they have taken shape from 1979 to 1987. Insofar as I have been an active participant in such efforts, it will invariably be an essay in self-criticism as well. The time is ripe for such an undertaking, for advocacy today finds itself poised at the edge of a paradox that is in part one of its making: on the one hand, public support for, and participation in, emergency relief efforts are at heights not seen for half a century; on the other, it is increasingly clear that such makeshift rescue operations are doomed to failure in the absence of a massive restoration of governmental housing and income assistance programs for the poor. The irony, I will argue, is that the imminent failure of the first may prove the most forceful demonstration of the necessity of the second.

Definitions and Dimensions of the Problem

For purposes of clarity and orientation, I should state at the outset that, in my view, homelessness is not a trait, or a property, or an affliction of persons. Nor is it an identity that certain marginal personages have honed to a fine eccentric edge. Instead, it is a circumstance—transient, episodic, or persisting, as the case may be—that presents a distinctive problem to be solved: where to spend the night. It may be solved for better or worse, in visible and in invisible ways, in jury-rigged or more lasting fashions. Public homelessness, the homelessness we see and can give names and numbers to, is only the manifest or declared tip of what is a much larger domain of need. Similarly, public shelter is only the apparent, self-identified piece of a vast assemblage of makeshift lodgings.

This approach to homelessness is something of a departure from a tradition that has its roots in the nineteenth-century campaigns to "eliminate" the tramp. At that time, the homeless man, as personified in the figure of the tramp, was considered "a barbarian, openly at war with society" (as social worker Mary Richmond put it). It wasn't just that their lifeways mimicked those of nomadic savages. The tramp was literally thought to be a reversion to precivilized (i.e., pre-waged labor) times, and his presence was felt to be a corrupting example to all those laboring men on whom civilization's hold was tenuous. Since then, the deficiency of the homeless man—of which his lack of shelter was only one symptom—has been variously construed. He has been seen as someone suffering from a genetic defect, variously linked to "nomadism" or "feeble-mindedness"; as a product of mistakes made in early development, resulting in an "undersocialized" being; as a slave to rum or dope; and as someone who shuns all social and familial entanglements, a "disaffiliated" man.[1] With respect to homeless women, the overriding concern has been their alleged moral turpitude.

By contrast, the position assumed here sees homelessness not so much as a new problem as it is one contemporary expression of a number of enduring problems. These include unemployment, the lack of supportive residences for the mentally ill, family break-up, inadequate welfare benefits, domestic violence, and migration—all of which may strain and attenuate the coping capacity of a household or individual. Homelessness, in this view, must be counted among the natural sequelae of such conditions during a time when housing has become an increasingly scarce and costly commodity.[2]

Much debate has been fired over the true dimensions of homelessness as a national problem. Few, however, would dispute the contention that the problem has grown markedly in recent years. Indeed, if one takes the Reagan Administration's reckonings at face value, there were as many as 90,000 more people homeless on a given night in January 1984 than had been the case when the President assumed office (U.S. Department of Housing and Urban Development, 1984). As it happens, this is roughly equivalent to the total number of shelter beds available nationwide that night. Thus, if one assumes perfect elasticity of supply and demand and no barriers of access whatever, the stock of emergency shelter was just adequate to handle the *net increase* in the pool of homeless people that occurred between 1981 and 1984. How the other quarter of a million people who were also thought by HUD to be homeless that night managed is not known.

Recent reports from city officials nationwide confirm that demand for emergency food and shelter assistance has continued to climb, despite the improved economic climate of the last three years (U.S. Conference of Mayors, 1986a, 1986b). To understand what is fueling the growth and persistence of this new homelessness, we would need to examine the forces underlying the dislocations in the urban ecology (and different dislocations in rural economies) as they have taken shape over the last 15 years. Of special relevance are changes in dominant economic activity, the composition of the labor force, and the dynamics of the housing market. In cities like New York, the combined forces of abandonment and gentrification threaten to transform urban space into progressively segregated zones of luxury and penury, with the divisions of color falling as might be expected (Marcuse, 1985; Hopper, Susser, and Conover, 1986).

It has become increasingly clear that the contemporary reality of homelessness accords poorly with received images of skid row. On at least six dimensions, the phenomenon today is singular:

1. Sheer scale: Conservative projections of shelter demand in New York City for the winter of 1988–89 show numbers surpassing 30,000; by contrast, the shelter burden in the city during the worst month of the Depression was around 21,000 (Hopper, 1987, Table 3). In other cities across the country, the numbers (while they may not rival Depression figures) are the highest in 50 years.

2. Visibility: Today's homeless poor are also a more visible and more widely dispersed feature of the urban landscape than has tended to be the case in the past. The organized, collective squatting of former times, which could take on the dimensions of rather large-scale settlements, has given way (with a few exceptions) to a visibility which is isolated, scattered, unorganized. In some areas, street begging (or "panhandling") has assumed aggressive postures of the sort that have traditionally brought down police repression.

3. Heterogeneity: With the exception of periods of severe depressions, homelessness in the past was chiefly a phenomenon of men, many of whom by choice or circumstances had led rather marginal lives all along. Today, the homeless poor include men, women, and children; some live alone, others—in some cities, the majority—as members of families. In some areas, mobility is the norm, while in others the homeless tend to be local. As a rule, they are younger and more ethnically diverse than their skid row counterparts of the 1950s and 1960s. It may not be too much to suggest that a region's homeless population is more and more a simple proxy for its poor.

4. Advocacy: Reform efforts in the past were led either by professional charity or religious groups, or by organizations of the unemployed themselves. Advocacy today can count a vast corps of volunteers, a seasoned core of professionals (often lawyers or academics), and, increasingly, nascent organizations of the homeless poor themselves among its ranks. If, in its fervor to make headway, advocacy has not avoided some

of the pitfalls of charity (as I will suggest), it has also inherited the conviction of some of its forebears that wider linkages to the society and economy at large must be made for any lasting reform to take place.

5. Housing: Arguably, at no time in the history of homelessness in this country has the scarcity of affordable housing played so central a part in the theater of homelessness. Indeed, were it not for that shortage, homelessness would be neither as common nor as persisting a condition as it has become.

6. Episodic character: Increasingly, today homelessness is not an endpoint or culmination of a long road to dissolution and penury. Instead it has become, in some areas at least, a recurring feature of life at the margins of subsistence. By extension, the "solutions" to homelessness devised between bouts of shelter appear to be highly provisional affairs. Far from resolving the underlying problem, these temporary arrangements (usually with friends or family) are signs of a general pattern of subsistence that is fundamentally makeshift in character.

In the face of this rather novel configuration of homelessness, what kind of success can advocates for the homeless poor claim?

Achievements of Advocacy

Whatever the achievements of advocacy, of course, it would be reckless to attribute them to the exertions of a few unreconstructed survivors from the sixties. Indeed, one of the most striking things about contemporary advocacy is how rapidly its ranks have diversified. Long-standing partisans for the poor (like the Catholic Worker movement) have found their efforts championed by members of the press, the pulpit, the academy, and by ordinary (and sometimes quite poor) households (e.g., *New York Times,* November 30, 1987:B1).[3]

The gains won by this expanded corps of advocates are especially clear in five areas.

1. First, and of most immediate importance, has been the gradual accumulation of resources—public, private, and volunteer—devoted to emergency food and shelter. The numbers of soup kitchens, shelters, drop-in centers, and outreach programs stand at post-Depression highs. So, too, does the number of ordinary men and women who volunteer to cook and serve a meal to shelter residents, or give up a night or two a month in their own beds to staff a small makeshift shelter at a local parish.

2. Second is the slow erosion of inherited stereotypes of homeless

people. Not that the stigma of skid row has been erased entirely; indeed, in some quarters, the old images thrive. The police chief of Los Angeles, for example, recently opined: " 'Homeless' has become a euphemistic catch-all for vagrants and transient alcoholics" (*New York Times,* January 22, 1987:A18). Still, it is fair to say that whenever the press has taken the trouble to investigate the detailed particulars of these lives, received notions about who is on the street and why fall quickly by the wayside.[4]

3. Litigation is a third area of success. In at least a dozen communities, class action suits have been filed and won regarding the right to shelter, the quality of public shelter, the right to vote, and the removal of barriers to emergency assistance (for a review, see Hayes, 1987).

4. Fourth, and the most important development in reframing the question of the homeless poor, has been the growing awareness of the centrality of affordable housing both to the resurgence of homelessness and to any lasting solution to it. The introduction of an analytic of housing to what had been a rhetoric of emergency relief has, more than any other factor, worked to wrest the interpretation of homelessness from the brace of pathology and to restore it, center stage, to the contemporary picture of poverty (see Hopper and Hamberg, 1986). In a related development, the realization that safe, accessible refuge is an indispensable adjunct to outreach efforts to the mentally disabled on the streets has taken on the character of preferred clinical practice (Lamb, 1984).

5. Finally, and strategically the most intriguing, has been a growing tendency of the homeless poor to take the reins of advocacy themselves. Local groups of homeless have staged demonstrations, conducted strikes at mandatory work programs, organized marches, occupied offices, and engaged in mass sleep-ins to dramatize the plight of their numbers. Organizers from the National Union of the Homeless have been crisscrossing the country for five years now, working to set up local chapters and agitating for an agenda of jobs and housing, and not merely emergency handouts. Homeless men, women, and children have been articulate participants at Congressional hearings on the issue. With assistance from grass-roots activists, others have taken pen and brush in hand to give vivid expression to the experience of the streets.[5] Still others run shelters, do outreach, and work on housing development projects.

Again, however one measures the successes of advocacy, they must be understood within the context of the cluster of factors that have influenced public receptivity to the issue. Homelessness has proven a power- _ ful focal point for the convergence of a wide array of dissatisfactions with contemporary social policy. In many cities, as noted earlier, its high visibility makes it difficult to ignore. Even where its local dimensions are less apparent, extensive media coverage has fostered widespread awareness of the issue. Vignettes recounting the travails of homeless individuals and families have come to sound more and more like the stories one might encounter within the confines of kin and friends. Then, too, in recent years the issue itself has emerged as a touchstone for opposition to the Reagan Administration's efforts to dismantle the legacy of the New Deal. The keynote address of Governor Mario Cuomo to the ill-fated Democratic Convention in 1984 was notable for its sounding of the "two cities" theme, in which the homeless and hungry figured prominently (see Cuomo, 1987).

Limitations and Setbacks

What, then, are the shortcomings of such efforts? The most dismaying failure of advocacy to date is also the most obvious: emergency relief hasn't met the need. There are still legions of homeless people making do without any but the most rudimentary, jury-rigged shelter. Despite all the effort, even this most basic and least disputed goal has yet to be realized. Where shelter has been provided, moreover, its tendency has been to become not a waystation en route to replacement quarters but a piece in what routinely appears as the puzzle of subsistence, to be solved by a variety of makeshifts. Finally, faced with a population of applicants for relief that departs radically from their skid row counterparts of the 1950s and 1960s, public shelter in many locales has yet to adjust itself to this new reality of need. It continues to be premised—as journalist Matthew Josephson put it the last time demand overwhelmed available supply—"on the theory of the bum" (Josephson, 1933).

There are three additional areas which, because they have not received the attention they deserve, should be considered here: the local character of entitlement, the appearance of regressive programmatic initiatives, and a new ideological twist on the notion of the "deserving poor."

Survival as a Local Entitlement

The precariousness of elemental rights was vividly demonstrated in a class action suit, *Price* v. *Cohen,* filed in Philadelphia. A 1982 revision of the state's Public Welfare Code had classified able-bodied individuals between 18 and 45 as "transitionally needy," and stipulated (with certain exceptions) that they were entitled to benefits for only three months in any calendar year. Nearly 68,000 people were removed from the state's welfare rolls before a district court ruled that the practice was unconstitutional. But on August 17, 1983, the Third Circuit Court of Appeals reversed the lower court's decision and upheld the regulations. It did so grudgingly, mindful of the likely negative consequences of its actions on the named plaintiffs.[6]

In reaching its decision, the court relied decisively on an earlier Supreme Court ruling, *Dandridge* v. *Williams* (1970). While it might, on "first impression," appear that "subsistence is implicitly protected by the Constitution," because it is the precondition for the exercise of all other rights, the court still ruled to the contrary. Citing *Dandridge*, it reaffirmed that no state is under an obligation to justify its social welfare policies, "even where the most basic economic needs of impoverished human beings are at stake" (*Opinion*, No. 83-1387:12).

A protest encampment in the state capitol rotunda followed; its participants were summarily evicted. By early fall, a fifth of those put up in Philadelphia's emergency shelters were estimated to be casualties of the new regulations (*New York Times*, September 18 and October 2, 1983). By the state's own reckoning, only 18 percent of those dropped from the welfare rolls found steady work in the ensuing six months (Commonwealth of Pennsylvania, 1984).

Programmatic Setbacks

An imminent return to the nineteenth-century workhouse is apparent in some communities. Able-bodied clients in New York City shelters are expected to work 20 hours a week in return for bed, board, and a "stipend" of $12.50. In October 1982, Sacramento County in California eliminated cash grants to able-bodied applicants altogether. Instead, it reverted to "indoor relief": rudimentary quarters in a barrack-like facility. Discipline was strict—no liquor or sex, no privacy, meals at appointed times, wake-up at 6:00 A.M., curfew at 9:00 P.M. Before such practices were challenged in court, the Bannon Street Shelter also required residents to request toothpaste and toilet paper on an as-needed basis before using the bathroom (Segal and Specht, 1983).

The county's motive was clear: to deter potential applicants for assistance at a time when such requests were rapidly rising. During the months in which the mandatory shelter/work program was in effect (before being rescinded by court order), new applications for relief fell by more than 50 percent (*San Francisco Chronicle,* April 9, 1983). Equally telling, however, in the first six months following the court order, during which time the program operated on a voluntary basis and applicants were offered a choice between a cash grant and berth at the shelter, Bannon Street continued to run at full capacity. Nor, county officials admitted, was there any way of knowing whether those who had been deterred formerly were any less desperate, any less ''worthy'' than those who accepted relief on the county's terms (D. Hart, personal communication, November 30, 1983). Humiliation is a less than discriminating sieve, and nobody has any idea of what happened to those who were not assisted.

Other institutional responses to homelessness have a decidedly hybrid character, emblematic of a period, perhaps, in which bureaucratic responsibility for this dependent population has yet to be fixed and proper ''classification'' of its needs remains a vexing issue. Psychiatric hospital buildings in New York City, for example, have been pressed into service as emergency shelters. More than a few ex-patients have thus found themselves shuttled back to the sites of their former confinement—this time as shelter clients rather than as patients. The converse has also occurred: a psychiatric inpatient unit in a Boston hospital found that it could cut operating costs by 14 percent if it converted to day hospital status and referred patients home each night. Those without an address of their own and lacking friends or family to put them up were quartered in what had been the hospital's gymnasium, rigged up to serve as a makeshift dormitory (Gudeman, Shore, and Dickey, 1983).

It may not be too much to suggest that one lesson to be derived from such institutional makeshifts is that the first recourse of the state will be to salvage otherwise discarded resources and put them in the service of emergency assistance. The danger, of course, is that in the absence of long-term alternatives these hastily assembled improvisations will take on an institutional life of their own. Thus does waste property come to the aid of waste people, without either altering the terms of its intrinsic value.

From Blame the Victim to Pity the Casualty

Not long ago, it was common for those in the corridors of power to dismiss expressions of concern for the homeless poor as misplaced hand-wringing. ''Some of those people,'' in President Reagan's own memorable words, ''are there, you might say, by their own choice.'' As addled or eccentric as it may be, so the apparent logic went, their exercise of free choice should still be countenanced. But by the spring of 1984, Secretary of Health and Human Services Margaret Heckler was sounding a different note. Homelessness, she contended, was not a new problem, but one "as old as time," usually "connected to the problem of alcohol or drug dependency." The addition of the mentally disabled complicates the picture, but does not fundamentally change its nature (Heckler, 1984). Homelessness, in this view, is still a problem of disturbed individuals, even if, as the 1987 White House budget proposal put it, one of "intense human suffering," rather than a signal of a breach in the fundamental needs-meeting mechanisms of this society.

Thus does outrage at our own inaction and neglect give way to pity for the victims of outrageous fortune. Questions about the provenance of such misery yield to biblical counsel about those "ye have always. . . ." And analysis of the underlying structures of impoverishment is replaced by nitpicking over the proper diagnostic categories to be applied. Safely ensconced within the confines of vice and disease, homelessness ceases to mock the state's pretense to business as usual.

What role have we advocates played in this transformation? An old formula for successful advocacy runs as follows: continuous renewal of the terms of demand coupled with unremitting criticism of all efforts to accommodate the problem without significant change. Isn't it true that we have at times let vigilance flag in the interest of incremental success? Haven't we fallen prey on occasion to the trap of packaging a difficult and disturbing reality in terms that are both nonstigmatizing and designed to elicit public support at large? "Homeless" may be a welcome substitution for a host of earlier epithets, but does it do justice to the complexity of the issues we face? Might not one of the unanticipated consequences of its use be the artificial simplification of a range of problems, the concerted import of which runs much deeper than mere lack of shelter? Don't we risk alienating an initially sympathetic public by portraying the issue as one of immediate and urgent relief of existing need—knowing full well that this is but the first and easiest step on a long road to reform? By sounding the theme of emergency relief, aren't we, wittingly or not, participating in the magic lantern game of a quick solution to homelessness?

Essentially the same nettlesome set of questions has been raised before, and it is to one type of response to them that I now turn.

Some Counsel from Forebears

As descendants of the great documentary tradition of the thirties, present-day advocates for the homeless are also heirs to its hazards. Chief among these is a reflexive, paternalistic impulse to eradicate the surface misery while leaving untouched the underlying structures of immiseration. The signs are all around us: the proliferation of emergency shelters and soup kitchens, the enormous outpouring of popular support for the cause, the extensive voluntary participation in shelter and feeding operations—in short, the larger part of the apparatus of relief that agitation and litigation have brought into existence. At least one commentator has remarked on the danger such success represents.

In assessing the emergence of homelessness as a social problem and its acquisition of newfound legitimacy, Mark Stern (1984) argues that the phenomenon may well spell the demise of the welfare rights movement of the 1960s. Not entitlement, but benevolence, is the watchword of much of the contemporary response to homelessness. In this, Stern detects a return to the Victorian tradition of voluntary charity and personalized relief. The substance of need is taken to be obvious, the style of assistance is direct and immediate, and—whether intended by those who offer food and shelter or not—humiliation of the recipient is the usual accompaniment. By extension, it is possible to argue that in this guise homeless relief functions as a disciplinary measure, one effect of which is to deter potential applicants for assistance and force them to make makeshift arrangements elsewhere (Hopper and Hamberg, 1986). Inadvertently, and over the objections of their champions, "the homeless may actually have functioned to reduce the willingness of Americans to explore the complexities of need in the 1980s" (Stern, 1984:299).

This is a harsh judgment, one that applies to my own work as much as anywhere else. It is also, it seems to me, an accurate one, so far as it goes. The necessary corrective, while onerous, is not impossible to imagine. Indeed, its essential outline may already be sketched. It derives, appropriately enough, from a neglected strain of that same documentary tradition of the thirties.

In James Agee's and Walker Evans's study of tenant farmers in Alabama, *Let Us Now Praise Famous Men*, that tradition achieved perhaps its finest realization. It was a troubled project. The book went through any number of rewritings before it was finally published. Winnowed out along the way was a "note" Agee had written that reveals the authors' deep suspicion of facile efforts to translate their scrupulous inventory of hardship and grace into prescriptions for social change. The note was subsequently recovered by historian William Stott. It reads in part as follows:

> Tenantry as such . . . does not particularly interest us, and the isolation of tenantry as a problem to be attacked and solved as if its own terms were the only ones, seems to us false and dangerous, productive, if of anything, chiefly of delusion, and further harm, and subtler captivity. (as cited in Stott, 1973:294)

This warning applies with particular force to the contemporary counterparts of Agee's poor white farmers: the delusion, harm, and subtler captivity are already apparent in the treatment of today's homeless poor. The restriction of federal efforts to time-limited relief operations enacted by voluntary organizations under the aegis (until recently) of the Federal Emergency Management Agency[7]; the re-emergence of the poorhouse, of mandatory work programs, and in many communities of the outlawed practice of ''moving on'' nonresident applicants for relief[8]; the continued resort to armories, school buildings, church basements, hotels, and warehouse shelters as, for the time being at least, the solution to the housing needs of the homeless poor[9]; the recycling of waste institutional space in a number of forms—all attest to the truth of Agee's conviction that a problem misperceived will generate further problems of its own making.

There is, however, another and complementary side to this story, one that makes for the paradox alluded to earlier. The critics may be right in seeing the proliferation of voluntary relief efforts as, in part at least, a return to a Victorian style of charity. But they miss, I think, the covert treacheries contained in such efforts. Put simply, there is nothing quite like a stint at a soup kitchen or shelter to convince someone both of the urgent need for such endeavors and of their utter insufficiency. This is a frequently enough reported observation to have acquired the status of a truism today. People who volunteer at such places are not mindless drones; instead, in my experience they tend to be those who don't allow themselves the uninformed detachment that so often passes for tacit approval of social policies. Once exposed to the realities of street life and to the desperately strained quality of the relief that is available, they are much less likely to fall for the bloodless abstractions that are so frequently trotted out in official pronouncements on the problem. They are much more likely to see shelters for what, at best, they are: minimally decent, stopgap measures whose only legitimate function is to enable people who might not otherwise make it to hang on a bit longer, while the larger decisions as to their ultimate fate are deliberated.

On occasion, such an experience takes root and produces a sudden, unbidden moment of kinship—of the sort reported by a Presbyterian elder at a Salt Lake City soup kitchen: "I look at these people and I think: I am one job and one divorce away from them" (*Iowa Press-Citizen,* May 7, 1983). (Increasingly, of course, the ranks of advocates are filled by those for whom the notion of kinship is not a sudden epiphany but a lived reality and a daily reckoning.)

It is from such groups, alive to the precariousness of everyday life for so many people and insistent that more than mere shelter be provided to remedy the situation of the homeless poor, that the political constituency of support for long-term solutions to homelessness may one day be forged.

In the meantime, advocates for the homeless must be tuned both to the requisites of human gesture—the only instrumentality through which dignity and respect can be conferred—and to the structures of political economy, where ultimately reside both the causes of and means for resolving contemporary homelessness.

As this chapter goes to press two developments offer confirmation of the trends recounted here, even as they give reason for hope. In New York, a group of homeless families in a Brooklyn hotel (Parents on the Move) have given notice that they will not participate in the city's relocation plan without assurances that this will not simply mean shuttling to yet another wretched hotel[10]; they have occupied the on-site office of the city's Crisis Intervention Services and are refusing to move. In Washington, D.C., the 101st Congress will be deliberating the fate of four bills to provide permanent housing for homeless people; the proposed appropriations range from $0.5 to $45 billion.

Acknowledgments

For helpful comments on an earlier draft of this chapter, I would like to thank Frank Caro, Sue Estroff, Kostas Gounis, Robert Hayes, and Louisa Stark.

Notes

1. For analysis and critique of these various depictions, see Hopper (1987).
2. For a full exposition of this argument, see Hopper and Hamburg (1986).

3. It is tempting to view this phenomenon as the late embodiment of what has been called the "moral economy" of the populace, a set of fundamental beliefs and values concerning the elemental rights of citizenship and their irreducibility to the logic of the market (e.g., Thompson, 1971).

4. On occasion, this realization can take a quite arresting turn. In late March of 1987, the following notice ran in the *New York Times* obituary section: "One of New York City's homeless died March 24, 1987, on 40th St. and Madison Ave. He was clean-up person on the block for over 15 years. May he have a better life." It was signed E. F. Markham, accountant.

5. The "Unforgotten Voices" project, organized by Deborah Mashibini under the joint auspices of the Coalition for the Homeless and Emmaus House in New York City, is a particularly notable example. The project has staged a number of formal poetry readings and exhibitions of art by homeless men and women, and an edited volume of writings is now available (Mashibini, 1987).

6. In the words of the court:

   Bleak and uncertain futures confront the named plaintiffs. Their sources of public assistance are either wholly exhausted or inadequate to maintain them. Each has already received the ninety day allowance permitted the transitionally needy under section 10, and will therefore be ineligible for further cash payments under the general assistance program until next year. . . . [G]iven the high unemployment rate, particularly in certain areas of Pennsylvania, it will be difficult for these persons to find work." (*Opinion,* No. 83-1387:6,7)

7. The most recent legislation, signed into law on July 22, 1987 as the Stewart B. McKinney Homeless Assistance Act, was originally entitled the Urgent Relief for the Homeless Act.

8. Sometimes, when applied to the mentally disabled on the streets, referred to as "Greyhound therapy" (e.g., *New York Times,* November 29, 1987:E8).

9. A recognition implicit in a recent proposal by the mayor of New York that anyone who works and yet resides in a city shelter should be required to pay "rent" (*New York Times,* Dec. 7, 1988:B9).

10. For a moving account of life in the hotels in which homeless families are lodged, see Kozol (1988).

9 Solutions to the Homeless Problem

CAROL L. M. CATON

We must ameliorate the miseries of our homeless. . . . But in doing so we must not make the situation worse. Today, it is inconceivable that a new medication would be introduced before large-scale clinical trials were conducted among diverse patient populations. Furthermore, once the drug became widely available we would continue to monitor its effectiveness and potential toxicity. . . .

Why do we not have similar criteria for our social experiments? In the case of deinstitutionalization, no large-scale efficacy trials were performed. Toxicity and adverse consequences were not monitored. We are only now beginning to identify who the homeless mentally ill are. Well-designed and replicated controlled experiments are necessary. Without such studies we will repeat our mistakes. And we are certain to cause new, unforeseeable hardships. Before we prematurely institute new public policies, we should collect the necessary data to rationally initiate social welfare system changes. By calling for careful studies, we do not advocate inaction until all the answers are known; we must deal with today's difficulties today. But unless we invest time, energy, money, and our good minds toward a solution, today's problem will remain for tomorrow.

Richard Jed Wyatt and Evan G. DeRenzo, Editorial, *Science*, December 12, 1986

Life support services, health and mental health care, education, vocational training, and long-term housing are just some of the creative efforts that have been initiated recently with public monies and through public/private partnerships to ameliorate the miseries of the homeless. But as new programs become established and reach an ever wider constituency of those in need, it is imperative that they be carefully studied and evaluated. While the resurgence of homelessness as a national problem was not anticipated, its presence in the 1980s and the public response to it have generated an opportunity to better understand the causes of this ancient plight and to identify effective prevention and management methods.

Homelessness: Blight on a Nation

Homelessness in the United States has become a significant social problem. The national scope of homelessness has made it a topic of Congressional hearings (House Committee on Banking, Finance, and Urban Affairs, Subcommittee on Housing and Community Development, Dec. 15, 1982 and Jan. 25, 1984; House Select Committee on Aging, Subcommittee on Housing and Consumer Interests, May 2, 1984; House Committee on Banking, Finance, and Urban Affairs, Subcommittee on Housing and Community Development, Feb. 4, 1987), numerous governmental reports at the local, state, and national level (Cuomo, 1983; U.S. Dept. of Housing and Urban Development, 1984; U.S. General Accounting Office, 1985; U.S. Conference of Mayors, January 1986, June 1986, December 1987), and a plethora of journalistic accounts (David Whitman in *U.S. News & World Report,* Feb. 29, 1988; Miller et al., *Newsweek,* March 21, 1988; Gita Mehta in *Vogue,* March 1988; *New York Times,* March 29, 1988; Marilyn Gardner in the *Christian Science Monitor,* April 1, 1988).

Although the absence of precise statistics has engendered a lively debate on the number of homeless Americans, there is widespread agreement that homelessness has increased steadily over the decade. The Department of Housing and Urban Development reported that the number of shelters for the homeless increased 66 percent between 1980 and 1984 (U.S. Dept. of Housing and Urban Development, 1984; U.S. General Accounting Office, 1985). Service providers have reported an ever larger number of homeless seeking shelter throughout the mid to late 1980s. New York City housed an average of 2,000 adults in January 1980, and over 9,000 by January 1988 (U.S. General Accounting Office, 1985; Barbanel, 1988). This figure did not include a count of homeless mothers and their children, a segment of the homeless population experiencing rapid growth in the late 1980s. Homeless families are sheltered in hotels and city-owned apartments, funded through a voucher system. The New York City Human Resources Administration has reported that 3,285 homeless families were lodged in city-contracted welfare hotels in January 1985, compared with 2,400 one year earlier (U.S. General Accounting Office, 1985). In Boston, the number of shelter beds increased by 141 percent in the period from 1984 through 1987, from 972 to 2,351 beds (U.S. Conference of Mayors, 1987).

In a 1987 survey of homeless in 26 American cities, the U.S. Conference of Mayors reported that in nearly every city surveyed the demand for emergency shelter increased by an average of 21 percent. Not one showed a decrease in demand. Although cities such as Boston, New York, Philadelphia, Detroit, and Washington, D.C., were able to meet the demand for shelter in 1987, an average of 23 percent of the demand for emergency shelter goes unmet. Indeed, governmental reviews perceive homelessness as an increasingly complex problem that is likely to persist for several years to come (U.S. General Accounting Office, 1985; U.S. Conference of Mayors, 1987).

The Public Response to Homelessness

Being without a home is the dark side of the American experience, the nightmare of what could become of us without opportunity, determination, or help from our fellow citizens. As homelessness has become more visible throughout the nation, the public response has been both negative and positive.

Reminiscent of efforts to "warn out" the homeless from Colonial towns two centuries ago, city officials in Phoenix, Arizona, dispensed with all programs providing overnight shelter so as to encourage the city's homeless men and women to seek refuge elsewhere (House Committee on Banking, 1982, p. 670). In addition, a bill was passed prohibiting the homeless from sleeping in public buildings, parks, streets, depots, and parking lots. Convictions carried fines, incarceration, or both. A similar bill introduced before the Baltimore city council was ultimately defeated largely through the efforts of advocates for the homeless (House Committee on Banking, 1982, p. 513; Bassuk and Lauriat, 1986).

In Fort Lauderdale, Florida, a municipal commissioner thought the city should institute a program of spraying garbage with poisonous substances to discourage destitute people from foraging in dumpsters and refuse containers (House Committee on Banking, 1982). On Manhattan's prosperous Upper East Side, community residents blocked plans to convert a neighborhood townhouse into a 24-hour drop-in center that would serve up to 75 people, providing them with psychiatric treatment, drug and alcohol counseling, and assistance with obtaining public entitlements, medical care, and housing. In the words of one community leader, the program would be "a magnet for undesirables" (*New York Times,* July 4, 1988, p. 27).

In spite of these hostile attitudes toward the homeless, which seem more characteristic of a previous era, much of the public response to the homeless seems to be more positive in the 1980s. Two constructive elements have been the attempt to understand why homelessness has resurfaced under conditions of relative peace and prosperity, and the humanitarian cry for action to assist those in such a wretched predicament. These themes are reflected in official public policy on a national level.

Defining the Problem

The early 1980s witnessed the publication of a growing number of reports (e.g., Baxter and Hopper, 1981; Hopper et al., 1982; Leepson, 1982; Rousseau and Shulman, 1982; Phoenix South Community Mental Health Center, 1983; Salerno, Hopper, and Baxter, 1984) describing the nature and extent of homelessness in urban centers. Following in short succession, a series of governmental reports probed the epidemiology of homelessness and offered policy recommendations (Cuomo, 1983; U.S. Dept. of Housing and Urban Development, 1984; U.S. General Accounting Office, 1985).

The National Governor's Association Task Force on the Homeless issued a report in 1983 (*1933/1983—Never Again, A Report to the National Governor's Association Task Force on the Homeless,* by Mario M. Cuomo) outlining recommendations for a national policy to overcome homelessness. Contending that emergency food and shelter programs are essential in the short run to meet the most immediate life-threatening needs of people without homes, this report sets forth recommendations for the provision of crisis shelters. Shelters must be open 24 hours a day throughout the year and should offer food, personal hygiene facilities, and transportation. But they should only be designed as temporary stops on the way to a more stable way of life. Services that offer hope for the future, such as access to job training and placement and income maintenance services, should be made available.

The National Governor's Association report recommended that each state set up a task force to closely examine the adequacy of existing policies in the following areas:

1. Number and quality of emergency shelters for youth, single men and women, families, and victims of domestic violence.
2. Regulations and enforcement procedures to ensure a minimal level of decency in shelters.
3. Planning for aftercare of the chronically mentally ill after discharge from public hospitals, including appropriate residential placement.
4. Basic living allowances for those on public assistance.
5. General relief regulations, especially those affecting single, able-bodied men and women.
6. Current housing policies, especially for low-income people.

The report urged that states also deal with the fundamental causes of homelessness and devise long-term solutions. It was suggested that each state provide capital funding for permanent housing for the homeless, bolstered by support services and health care where needed. Moreover, the report states that, at the national level, a massive jobs program could provide employment for those with skills or training for those whose job skills are either obsolete or nonexistent.

Policies and Programs

Emergency Food and Shelter

Early efforts to assist the homeless focused primarily on providing emergency relief at the local level. Public Law 98-8 (March 24, 1983) provides for an emergency food and shelter program to be administered by the Federal Emergency Management Agency (FEMA). The sum of $100 million was appropriated in 1983, half of which was provided as a grant for use by a National Board chaired by FEMA but including representatives from voluntary organizations such as the United Way of America, the Salvation Army, the National Council of Churches, the National Conference of Catholic Charities, the Council of Jewish Federations, and the American Red Cross. The remaining $50 million was allocated to states to distribute. Since its inception, the FEMA program has assisted 21 cities in providing shelter and other services to homeless individuals (U.S. Conference of Mayors, 1987).

In November 1983, Congress enacted Public Law 98-181, which authorized $60 million for the U.S. Department of Housing and Urban Development to disburse to states and localities, Indian tribes, and nonprofit organizations to operate programs for the homeless. Such grants have been used to rehabilitate and operate shelter facilities.

Other federal agencies have contributed to emergency efforts for the homeless. The Department of Housing and Urban Development made available agency-held single-family properties to local governments for use as emergency shelters for homeless families and encouraged public housing authorities to give homeless people emergency priority for placements in public housing.

In 1983, the Department of Defense provided $8 million for the renovation or repair of military facilities for sheltering the homeless. The General Services Administration leased one of its buildings for use as a shelter (Washington, D.C.) and allowed food banks to be eligible to receive surplus items, such as refrigerators and other kitchen appliances.

ACTION, which coordinates volunteer activities on a national level, has provided volunteers to help prepare, cook, and serve hot meals in soup kitchens and shelters. Volunteers also collect food donations from groceries, drugstores, churches, and schools, and distribute them to agencies that serve the needy. In addition, they are involved in food banks and gleaning operations to obtain surplus fruits and vegetables from food stores and markets.

The Stewart B. McKinney Homeless Assistance Act

In recognition of the severity and scope of homelessness in the United States and the need for comprehensive federal actions, the Stewart B. McKinney Homeless Assistance Act (Public Law 100-77) was passed on July 22, 1987, allocating $355 million in fiscal year 1987 to fund crisis programs and begin to address long-term solutions. By the end of 1987, most major cities had applied for federal funds under this new program (U.S. Conference of Mayors, 1987).

The McKinney Act specifies that an Interagency Council on the Homeless, chaired by the Secretary of the Department of Housing and Urban Development, be established and include the heads of the ten cabinet departments and the representatives of other federal agencies providing assistance to the homeless, such as FEMA and ACTION. The Council is mandated to review, coordinate, and monitor federal activities and programs for the homeless, to collect and disseminate information, and to provide technical assistance to state and local governments and nonprofit organizations through the ten federal regions.

The McKinney Act provides for a broader range of housing and other assistance than that specified in previous legislation. New programs and activities include a wide variety of housing assistance for homeless families and individuals. In fiscal year 1987, over $180 million was appropriated for the Emergency Shelter Grant Program, Transitional Housing, Permanent Housing for the Handicapped, federal loans for rehabilitation of single-room occupancy dwellings, and supplemental assistance for facilities to assist the homeless. Title V of the McKinney Homeless Assistance Act requires that the Department of Housing and Urban Development, the Department of Health and Human Services, and the General Services Administration work together in identifying underutilized public buildings and properties that might be suitable for use in assisting these people.

Other efforts sponsored by the Department of Housing and Urban Development to increase opportunities for the homeless include the Community Development Block Grant Entitlement Program Assistance for the Homeless. Under this program, communities have broad discretion, directly or through charitable organizations, to institute a variety of activities benefitting the homeless. The U.S. Conference of Mayors (1987) has reported that as of late 1987, 19 cities have made use of the Community Development Block Grant Program. In fiscal year 1987, St. Louis, Missouri, obtained a $1.3 million-grant in Community Development Block Grant funds to build a 200-bed facility for the homeless expected to assist between 400 and 1,200 people each year. In Portland, Oregon, $125,800 was allocated to the American Red Cross to cover emergency short-term housing through housing vouchers for about 9,000 persons.

The Urban Development Action Grant Program provides grants, awarded through national competition, to aid economic recovery in cities and urban counties undergoing severe economic duress. Under this program, Los Angeles, California, received $1.6 million as a loan for the Volunteers of America, a nonprofit organization, to renovate the old El Ray Hotel in the skid row community and convert it into a neighborhood revitalization center providing housing, detoxification facilities, and a full range of social services for the homeless.

The Stewart B. McKinney Homeless Assistance Act also appropriated $133 million in fiscal year 1987 for health care, alcohol and drug abuse rehabilitation, and mental health services, as well as emergency community programs to be administered through the Department of Health and

Human Services. A major effort of the Department of Health and Human Services in connection with the Stewart B. McKinney Homeless Assistance Act is the Block Grant Program for Services to Homeless Individuals Who Are Chronically Mentally Ill. Congress appropriated $32.2 million in fiscal year 1987 to be allocated to the states to support outreach services, community mental health services, referrals to health services and substance abuse treatment programs, staff training, case management, and support services in residential settings.

Other activities include pilot projects for the homeless persons who are either mentally ill or in need of substance abuse treatment, and for runaway and homeless youths and their families. The Department of Health and Human Services also sponsors the Community Support Program, which supports mental health services pilot programs for grants through state mental health authorities for outreach, case management, and residential assistance for the homeless mentally ill. Approximately $7.5 million were allocated in 1987 for outreach literacy programs, to be coordinated with existing volunteer programs in the area. Moreover, funding was set aside to ensure that homeless children and youth have access to public education and that homeless adults have job training opportunities.

Public/Private Partnership

Current legislation on homelessness encourages the public and private sectors to work together in developing effective models for assisting the homeless, and stimulates local innovation and initiative. An example of such an effort is the Program for the Chronically Mentally Ill Homeless, sponsored by the Robert Wood Johnson Foundation, the Department of Housing and Urban Development, and the Department of Health and Human Services. Its aim is to support community-wide projects with a health, mental health, social services, and housing component geared to helping the chronically mentally ill function more effectively day to day in a community setting, avoiding institutionalization when possible. The Foundation is donating about $28 million in grants and low-interest loans to eight cities: Philadelphia, Baltimore, Cincinnati, Columbus, Charlotte, Denver, Austin, and Honolulu. The state of Ohio is providing capital funding for a ninth city. This program, cosponsored by the National Governor's Association, the U.S. Conference of Mayors, and the National Association of Counties, will provide a continuum of care that will include at least 3,600 to 5,400 housing units and day treatment services for the chronically mentally ill (U.S. Dept. of Housing and Urban Development, 1987). The Department of Health and Human Services has committed $2 million to help evaluate the demonstration.

Because of the large response to this demonstration project, the Robert Wood Johnson Foundation has allocated an additional $10 million to another project, the Mental Health Services Demonstration Program. This program provides smaller scale demonstration funding for cities not participating in the Program for the Chronically Mentally Ill and is designed to implement case management and other services, as well as various financing approaches.

Model Programs to Help the Homeless

It is ultimately at the local level where efforts to help the homeless become tangible in terms of shelter, food, and human service programs. Many localities have developed a partnership of public and private agencies to provide services to this population. In New York City, publicly funded and operated shelters exist side by side with shelters operated by religious or nonprofit agencies. Crisis shelter and life-support services, an initial priority for the homeless, are slowly being supplemented by long-term housing programs, addressing the widely held view that shelters are only a temporary solution to the homeless problem (Bassuk and Lauriat, 1986).

Housing

Working with voluntary agencies and in some cases using federal funding opportunities, cities hard hit by homelessness have begun to develop long-term efforts to increase the availability of housing for the poor. In New York City the Mayor's $4.2 Billion Ten-Year Plan will utilize $2 billion of the city's capital funds and private-sector participation to produce, upgrade, and preserve 250,000 vacant and occupied units for homeless and low-, moderate-, and middle-income individuals and families. Two rehabilitation programs in the plan, the Vacant Building Program and the Construction Management Program, are currently under way and involve the rehabilitation of vacant buildings owned and managed by the City's Housing Preservation and Development Department. Rehabilitation efforts will also be undertaken in cooperation with the Local Initiative Support Corporation and the Enterprise Foundation, a private foundation which provides funding for innovative housing programs. A new construction program, the Affordable Housing Program, will also be initiated.

In Norfolk, Virginia, the Old Huntersville Project involves the renovation and sale of houses to low-income people. Carried out through the Enterprise Foundation, volunteers provide labor and donate materials.

Philadelphia's Family Stabilization Program subsidizes units in apartments and houses for families in shelters. The city also sponsors subsidized housing for the mentally ill.

Through homesteading programs, cities such as Washington, D.C., and Portsmouth offer home ownership opportunities for renters to purchase foreclosed property under lien to the local government. Such first-time homeowners are also eligible for grants for housing rehabilitation.

Boston's Housing Partnership, a consortium of private, community, and government leaders acting as an umbrella development organization, facilitates the rehabilitation and expansion of affordable housing. The Bricklayer's and Laborer's Union Projects involve the construction of new homes sold at cost, less than 50 percent of market value, through a lottery system.

Kansas City's Justin Place and Quality Heights are public/private developments involving local developers, neighborhood groups, and financiers. At Justin Place, 40 percent of the units will be designated for low- to moderate-income persons, with rent not to exceed 30 percent of income. At Quality Heights, a development for families, rents will range from $180 to $290 per month.

San Francisco subsidizes housing for the frail, elderly, and mentally ill among the homeless population through renovations carried out with the Department of Housing and Urban Development, state, and community development funds.

St. Paul's More Than Shelter Program is a public/private partnership to develop at below market rents subsidized housing units for the working poor and subsidized single-room occupancy units, as well as rehabilitate existing single-room occupancy units (U.S. Conference of Mayors, 1987).

Health Care

The Robert Wood Johnson Foundation and the Pew Memorial Trust, in collaboration with the U.S. Conference of Mayors, have sponsored the Health Care for the Homeless Program which has been implemented in 18 cities. In most cases, programs are at shelters and other sites where the homeless can be easily reached. Boston received a grant for $1.5

million for health-care teams to travel to area shelters. In Detroit, on-site primary care and casework services are offered at eight locations. A medical team makes scheduled visits to shelters, drop-in centers, and soup kitchens in the target service area within the central city. The team consists of a physician, public health nurse, social worker, outreach worker, and a driver. Medical problems that cannot be diagnosed or treated at the mobile sites are referred to a stationary team for further evaluation and hospitalization, if necessary. The team social worker expedites receipt of other needed services such as clothing, shelter, counseling, legal aid, and entitlements. A once-a-week clinic is operated at a stationary site at the Detroit Receiving Hospital/University Health Center. It is notable that in the first six months of this program's operation, nearly 25 percent of patients appeared to have a psychiatric disorder, such as schizophrenia, depression, or personality disorder (U.S. Conference of Mayors, June 1986).

Multiservice Centers

New Orleans has developed a multiservice center for the homeless in another example of cooperation between public and private sectors. The center provides day shelter, facilities for showering and laundry, mail and telephone access, clothing, emergency assistance, employment assistance, screening for health and mental health needs, legal aid, and assistance in finding permanent housing. Program staff includes persons who were formerly homeless and is supplemented by a network of voluntary agencies providing a range of services to indigent and disabled persons (U.S. Conference of Mayors, June 1986).

Employment Programs

The New York City Shelter Work Experience Program operates in most of the 25 shelters for homeless adults in the city. It is designed to give all shelter residents who are physically and mentally capable of working the opportunity to contribute productively to the day-to-day operation of the environments in which they live. Work activities include cleaning and maintenance of shelter buildings and grounds, and the opportunity to perform valuable community service such as cleaning local parks. Work assignments are part-time (20 hours per week), leaving time for job interviews and other appointments. Participants qualify for a stipend of $12.50 per week, in addition to room, board, and all other services provided by the shelter. While the Work Experience Program is not designed as an employment program, it allows clients to learn and maintain attitudes and skills necessary for competitive employment (U.S. Conference of Mayors, June 1986).

To help build confidence and self-esteem, the Washington, D.C., adult emergency centers offer residents job counseling, social skills training (such as filling out job applications), and assistance with entitlements and permanent housing applications. As an indicator of success, in 1985 over 300 homeless men were placed in full- or part-time employment through programs of this nature (U.S. Conference of Mayors, June 1986).

Self-Help Groups

The homeless mentally ill are frequently seen as resistant to treatment because they refuse mental health treatment and other services. Indeed, it is not uncommon for mental health professionals to meet with rejection when reaching out to homeless people. Reasons for this may vary, but some homeless are not ready for mental health services until their basic life-support needs have been met. Others indicate that they have had bad experiences with the mental health system, or do not see themselves as ill and in need of care.

Self-help programs have been proposed as a way of reaching the hard-to-reach mentally ill in the homeless population. New mental health programs established in connection with the Stewart B. McKinney Homeless Assistance Act have been encouraged to include a self-help component (Notes from CHAMP, July 1988). Areas where self-help has proven effective for the homeless include drop-in social clubs, financial benefits and other advocacy programs, temporary and transitional housing placement, street outreach programs, and multiservice community centers.

Efforts at Treating the Homeless

Research on the homeless problem is challenged by the very nature of homelessness. The homeless population is made up of a heterogeneous group of men, women, and children with different reasons for being without a home and varied personal resources and needs that are often unique. Some are mentally ill, but most are not; some abuse alcohol and other drugs, others do not; most are poor and unemployed, but some are not without job skills; some are homeless for days or weeks, while others are homeless as a way of life; many use shelters, but a significant number shun official crisis shelter programs, preferring instead to live in public places.

The condition of being without a home is often associated with a plethora of other personal or social ills. Indeed, the problem of homelessness is interwoven into the fabric of urban poverty. Attempts to isolate the thread of homelessness often reveal connections to mental and physical illness and disability, criminality, poor education, and limited employment skills. Treating the condition often involves not only the provision of total life-support services, but addressing the underlying issues that interfere with a person's ability to function independently. In some cases homelessness could be remedied by housing alone, but in other cases housing is only one element in a blueprint for survival.

Understanding the Genesis of Homelessness

There is a critical need for information about how homelessness evolves out of a person's life experiences and is related to both personal and large-scale social and economic issues. Rossi and his colleagues (1987) contend that "literal" homelessness is usually associated with extreme poverty and an inadequate supply of low-cost housing, especially for single persons. Socially isolated persons without access to the resources of a larger household who have been impoverished for long periods of time are the pool of individuals most vulnerable to becoming homeless. As Rossi states, the "homeless are therefore best seen as the long-term very poor who cannot be taken care of by friends and family (or are rejected by them) and who have been unable for a variety of reasons to establish households of their own" (Rossi et al., 1987, p. 1340). Mental and physical disabilities can interfere both with employment prospects and with the supportive network of family and friends.

Taking the Chicago General Assistance population, which numbers about 100,000 people, as a rough estimate of the extremely poor population of Chicago, Rossi and his researchers (1987) found that the literal homeless in Chicago constitute only about 3 percent of the population of extremely poor. To understand the evolution of homelessness among these 3 percent, Rossi's study looked at how the 97 percent of Chicago's extremely poor avoided that situation. Although the definitive research is yet to be done, Rossi et al. (1987) speculate that extremely poor people avoid homelessness by either overspending on housing or by receiving housing and other support from family or friends.

Surveys of the adult homeless in the United States have established that the seriously mentally ill are legion among this population (Bassuk, Rubin, and Lauriat, 1984; Crystal et al., 1986; Roth and Bean, 1986; Rossi et al., 1987). Many believe that the mentally ill who are homeless are in that situation because they have slipped through the mental health bureaucracy or have been poorly served by it (Goleman, 1987, 1988). It has been alleged that mental health deinstitutionalization policies have resulted in patients being discharged from hospitals without adequate housing placement, ongoing supervision, or referral to community-based aftercare treatment (Talbott, 1979; Baxter and Hopper, 1981; Bassuk, 1984; U.S. Dept. of Housing and Urban Development, 1984; Mechanic and Aiken, 1987). This contention has never been rigorously explored, and the majority of the chronically mentally ill treated in the era of deinstitutionalization have been able to sustain living in the community without becoming homeless. The connections between homelessness in this population and the factors commonly implicated in the general homeless problem—that is, economic duress resulting from inflation and high unemployment, the lack of housing for the poor, and deinstitutionalization (Bassuk, 1984; Lamb, 1984; U.S. Dept. of Housing and Urban Development, 1984; U.S. General Accounting Office, 1985; Bassuk and Lamb, 1986)—are not well understood. Effective solutions must ultimately emerge from a scientific understanding of homelessness and its causes (Holden, 1986; Barbanel, 1988). A clearer understanding of the evolution of homelessness might lead to the prevention of homelessness for some and earlier intervention for others, forestalling the development of chronic homelessness so prevalent in our urban shelters (Crystal et al., 1986).

Understanding the Efficacy of Proposed Solutions

Humanitarian concern for the plight of the homeless is manifest in new federal legislation and an array of publicly and privately funded efforts in cities and towns. It is critically important to study and evaluate how well these new programs work. As Wyatt and DeRenzo (1986) point out, well-designed and replicated controlled experiments of new interventions are necessary. Although designing studies of community programs poses many problems, established work demonstrates that such experimental evaluations are feasible and yield valuable insights (Paul and Lentz, 1977; Stein and Test, 1980; Wyatt and DeRenzo, 1986; and others).

Programs for the homeless should be studied experimentally, with random assignment to intervention and control groups (Campbell and Stanley, 1963; Judd and Kenny, 1981; Cronbach, 1983). Depending on the type of intervention being studied, control groups can consist of usual treatment or management procedures in place of no treatment. In studying the efficacy of a new housing program for the homeless mentally ill, Lipton, Nutt, and Sabatini (1988) selected patients ready for discharge from a psychiatric inpatient unit and randomly assigned them to an experimental community residence. Control subjects received individual housing placement arranged through usual discharge planning.

There is no substitute for extensive day-to-day experience with the operation of a program when designing and executing research on its efficacy. It is often necessary to tailor a research design to suit the demands of a particular setting or situation. Such a challenge can be met without compromising scientific rigor. While giving standard prescriptions for such studies would be unwise in light of the heterogeneity of programs for the homeless, the following guidelines have general relevance.

Specifying the Target Group

Evaluation of special programs for the homeless requires specification of the constituency for whom the program is intended, be it mothers and children or the chronically mentally ill. This allows the target group of homeless to be classified into subgroups on the basis of need. The programs' goals, whether health screening, transitional housing, or vocational rehabilitation, can then be clearly delineated. It is interesting that many of the new programs for the homeless, particularly those based at shelters, attempt to meet the multiple needs of their clients for basic life supports, social services, and health or mental health care. Such programs can be viewed as programs within programs when designing an evaluation approach.

Studying Access to Programs

A critical aspect of program evaluation is determining who among those in the intended target group are able to obtain access to the program. Accessibility is accomplished through referrals, transmission of information about the program to prospective clients, and the program's own admission criteria and selection process. It is well known that some model programs are highly selective, eliminating from consideration those with particularly undesirable traits, such as substance abuse, a history of criminality, or chronic unemployment. Identifying the clinical and social characteristics of those who do not gain access to programs, as well as those who are offered access but refuse to participate, is important in determining the portion of the homeless population reached by the program. The chronically homeless with several, complicated needs are particularly difficult to help, and it is possible that for them one of their difficulties is in taking advantage of available care.

Describing Treatment Process and Goals

Once people gain admission to a program, how do they make use of it? Do they participate regularly or only sporadically? Some individuals adjust well to being a program member, but when leaving the program may experience difficulty at moving to a status of greater self-reliance.

Describing what happens in a program is important in determining whether goals have been met and the ultimate success or failure of the program. The desired outcome of a program for the homeless might typically involve multiple dimensions, such as treatment adherence (keeping the client involved in a program in which he or she can be well supervised, keeping the client out of trouble and off the streets), a higher level of adjustment in terms of social or financial independence, and efficacy in preventing costly hospitalizations or crisis care (Piasecki, Pittinger, and Rutman, 1978; Taintor, Widem, and Barrett, 1984; Gudeman and Shore, 1985).

Refining Outcome Measurements

Measurements of outcome should be standardized across studies as much as possible, using a common battery of research instruments to measure dependent variables such as employment, stability of living arrangements, use of hospital and community services, and life satisfaction. A common set of research instruments facilitates the comparison of findings from one study to another.

Short-Term and Long-Term Follow-up

Baseline measurement of all dependent variables permits careful study of the effects of treatment while it is in progress. Assessment of outcome at termination and at follow-up several months or even years later is critical in evaluating the long-term effects of psychosocial therapies. Evidence from studies of psychosocial treatment of schizophrenic populations, such as Stein and Test's (1980) Training in Community Living Program and Paul and Lentz's (1977) investigation of social learning, indicates that advances made tend to diminish once the intervention is withdrawn. May (1974) has underscored the practical problems of conducting long-term follow-up; investigators may lose track of subjects or subjects may refuse later follow-up treatment. Nevertheless, if such procedures as obtaining addresses and telephone numbers of key relatives and making periodic telephone or mail contact with the patient are built into the study design, long-term follow-up will be easier.

Experiments at Multiple Sites

Most treatment research projects have been carried out in a single location. Although it is administratively more complex to organize research at more than one site, the advantages of doing so are obvious. The study of ten day-treatment programs reported by Linn's group (1979) produced findings that could not possibly have emerged from the study of a single program. In exploring outcome in relation to treatment approach, these investigators discovered that patients treated in day hospital programs with a rehabilitation orientation achieved superior adjustment to those treated with traditional psychotherapies.

Conducting experimental programs at multiple sites enhances understanding of how the programs can be adapted to new settings, countering the arguments of Suchman (1967), Mechanic (1978), and Bachrach (1980) that such ''model programs'' are merely hypotheses and cannot be generalized.

In summary, the complexity of the contemporary homeless problem in the United States, with its connections to extreme poverty and individual disability, have led experts to warn that a quick and easy solution is unlikely. A process must evolve in which clinical and humanitarian efforts work in concert to successfully confront the age-old problem of homelessness as it exists in the modern industrial era. The promising new programs developed in the 1980s are a good beginning, but a sustained effort is needed to bring about effective prevention and management approaches to benefit current and future generations.

References

Chapter 1

Advisory Social Service Committee of the Municipal Lodging House, New York City, September 1915.

Anderson, N. (1923). *The Hobo: The Sociology of the Homeless Man.* Chicago: University of Chicago Press.

Arnhoff, F. N. (1975). Social consequences of a policy toward mental illness. *Science* 188:1277.

Aydelotte, F. (1913). *Elizabethan Rogues and Vagabonds.* Oxford: Clarendon Press.

Bahr, H. M. (1968). *Homelessness and Disaffiliation.* New York: Columbia University Bureau of Applied Social Research.

Bahr, H. M. (1970). *The Disaffiliated Man, Essays and Bibliography on Skid Row, Vagrancy, and Outsiders.* Toronto: University of Toronto Press.

Barbanel, J. (1988). Number of homeless far below shelter forecasts. The *New York Times,* Jan. 26, 1988.

Bassuk, E. L., L. Rubin, A. Lauriat (1984). Is homelessness a mental health problem? *American Journal of Psychiatry* 141:1546.

Bassuk, E. L., and H. R. Lamb (1986). Homelessness and the implementation of deinstitutionalization, in *New Directions in Mental Health Services* (E. L. Bassuk, ed.). San Francisco: Jossey-Bass, vol. 30, p. 7.

Baxter, E., and K. Hopper (1981). *Private Lives/Public Spaces: Mentally Disabled Adults on the Streets of New York City,* Interim Report #2. New York: Community Services Society Institute for Social Welfare Research.

Blumberg, L. (1961). *What To Do About the Men on Skid Row: Report of the Greater Philadelphia Movement to the Redevelopment Authority of the City of Philadelphia.* Philadelphia: Greater Philadelphia Movement.

Bogue, D. J. (1961). *The Homeless Man on Skid Row.* Chicago: Tenants Relocation Bureau, City of Chicago.

Bogue, D. J. (1963). *Skid Row in American Cities.* Chicago: University of Chicago Press, p. 8.

Bryant, B. (1981). Special foster care: a history and rationale. *Journal of Clinical Child Psychology* 10:8.

Caplow, T., K. A. Lovald, and S. E. Wallace (1958). *A General Report on the Problem of Relocating the Population of the Lower Loop Redevelopment Area*. Minneapolis: Minneapolis Housing and Redevelopment Authority.

Carmody, D. (1984). Struggles in a welfare hotel recounted. The *New York Times,* Sept. 30, 1984, p. 37.

Cross, W. T., and D. E. Cross (1937). *Newcomers and Nomads in California.* Stanford: Stanford University Press.

Crystal, S., and M. Goldstein (1984). *Correlates of Shelter Utilization.* New York: City of New York Human Resources Administration.

Culver, B. F. (1933). Transient unemployed men. *Sociology and Social Research* 17:519.

Cuomo, M. M. (1983). 1933/1983—Never Again. A Report to the National Governor's Association Task Force on the Homeless, Portland, Me.

Department of Health and Human Services Steering Committee on the Chronically Mentally Ill (1980). Toward a national plan for the chronically mentally ill. Washington, D.C.: U.S. Dept. HHS, December.

Deutsch, A. (1937). *The Mentally Ill in America: A History of Their Care and Treatment from Colonial Times.* New York: Columbia University Press.

Dunham, H. W. (1953). *Homeless Men and Their Habitats.* Detroit: Wayne State University Press.

Golden, S. In preparation. Homeless women have always existed, in *The Women Outside,* Ch. 3.

Goldman, H. H., and J. P. Morrissey (1985). The alchemy of mental health policy: homelessness and the fourth cycle of reform. *Am. J. Public Health* 75:727.

Grice, E. (1977). *Rogues and Vagabonds: Or, the Actor's Road to Respectability.* Lavenham: T. Dalton.

Grob, G. N. (1973). *Mental Institutions in America: Social Policy to 1875.* New York: Free Press.

Henry, G. W. (1941). Mental hospitals, in *A History of Medical Psychology* (G. Zilboorg, ed.). New York: Norton, p. 558.

Hoffman, S. P. (1982). *Who Are the Homeless?* New York: New York City Regional Office, New York State Office of Mental Health.

Holden, C. (1986). Homelessness: Experts differ in root causes. *Science* 232:569, May 2, 1986.

Hotten, J. C. (1860). *The Book of Vagabonds and Beggars.* London: John Camden Hotten, Piccadilly.

Joint Economic Committee, Congress of the United States (June 15, 1984). Estimating the effects of economic changes on national health and social well-being. Washington, D.C.: U.S. Government Printing Office.

Kasinitz, P. (1984). Gentrification and homelessness: the single room occupant and the inner city revival. *The Urban and Social Change Review* 17:9.

Klerman, G. L. (1977). Better but not well: social and ethical issues in deinstitutionalization of the mentally ill. *Schizophrenia Bull.* 3:617.

Lamb, H. R. (1984). Deinstitutionalization and the homeless mentally ill, in *The Homeless Mentally Ill* (H. R. Lamb, ed.). Washington, D.C.: American Psychiatric Association, Ch. 3, p. 55.

Leepson, M. (1984). The homeless: a growing national problem. *Editorial Research Reports,* Vol. II, No. 16, Oct. 29.

London, J. (1970). *The Road.* Santa Barbara: Peregrine.

Low Income Housing Information Service (1984). Analysis of the federal government's annual housing survey, cited in E. L. Bassuk, *The Homelessness Problem. Scientific American,* 251:40–45, July, p. 41.

Martin, M. A. (1987). Homeless women: an historical perspective, in *On Being Homeless: Historical Perspectives* (R. Beard, ed.). New York: Museum of the City of New York, p. 32.

McCook, J. J. (1893). A tramp census and its revelations. *Forum* 15:753.

McEntire, D. (1952). *Population and Employment Survey of Sacramento's West End.* Sacramento: Redevelopment Agency of the City of Sacramento.

New York City Welfare Council (1949). *Homeless Men in New York City.* New York: Welfare Council.

New York Times. May 27, 1984, p. 46.

New York Times. Sept. 15, 1984, p. 1.

New York Times. Proposals for Mentally Disabled Would Ease Eligibility for U.S. Aid. Dec. 9, 1984, p. 1.

Pound, J. (1971). *Poverty and Vagrancy in Tudor England.* London: Longman.

Reed, E. F. (1934). Federal transient program: an evaluative survey, May to July, 1934. New York: Committee on Care of the Transient and Homeless, p. 18.

Reich, R., and L. Siegel (1978). The emergence of the Bowery as a psychiatric dumping ground. *Psychiatric Quarterly* 50:191.

Ribton-Turner, C. J. (1887). *A History of Vagrants and Vagrancy and Beggars and Begging.* London: Chapman and Hall.

Ringenbach, P. T. (1973). *Tramps and Reformers 1873–1916: The Discovery of Unemployment in New York.* Westport, Conn.: Greenwood Press.

Roseman, A. (1935). *Shelter Care and the Local Homeless Man.* Chicago: Public Administration Service, Vol. 46, p. 5.

Rossi, P. H., G. A. Fisher, and G. Willis (1986). *The Condition of the Homeless of Chicago.* Amherst: University of Massachusetts Social and Demographic Research Institute, September 1986.

Rossi, P. H., J. D. Wright, G. A. Fisher, and G. Willis (1987). The urban homeless: estimating composition and size. *Science* 235:1336.

Rothman, D. J. (1971). *The Discovery of the Asylum*. Boston: Little Brown.

Rothman, D. J. (1987). The first shelters: the contemporary relevance of the almshouse, in *On Being Homeless: Historical Perspectives* (R. Beard, ed.). New York: Museum of the City of New York, p. 10.

Salerno, D., K. Hopper, and E. Baxter (1984). *Hardship in the Heartland: Homelessness in Eight U.S. Cities*. New York: Community Service Society of New York.

Segal, S. P., J. Baumohl, and E. Johnson (1977). Falling through the cracks: mental disorder and social margin in a young vagrant population. *Social Problems* 24:387.

Shaffer, D., and C. L. M. Caton (1984). Runaway and homeless youth in New York City: a report to the Ittleson Foundation. New York: Division of Child Psychiatry, Department of Psychiatry, College of Physicians and Surgeons, Columbia University.

Shakespeare, *King Lear* III, 4.

Siegal, H. A., and J. A. Inciardi (1982). The demise of skid row. *Society*, January–February.

Smith, J. T. (1970). *Vagabondia; Or, Anecdotes of Mendicant Wanderers*. Los Angeles: Sherwin & Freutel.

Solenberger, A. W. (1911). *One Thousand Homeless Men*. New York: Russell Sage Foundation. (Printed in Philadelphia by press of Wm. F. Fell, Co.)

Talbott, J. A. (1979). Deinstitutionalization: avoiding the disasters of the past. *Hospital and Community Psychiatry* 30:621.

U.S. Senate, Subcommittee of the Committee on Manufacturers, Seventy-second Congress, second session, on S-5125. (1933). "Relief for Unemployed Transients," testimony of Nels Anderson, Jan. 24, 1933, p. 65.

Wallace, S. E. (1965). *Skid Row as a Way of Life*. Totowa, N. J.: The Bedminster Press.

Chapter 2

Adams, G. R., and G. Munro (1979). Portrait of the North American runaway: a critical review. *J. Youth and Adolescence* 8:359.

Bahr, H. M. (1968). *Homelessness and Disaffiliation*. New York: Columbia University Bureau of Applied Social Research.

Bahr, H. M. (1973). *An Introduction to Disaffiliation*. New York: Oxford University Press.

Bassuk, E. L., L. Rubin, and A. S. Lauriat (1986). Characteristics of sheltered homeless families. *Am. J. Public Health* 76:1097.

Behavioral Research and Evaluation Corporation (BREC) (1975). Boulder, Col.: Unco, Inc.

Beyer, M. (1974). Psychosocial problems of adolescent runaways. Ph.D. dissertation, Yale University, 74:25718, 35/05-B:2420.

Bogue, D. J. (1961). *The Homeless Man on Skid Row*. Chicago: Tenants Relocation Bureau, City of Chicago.

Bureau of the Census (1982). *Statistical Abstract of the United States, 1982–83*, 103rd ed. Washington, D.C.: U.S. Bureau of Commerce.

Crystal, S., and M. Goldstein (1984). *Correlates of Shelter Utilization*. New York: City of New York Human Resources Administration.

Crystal, S., M. Goldstein, R. Levitt, and L. Bloom (1982). Chronic and situational dependency. New York: City of New York Human Resources Administration, May 1982.

Cuomo, M. M. (1983). 1933/1983—Never Again. A Report to the National Governor's Association Task Force on the Homeless, Portland, Me.

Farr, R. K., P. Koegel, and A. Burnam (1986). A study of homelessness and mental illness in the skid row area of Los Angeles. Los Angeles County: Department of Mental Health, March 1986.

Fischer, P. J., S. Shapiro, W. R. Breakey, J. C. Anthony, and M. Kramer (1986). Mental health and social characteristics of the homeless: a survey of mission users. *Am. J. Public Health* 76:519.

Golden, S. In preparation. Homeless women have always existed, in *The Women Outside*, Ch. 3.

Gullotta, T. P. (1979). Leaving home: family relationships of the runaway child. *Social Casework* 60:111.

Hombs, M. E., and M. Snyder (1982). *Homelessness in America; A Forced March to Nowhere*. Washington, D.C.: The Community for Creative Nonviolence.

Leavitt, R. L. (ed.) (1981). *Homeless Welfare Families: A Search for Solutions*. New York: Community Council of Greater New York.

Leventhal, T. (1963). Control problems in runaway children. *Arch. Gen. Psychiat.* 9:122.

Martin, M. A. (1987). Homeless women: an historical perspective, in *On Being Homeless: Historical Perspectives* (R. Beard, ed.). New York: Museum of the City of New York, p. 32.

National Center for Health Statistics (1975). *Data from the National Health Survey: Parent Ratings of Behavioral Patterns of Children*. Washington, D.C.: U.S. Vital and Health Statistics, U.S. Department of Health, Education and Welfare Publications, No. (HSM), 72-1010, Series (11) 108.

Opinion Research Corporation (1976). National Statistical Survey on Runaway Youth Part 1. (Paper prepared for the Office of the Secretary, Department of Health, Education and Welfare.) Princeton, N.J.: Opinion Research Corporation.

Phillips, M. H., D. Kronenfeld, V. Middleton-Jeter, A. Jacoby, M. Pla-Brown, N. DeChillo, and M. Allan (1981). The forgotten ones: Treatment of single parent multi-problem families in a residential setting. New York: Henry Street Settlement Urban Life Center, February 1981.

Riemer, N. D. (1940). Runaway children. *Am. J. Orthopsychiat.* 10:522.

Roberts, A. R. (1982). Adolescent runaways in suburbia: a new typology. *Adolescence* 17:387.

Robins, L. N., and P. O'Neal (1959). The adult prognosis for runaway children. *Am. J. Orthopsychiat.* 29:752.

Rossi, P. H., G. A. Fisher, and G. Willis (1986). *The Condition of the Homeless of Chicago.* Amherst: University of Massachusetts Social and Demographic Research Institute, September 1986.

Rossi, P. H., J. D. Wright, G. A. Fisher, and G. Willis (1987). The urban homeless: estimating composition and size. *Science* 235:1336.

Roth, D., and G. J. Bean (1986). New perspectives on homelessness: findings from a statewide epidemiological study. *Hospital Community Psychiat.* 37:712.

Shaffer, D., and C. L. M. Caton (1984). Runaway and homeless youth in New York City: a report to the Ittleson Foundation. New York: Division of Child Psychiatry, Department of Psychiatry, College of Physicians and Surgeons, Columbia University.

Shellow, R., J. R. Schamp, E. Liebow, and E. Unger (1967). Suburban runaways of the 1960s. *Monographs of the Society for Research in Child Development* 111:32.

Simpson, J. H., M. Kilduff, and C. D. Blewett (1984). Struggling to survive in a welfare hotel. New York: Community Service Society of New York.

Solenberger, A. W. (1911). *One Thousand Homeless Men.* New York: Russell Sage Foundation. (Printed in Philadelphia by press of Wm. F. Fell, Co.)

Stierlin, H. (1973). A family perspective on adolescent runaways. *Arch. Gen. Psychiat.* 29:56.

U.S. Department of Housing and Urban Development (1984). A Report to the Secretary on the Homeless and Emergency Shelters. Washington, D.C.: Office of Policy Development and Research.

Wallace, S. E. (1965). *Skid Row as a Way of Life.* Totowa, N.J.: The Bedminster Press.

Williams, A. D. (1979). A comparison study of family dynamics and personality characteristics of runaways and non-runaways. *Dissertation Abstracts International* 39:5096-B.

Wolk, S., and J. Brandon (1977). Runaway adolescents' perceptions of parents and self. *Adolescence* 12:175.

Chapter 4

Arce, A. A., M. Tadlock, M. J. Vergare, and S. H. Shapiro (1983). A psychiatric profile of street people admitted to an emergency shelter. *Hospital and Community Psychiatry* 34:812.

Bachrach, L. L. (1984). The homeless mentally ill and mental health services: an analytical review of the literature, in *The Homeless Mentally Ill* (H. R. Lamb, ed.). Washington, D.C.: American Psychiatric Association, Ch. 2, p. 11.

Barrow, S., and A. Lovell (1982). Evaluation of Project Reach-Out, 1981–1982. New York: New York State Psychiatric Institute.

Bassuk, E. L., L. Rubin, and A. Lauriat (1984). Is homelessness a mental health problem? *Am. J. psychiat.* 141:1546.

Bassuk, E. L., L. Rubin, and A. S. Lauriat (1986). Characteristics of sheltered homeless families. *Am. J. Public Health* 76:1097.

Breakey, W. R. (1987). Treating the homeless. *Alcohol Health and Research World* 11:42.

Crystal, S., and M. Goldstein (1984). *Correlates of Shelter Utilization.* New York: City of New York Human Resources Administration.

Crystal, S., M. Goldstein, R. Levitt, and L. Bloom (1982). Chronic and situational dependency. New York: City of New York Human Resources Administration, May 1982.

Crystal, S., S. Ladner, and R. Towber (1986). Multiple impairment patterns in the mentally ill homeless. *Int. J. Mental Health* 14:61.

Farr, R. K., P. Koegel, and A. Burnam (1986). A study of homelessness and mental illness in the skid row area of Los Angeles. Los Angeles County: Department of Mental Health, March 1986.

Fischer, P. J., S. Shapiro, W. R. Breakey, J. C. Anthony, and M. Kramer (1986). Mental health and social characteristics of the homeless: a survey of mission users. *Am. J. Public Health* 76:519.

Goldfinger, S. M., and L. Chafetz (1984). Developing a better service delivery system for the homeless mentally ill, in *The Homeless Mentally Ill* (H. R. Lamb, ed.). Washington, D.C.: American Psychiatric Association, Ch. 5, p. 91.

Hoffman, S. P., D. Wenger, J. Nigro, and R. Rosenfeld (1982). *Who Are the Homeless?* New York: New York State Office of Mental Health.

Jones, B. E. (ed.) (1986). *Treating the Homeless: Urban Psychiatry's Challenge.* Washington, D.C.: American Psychiatric Press.

Lamb, H. R. (1984). Deinstitutionalization and the homeless mentally ill, in *The Homeless Mentally Ill* (H. R. Lamb, ed.). Washington, D.C.: American Psychiatric Association, Ch. 3, p. 55.

Levine, I. S. (1984). Service programs for the homeless mentally ill, in *The*

Homeless Mentally Ill (H. R. Lamb, ed.). Washington, D.C.: American Psychiatric Association, Ch. 9, p. 173.

Lipton, F. R., and A. Sabatini (1984). Constructing support systems for homeless chronic patients, in *The Homeless Mentally Ill* (H. R. Lamb, ed.). Washington, D.C.: American Psychiatric Association, Ch. 8, p. 153.

Lipton, F. R., A. Sabatini, and S. E. Katz (1983). Down and out in the city: the homeless mentally ill. *Hospital and Community Psychiatry* 34:817.

Morse, G., and R. J. Calsyn (1986). Disturbed homeless people in St. Louis: needy, willing, but underserved. *Int. J. Mental Health* 14:74.

Pepper, B. M., C. Kirshner, and H. Ryglewicz (1981). The young adult chronic patient: overview of a population. *Hospital and Community Psychiatry* 32:463.

Rossi, P. H., G. A. Fisher, and G. Willis (1986). *The Condition of the Homeless of Chicago.* NORC: University of Chicago.

Roth, D., and G. J. Bean (1986). New perspectives on homelessness: findings from a statewide epidemiological study. *Hospital and Community Psychiatry* 37:712.

Schwartz, S. R., and S. M. Goldfinger (1981). The new chronic patient: clinical characteristics of an emerging subgroup. *Hospital and Community Psychiatry* 32:470.

Shaffer, D., and C. L. M. Caton (1984). Runaway and homeless youth in New York City: a report to the Ittleson Foundation. New York: Division of Child Psychiatry, Department of Psychiatry, College of Physicians and Surgeons, Columbia University.

Snow, D. A., S. G. Baker, and L. Anderson (1986). The myth of pervasive mental illness among the homeless. *Social Problems* 33:407.

Struening, E. L. (1986). A study of residents of the New York City shelter system. Report to the New York City Department of Mental Health, Mental Retardation, and Alcoholism Services. New York: New York State Psychiatric Institute, Epidemiology of Mental Disorders Research Department.

Chapter 5

Alcoholism (1984). UCLA School of Medicine Conference (L. J. West, moderator). *Ann. Intern. Med.* 100:405.

Alstrom, C. H., R. Lindelius, and I. Salum (1975). Mortality among homeless men. *Br. J. Addictions* 70:245.

American Diabetes Association (1984). *The Physicians Guide to Type II Diabetes.* Alexandria, Va.: American Diabetes Association.

American Thoracic Society/Centers for Disease Control (1983). Treatment of tuberculosis and other mycobacterial diseases. *Amer. Rev. Resp. Dis.* 127:790.

Anderson, A. R., J. S. Christiansen, J. K. Anderson, S. Kreiner, and T. Deckert

(1983). Diabetic nephropathy in type I (insulin-dependent) diabetes: an epidemiologic study. *Diabetologica* 25:496.

Anderson, N. (1923). *The Hobo*. Chicago: University of Chicago Press.

Arce, A. A., M. Tadlock, M. J. Vergare, and S. H. Shapiro (1983). A psychiatric profile of street people admitted to an emergency shelter. *Hospital and Community Psychiatry* 34:812.

Aronstein, W. S., and F. Arnett (1985). Antiinflammatory and immunosuppressive drugs, in *Manual of Drug Therapy* (D. A. Scheinberg and L. Scheinberg, eds.). New York: Raven Press, p. 264.

Asander, H. (1980). A field investigation of homeless men in Stockholm. *Acta Psychiatr. Scand.* 61:3, Suppl. 281.

Babigian, H. M. (1985). Schizophrenia: epidemiology, in *Comprehensive Textbook of Psychiatry/IV* (H. I. Kaplan and B. J. Sadock, eds.). Baltimore/London: Williams & Wilkins, p. 649.

Barbanel, J. (1988). Crack use pervades life in a shelter. The *New York Times,* Feb. 18, 1988, p. A1.

Bargmann, E. (1985). Washington D.C.: the Zacchaeus Clinic—a model of health care for homeless people, in *Health Care of Homeless People* (P. W. Brickner, L. K. Scharer, B. Conanan, A. Elvy, and M. Savarese, eds.). New York: Springer, p. 323.

Barnes, D. M. (1988). Health workers and AIDS: questions persist. *Science* 241:161.

Barry, M. A., C. Wall, L. Shirley, J. Bernardo, P. Schwingl, E. Brigandi, and G. A. Lamb (1986). Tuberculosis screening in Boston's homeless shelters. *Public Health Rep.* 101:487.

Bassuk, E. (1983). Summary of clinical data on the homeless, in *Health Care of Homeless People* (P. W. Brickner, L. K. Scharer, B. Conanan, A. Elvy, and M. Savarese, eds.). New York: Springer, p. 9.

Bergenan, H., S. Borg, and T. Hindmarsh (1980). Computerized tomography of the brain and neuropsychiatric assessment of male alcoholic patients and a random sample of the general population. *Acta Psychiatr. Scand.* (suppl.) 286:77.

Bernstein. J. G. (1983). *Handbook of Drug Therapy in Psychiatry*. Littleton, Mass.: Wright-PSG.

Bogue, D. J. (1963). *Skid Row in American Cities*. Chicago: University of Chicago Press.

Braun, M. M., B. I. Truman, B. Maguire, G. T. DiFerdinando, G. Wormser, R. Broaddus, and D. L. Morse (1989). Increasing incidence of tuberculosis in a prison inmate population; association with HIV infection. *JAMA* 261:393.

Brickner, P. W. (1985). Health issues in the care of the homeless, in *Health Care of Homeless People* (P. W. Brickner, L. K. Scharer, B. Conanan, A. Elvy, and M. Savarese, eds.). New York: Springer, p. 3.

Brickner, P. W., D. Greenbaum, A. Kaufman, F. O'Donnell, J. T. O'Brien,

R. Scalice, J. Scandizzo, and T. Sullivan (1972). A clinic for male dere-licts: a welfare hotel project. *Ann Int. Med.* 77:565.

Brickner, P. W., and A. Kaufman (1973). Heart disease in homeless men. *Bull N.Y. Acad. Med.* 49:475.

Brickner, P. W., L. K. Scharer, B. Conanan, A. Elvy, and M. Savarese (eds.) (1985). *Health Care of Homeless People.* New York: Springer.

Burkhart, C. (1983). Scabies: an epidemiologic assessment. *Ann. Int. Med.* 98:498.

Cahill, G. F., Jr. (1986). Metabolism: hypoglycemia, in *Scientific American Medicine* (E. Rubenstein and D. D. Federman, eds.). New York: Scientific American Inc., p. 1.

Cahill, G. F., Jr., R. A. Arky, and A. J. Perlman (1986). Metabolism: diabetes mellitus, in *Scientific American Medicine* (E. Rubenstein and D. D. Federman, eds.). New York: Scientific American Inc., p. 1.

Carlen, P. L., and D. A. Wilkenson (1980). Alcoholic brain damage and revers-ible defects. *Acta. Psychiatr. Scand.* (suppl.) 286:103.

Cassem, N. H. (1979). Psychiatry: alcoholism, in *Scientific American Medicine* (E. Rubenstein and D. D. Federman, eds.). New York: Scientific Ameri-can Inc., p. 1.

Celantano, D. D., R. M. Martinez, and D. V. McQueen (1981). The association of alcohol consumption and hypertension. *Prevent. Med.* 10:590.

Centers for Disease Control (1986). Tuberculosis and acquired immune deficiency syndrome—Florida. *MMWR* 35:587.

Cerda, J. J., and F. P. Brooks (1967). Relationships between steatorrhea and an insufficiency of pancreatic secretion in the duodenum in patients with chronic pancreatitis. *Am. J. Med. Sci.* 253:38.

Chafetz, M. E. (1975). Alcoholism and alcoholic psychoses, in *Comprehensive Textbook of Psychiatry/II* (A. M. Freedman, H. I. Kaplan, and B. J. Sa-dock, eds.). Baltimore/London: Williams and Wilkins, p. 1331.

Chavkin, W., M. S. Kristal, C. Seabron, and P. E. Guigli (1987). The reproduc-tive experience of women living in hotels for the homeless in New York City. *N.Y.State J. Med.* 87:10.

Cohen, S. (1977). Angel dust. *JAMA* 238:515.

Cousins, A. (1983). Profile of homeless men and women using an urban shelter. *J. Emergency Nursing* 9:133.

Cutler, R. W. P. (1983). Neurology: metabolic and nutritional disorders, in *Sci-entific American Medicine* (E. Rubenstein and D. D. Federman, eds.). New York: Scientific American Inc., p. 1.

Cutler, R. W. P. (1986). Neurology: cerebrovascular diseases, in *Scientific Amer-ican Medicine* (E. Rubenstein and D. D. Federman, eds.). New York: Scientific American Inc., p. 1.

Daley, S. (1987). Tuberculosis cases spreading in New York City's shelters. The *New York Times,* March 30, 1987, p. B1.

DeFronzo, R. A., E. Ferrannini, and V. Koivisto (1983). New concepts in the pathogenesis and treatment of non-insulin-dependent diabetes mellitus. *Am J. Med.* 74(1A):52.

Department of Health and Human Services (1986). Highlights of the 1985 National Household Survey on Drug Abuse. Rockville, Md.: National Institute on Drug Abuse.

DeSanctis, R. W. (1987). Cardiovascular medicine: cardiomyopathies, in *Scientific American Medicine* (E. Rubenstein and D. D. Federman, eds.). New York: Scientific American Inc., p. 1.

Drapkin, A., and R. Matz (1967). Hyperosmolar dehydration and coma in diabetes mellitus. *N.Y. State J. Med.* 67:823.

Drapkin, A., and J. Reed (1963). Alcohol induced hypoglycemia. *Diabetes* 12:367 (abstract).

Edsall, J., J. G. Collins, and J. A. Gray (1970). The reactivation of tuberculosis in New York City in 1967. *Am. Rev. Respir. Dis.* 102:725.

Edwards, L. B., V. T. Livesay, F. A. Acquaviva, and C. E. Palmer (1971). Height, weight, tuberculous infection and tuberculous disease. *Arch. Environ. Health* 22:106.

Encyclopaedia Britannica (1771). Edinburgh: A. Bell and C. Macfarquhar, Vol. III, p. 58.

Fanta, C. H., and R. H. Ingram, Jr. (1988). Respiratory medicine: chronic obstructive diseases of the lung, in *Scientific American Medicine* (E. Rubenstein and D. D. Federman, eds.). New York: Scientific American Inc., p. 1.

Farber, E. M., and E. A. Abel (1979). Dermatology: parasitic infestations, in *Scientific American Medicine* (E. Rubenstein and D. D. Federman, eds.). New York: Scientific American Inc., p. 2.

Farr, R. K., P. Koegel, and A. Burnam (1986). A study of homelessness and mental illness in the skid row area of Los Angeles. Los Angeles County: Los Angeles County Department of Mental Health, March 1986.

Fennelly, C., S. Kloppfleisch, M. E. Hombs, and A. P. Russo (1979). The vexing problem of street people. *Public Welfare* 37:7.

Filardo, T. (1985). Chronic disease management in the homeless, in *Health Care of Homeless People* (P. W. Brickner, L. K. Scharer, B. Conanan, A. Elvy, and M. Savarese, eds.). New York: Springer, p. 19.

Fineberg, H. V. (1988). The social dimensions of AIDS. *Scientific American* 259:128.

Friedberg, C. K. (1966). *Diseases of the Heart.* Philadelphia and London: W. B. Saunders, p. 1000.

Gawin, F. H., and H. D. Kleber (1986). Abstinence symptomatology and psychiatric diagnosis in cocaine abusers: clinical observations. *Arch. Gen. Psychiatry* 43:107.

Goldfrank, L. (1985). Exposure: thermoregulatory disorders in the homeless patient, in *Health Care of Homeless People* (P. W. Brickner, L. K. Scharer,

B. Conanan, A. Elvy, and M. Savarese, eds.). New York: Springer, p. 57.

Gong, H., S. Fligiel, D. P. Tashkin, and R. G. Barbers (1987). Tracheobronchial changes in habitual, heavy smokers of marijuana with and without tobacco. *Am. Rev. Resp. Dis.* 136:142.

Goodwin, D. W. (1985). Alcoholism and alcoholic psychosis, in *Comprehensive Textbook of Psychiatry/IV* (H. I. Kaplan and B. J. Sadock, eds.). Baltimore/London: Williams and Wilkins, p. 1016.

Graham, S., and L. G. Reeder (1972). Social factors in the chronic diseases, in *Handbook of Medical Sociology* (H. E. Freeman, S. Levine, and L. G. Reeder, eds.). Englewood Cliffs, N.J.: Prentice-Hall, p. 63.

Gray, G. M. (1985). Gastroenterology: peptic ulcer diseases, in *Scientific American Medicine* (E. Rubenstein and D. D. Federman, eds.). New York: Scientific American Inc., p. 2.

Green, R. W. (1985). Infestations: scabies and lice, in *Health Care of Homeless People* (P. W. Brickner, L. K. Scharer, B. Conanan, A. Elvy, and M. Savarese, eds.). New York: Springer, p. 36.

Gregory, P. B. (1984). Gastroenterology: cirrhosis of the liver, in *Scientific American Medicine* (E. Rubenstein and D. D. Federman, eds.). New York: Scientific American Inc., p. 1.

Grinspoon, L., and J. B. Bakalar (1985). Drug dependence: non-narcotic agents, in *Comprehensive Textbook of Psychiatry/IV* (H. I. Kaplan and B. J. Sadock, eds.). Baltimore/London: Williams and Wilkins, p. 1003.

Haber, E., and E. E. Slater (1979). Cardiovascular medicine: high blood pressure, in *Scientific American Medicine* (E. Rubenstein and D. D. Federman, eds.). New York: Scientific American Inc., p. 1.

Hancock, W. E. (1983). Cardiovascular medicine: coronary artery disease—epidemiology and prevention, in *Scientific American Medicine* (E. Rubenstein and D. D. Federman, eds.). New York: Scientific American Inc., p. 1.

Hancock, W. E. (1985). Cardiovascular medicine: diseases of the aorta and large vessels, in *Scientific American Medicine* (E. Rubenstein and D. D. Federman, eds.). New York: Scientific American Inc., p. 1.

Harwood, H. J., P. L. Kristiansen, and J. V. Zachal (1985). *Social and Economic Costs of Alcohol Abuse and Alcoholism*. Research Triangle Park, N.C.: Research Triangle Institute. (Issue Report No. 2.)

Harwood, H. J., D. M. Napolitano, P. L. Kristiansen, and J. J. Collins (1984). *Economic Costs to Society of Alcohol and Drug Abuse and Mental Illness, 1980*. Research Triangle Park, N.C.: Research Triangle Institute. (Publication No. RTI/2734/00-01 FR.)

Haseltine, W. A., and F. Wong-Staal (1988). The molecular biology of the AIDS virus. *Scientific American* 259:52.

Health and Public Policy Committee (1986). The American College of Physicians, and The Infectious Disease Society of America: Acquired Immune Deficiency Syndrome (Position Paper). *Ann. Intern. Med.* 104:575.

The Health Consequences of Smoking: Nicotine Addiction: A Report of the Surgeon General (1988). U.S. Dept. of Health and Human Services publication (PHS) 88-8406. Rockville, Md.: Office on Smoking and Health.

Heyward, W. L., and J. W. Curran (1988). The epidemiology of AIDS in the United States. *Scientific American* 259:72.

Human Resources Administration (1980). Memorandum: Keener program medical survey report, 10/80.

Hunngren, A., and P. Reizenstein (1969). Studies in dumping syndrome: V. Tuberculosis in gastrectomized patients. *Amer. J. Dig. Dis.* 14:700.

Hypertension Detection and Follow-up Program (1979). I. Reduction in mortality in persons with high blood pressure including mild hypertension. *JAMA* 242:2562.

Iseman, M. (1985). Tuberculosis: an overview, in *Health Care of Homeless People* (P. W. Brickner, L. K. Scharer, B. Conanan, A. Elvy, and M. Savarese, eds.). New York: Springer, p. 151.

Jaffe, J. H. (1985). Drug dependence, in *Comprehensive Textbook of Psychiatry/ IV* (H. I. Kaplan and B. J. Sadock, eds.). Baltimore/London: Williams and Wilkins, p. 991.

Jenicke, M. A. (1987). Psychiatry: drug abuse, in *Scientific American Medicine* (E. Rubenstein and D. D. Federman, eds.). New York: Scientific American Inc., p. 1.

Kaplan, N. M. (1982). *Clinical Hypertension,* 3rd ed. Baltimore: Williams and Wilkins, p. 10.

Kellogg, R. F., O. Pianteri, B. Conanan, P. Doherty, W. J. Vicic, and P. W. Brickner (1985). Hypertension: a treatment and screening program for the homeless, in *Health Care of Homeless People* (P. W. Brickner, L. K. Scharer, B. Conanan, A. Elvy, and M. Savarese, eds.). New York: Springer, p. 109.

Kelly, J. T. (1985). Trauma: with the example of San Francisco's shelter programs, in *Health Care of Homeless People* (P. W. Brickner, L. K. Scharer, B. Conanan, A. Elvy, and M. Savarese, eds.). New York: Springer, p. 77.

Khurana, R. R., D. Younger, and J. R. Ryan (1973). Characteristics of pneumonia in diabetics. *Clin. Res.* 21:629 (abstract).

Kissen, D. M. (1957). Relapse in pulmonary tuberculosis due to specific psychological causes. *Health Bull. (Edinburgh)* 15:12.

Klatsky, A. L. (1979). Alcohol and cardiovascular disorders. *Primary Cardiology* 10:76.

Kolata, G. (1988). Many with AIDS said to live in shelters in New York City. The *New York Times,* April 4, 1988, p. B1.

Kreck, M. J. (1973). Medical safety and side effects of methadone in tolerant individuals. *JAMA* 223:665.

Kuretsky, J. (1985). National survey of HTLV-III in blood banks and plasma antibody screening centers. Bethesda, Md.: National Institutes of Health.

Lambert, B. (1988). New York faulted on tuberculosis. The *New York Times,* Jan. 24, 1988, p. A1.

Leads from the Morbidity and Mortality Weekly Report (1985). Drug resistant tuberculosis among the homeless—Boston. *JAMA* 254:735.

Leads from the MMWR (1987a). Tuberculosis provisional data—United States, 1986. *JAMA* 257:2704.

Leads from the MMWR (1987b). Tuberculosis control among homeless populations. *JAMA* 257:2886.

Leads from the MMWR (1987c). Multi-drug resistant tuberculosis—North Carolina. *JAMA* 257:743.

Leads from the MMWR (1987d). Update: Human immunodeficiency virus in health-care workers exposed to blood of infected patients. *JAMA* 257:3032.

Leads from the MMWR (1989). Relationship of syphilis to drug use and prostitution—Connecticut and Philadelphia, Pennsylvania. *JAMA* 261:353.

Li, F. P. (1986). Oncology: cancer epidemiology and prevention, in *Scientific American Medicine* (E. Rubenstein and D. D. Federman, eds.). New York: Scientific American Inc., p. 1.

Lifson, A. R., K. G. Castro, E. McCay, and H. W. Jaffe (1986). National surveillance of AIDS in health care workers. *JAMA* 256:3231.

Mann, J. M., J. Chin, P. Piot, and T. Quinn (1988). The international epidemiology of AIDS. *Scientific American* 259:82.

Marwick, C. (1985). The sizeable homeless population: a growing challenge for medicine. *JAMA* 253:3217.

McAdam, J., P. W. Brickner, R. Glicksman, D. Edwards, B. Fallon, and P. Yanowitch (1985). Tuberculosis in the SRO/homeless population, in *Health Care of Homeless People* (P. W. Brickner, L. K. Scharer, B. Conanan, A. Elvy, and M. Savarese, eds.). New York: Springer, p. 157.

McBride, K., and R. J. Mulcare (1985). Peripheral vascular disease in the homeless, in *Health Care of Homeless People* (P. W. Brickner, L. K. Scharer, B. Conanan, A. Elvy, and M. Savarese, eds.). New York: Springer, p. 121.

McLellan, A. T., G. E. Woody, and L. P. O'Brien (1979). Development of psychiatric illness in drug abusers. *N. Eng. J. Med.* 301:310.

MMWR (1984). Tuberculosis—United States. 33:77.

MMWR (1985). Education and foster care of children infected with human T-lymphotropic virus type III/lymphadenopathy associated virus. 34:517.

MMWR (1986). Apparent transmission of human T-lymphocyte virus type III/ lymphadenopathy associated virus from a child to a mother providing health care. 35:76.

Muschenheim, C. (1967). Diseases due to mycobacterium, in *Cecil-Loeb Text-*

book of Medicine (P. B. Beeson and W. W. McDermott, eds.). Philadelphia/London: W. B. Saunders, p. 259.

Nardell, E., B. McInnis, B. Thomas, and S. Wiedhaus (1986). Exogenous reinfection with tuberculosis in a shelter for the homeless. *N. Eng. J. Med.* 315:1570.

National Center for Health Statistics (1984). Advance report of final mortality statistics, 1981. Monthly Vital Statistics Report, DHHS, Pub. No. (PHS) 84-1120. Washington, D.C.: Public Health Service.

National Committee on Detection, Evaluation, and Treatment of High Blood Pressure (1984). The 1984 report of the joint committee. *Arch. Int. Med.* 144:1045.

New York State Psychiatric Institute (1981–82). Evaluation of Goddard-Riverside project Reachout. New York: CSS Evaluation Program, NYS Psychiatric Institute.

New York State Psychiatric Institute (1983). Community support system preliminary report. New York: CSS Evaluation Program, NYS Psychiatric Institute.

O'Brien, C. P., G. E. Woody, and A. T. McLellan (1981). Long-term consequences of opiate dependence. *N. Eng. J. Med.* 304:1098.

Oryshkevich, B. A. (1989). New York City's health care crisis: AIDS, the poor, and limited resources (letter). *JAMA* 261:378.

Osler, W. (1916a). *The Principles and Practice of Medicine.* New York and London: D. Appleton, p. 846.

Osler, W. (1916b). *The Principles and Practice of Medicine.* New York and London: D. Appleton, p. 154.

Parson, O. A. (1975). Brain damage in alcoholics: altered states of consciousness, in *Alcohol Intoxication and Withdrawal: Experimental Studies II* (M. M. Gross, ed.). New York: Plenum Press, p. 569.

Perlow, W., E. Baraona, and C. S. Lieber (1977). Symptomatic intestinal disaccharidase deficiency in alcoholics. *Gastroenterology* 71:680.

Pierce, J. P., M. C. Fiore, T. E. Novotny, E. J. Hatziandreu, and R. M. Davis (1989). Trends in cigarette smoking in the United States; projections to the year 2000. *JAMA* 261:61.

Powers, A. C., and G. S. Eisenbarth (1985). Autoimmunity to cells in diabetes mellitus. *Ann. Rev. Med.* 36:533.

Redfield, R. R., and D. S. Burke (1988). HIV infection: the clinical picture. *Scientific American* 259:90.

Reich, T. (1988). Biologic marker studies in alcoholism. *N. Eng. J. Med.* 318:180.

Reichman, L. B., C. P. Felton, and J. R. Edsall (1979). Drug dependence, a possible new risk factor for tuberculosis disease. *Arch. Int. Med.* 139:337.

Renner, J. A., Jr. (1978). Drug addiction, in *Handbook of General Hospital Psychiatry* (T. P. Hackett and N. H. Cassem, eds.). St. Louis, Mo.: C. V. Mosby, p. 29.

Rich, A. R. (1951). *The Pathogenesis of Tuberculosis,* 2nd ed. Springfield, Ill.: Charles T. Thomas.

Romeyn, J. A. (1970). Exogenous reinfection in tuberculosis. *Am. Rev. Respir. Dis.* 101:923.

Ron, A., and D. E. Rogers (1988). New York City's health care crisis: AIDS, the poor, and limited resources. *JAMA* 260:1453.

Ron, A., and D. E. Rogers (1989). New York City's health care crisis: AIDS, the poor, and limited resources (Letter). *JAMA* 261:378.

Rubin, R. H. (1987). Acquired immune deficiency syndrome, in *Scientific American Medicine* (E. Rubenstein and D. D. Federman, eds.). New York: Scientific American Inc., p. 1.

Rubin, R. H. (1988). Infectious disease: infection in the immunosuppressed host, in *Scientific American Medicine* (E. Rubenstein and D. D. Federman, eds.). New York: Scientific American Inc., p. 1.

Schwartz, R. H. (1983). Marijuana, a crude drug with a spectrum of underappreciated toxicity. *Pediatrics* 73:455.

Sebastian, J. G. (1985). Homelessness: a state of vulnerability. *Fam. Community Health* 3:11.

Simon, M. B. (1984). Infectious diseases: mycobacterium, in *Scientific American Medicine* (E. Rubenstein and D. D. Federman, eds.). New York: Scientific American Inc., p. 1.

Slavinsky, A. T., and A. Cousins (1982). Homeless women. *Nurs. Outlook* 30:358.

Slutkin, G. (1986). Management of tuberculosis in urban homeless indigents. *Public Health Rep.* 101:481.

Smith, J. W., F. I. Marcus, and R. Serokman, with the Multicenter Postinfarction Research Center (1984). Prognosis of patients with diabetes mellitus after myocardial infarction. *Am. J. Cardiol.* 54:718.

Solenberger, A. W. (1911). *One Thousand Homeless Men.* New York: Russell Sage Foundation.

Srikanta, S., O. P. Gunda, A. Rabizadeh, J. S. Soeldner, and G. S. Eisenbarth (1985). First-degree relatives of patients with type I diabetes mellitus: islet-cell antibodies and abnormal insulin secretion. *N. Eng. J. Med.* 313:461.

Stead, W. W. (1967). Pathogenesis of a first episode of chronic pulmonary tuberculosis in man: recrudescence of residuals of the primary infection or exogenous reinfection? *Am. Rev. Respir. Dis.* 95:729.

Stead, W. W., and J. H. Bates (1980). Epidemiology and prevention of tuberculosis, in *Pulmonary Diseases and Disorders* (A. P. Fishman, ed.). New York: McGraw-Hill, p. 1234.

Stricof, R. L., and D. L. Morse (1986). HTLV-III/LAV seroconversion following a deep intramuscular needlestick injury (Letter). *NEJM* 314:1115.

Sunderdam, G., R. J. McDonald, T. Maniatis, J. Oleske, and L. B. Reichman (1986). Tuberculosis as a manifestation of the acquired immune deficiency syndrome (AIDS). *JAMA* 256:362.

Tashkin, D. P., A. H. Coulson, V. A. Clark, M. Simmons, L. B. Bourque, S. Duann, G. H. Spivey, and H. Gong (1987). Respiratory symptoms and lung function in habitual heavy smokers of marijuana alone, smokers of marijuana and tobacco smokers of tobacco alone, and non-smokers. *Am. Rev. Respir. Dis.* 135:209.

ten Dam, H. G., and A. Pio (1982). Pathogenesis of tuberculosis and effectiveness of BCG vaccination. *Tubercle* 63:225.

Thompson, A. D. (1980). There may yet be time to save your brain (editorial). *Brit. J. Alcohol and Alcoholism* 15(3):89.

United States Department of Housing and Urban Development (1984). A report to the secretary on the homeless and emergency shelters. Washington, D.C., Office of Policy Development and Research.

Vaillant, G. E. (1978). Alcoholism and drug dependence, in *The Harvard Guide to Modern Psychiatry* (A. M. Nicholi, Jr., ed.). Cambridge, Mass.: Harvard University Press, p. 567.

Vermund, S. H., R. Belmar, and E. Drucker (1987). Homelessness in New York City: the youngest victims. *N.Y. State J. Med.* 87:3.

Veteran's Administration Cooperative Study Group on Antihypertensive Agents (1967). Effects of treatment on morbidity in hypertension. I. Results in patients with diastolic blood pressures averaging 115–129 mmHg. *JAMA* 202:116.

Veteran's Administration Cooperative Study Group on Antihypertensive Agents (1970). Effects of treatment on morbidity in hypertension. II. Results in patients with diastolic blood pressures averaging 90–114 mmHg. *JAMA* 213:1143.

Viberti, G. C., R. D. Hill, R. J. Jarret, A. Argyropoulos, U. Mahmud, and H. Keen (1982). Microalbuminuria as a predictor of clinical nephropathy in insulin-dependent diabetes mellitus. *Lancet* 1:1430.

Winick, M. (1985). Nutritional and vitamin deficiency states, in *Health Care of Homeless People* (P. W. Brickner, L. K. Scharer, B. Conanan, A. Elvy, and M. Savarese, eds.). New York: Springer, p. 103.

Wojak, J. C., and E. S. Flamm (1987). Intracranial hemorrhage and cocaine use. *AHA Focus Series: Stroke* 1:41.

Wolf, L. S. (1985). Diseases of the homeless. *JAMA* 254:1903 (letter).

Wolf, P. A., R. B. D'Agostino, W. B. Kannel, R. Bonito, and R. J. Belanger (1988). Cigarette smoking as a risk factor for stroke. *JAMA* 259:1025.

Wu, T., D. P. Tashkin, B. Djahed, and J. E. Rose (1988). Pulmonary hazards of smoking marijuana as compared with tobacco. *N Eng. J. Med.* 318:347.

Zimmerman, E. H., G. M. Gustafson, and H. G. Kemp, Jr. (1987). Recurrent myocardial infarction associated with cocaine abuse in a young man with normal coronary arteries: evidence for coronary artery spasm culminating in thrombosis. *J. Am. Coll. Cardiol.* 9:964.

Chapter 6

Baganz, P. C., A. E. Smith, R. Goldstein, and N. K. Pou (1971). The YMCA as a halfway facility. *Hospital and Community Psychiatry* 22:156.

Barbanel, J. (1988). Crack use pervades life in a shelter. The *New York Times,* Feb. 18, 1988, p. A1.

Baxter, E. (1980). Geel, Belgium: a radical model for the integration of deviancy, in *Proceedings in Overcoming Public Opposition to Community Care for the Mentally Ill* (R. Baron, I. D. Rutman, and B. Klaczynska, eds.). Philadelphia: Horizon House, p. 67.

Baxter, E., and K. Hopper (1981). *Private Lives/Public Spaces: Mentally Disabled Adults on the Streets of New York City,* Interim Report #2. New York: Community Services Society Institute for Social Welfare Research.

Beatty, L. S., and M. Seeley (1980). Characteristics of operators of adult foster homes. *Hospital and Community Psychiatry* 31:771.

Bennett, W. A. (1964). Students, patients share halfway house. *Rehab. Rec.* 5:21.

Bowen, W. T., and T. J. Fry (1971). Group living in the community for chronic patients. *Hospital and Community Psychiatry* 22:205.

Brown, G. W., J. L. T. Birley, and J. K. Wing (1972). Influence of family life on the course of schizophrenic disorders: a replication. *Br. J. Psychiat.* 121:241.

Budson, R. D. (1978). *The Psychiatric Halfway House.* Pittsburgh: University of Pittsburgh Press.

Budson, R. D. (1981). Challenging themes in community residential care systems, in *Issues in Community Residential Care, New Directions for Mental Health Services.* (R. D. Budson, ed.). San Francisco: Jossey-Bass, Vol. 11, p. 105.

Budson, R. D., M. C. Grob, and J. E. Singer (1978). A follow-up study of Berkeley House, a psychiatric halfway house, in *The Psychiatric Halfway House* (R. D. Budson, ed.). Pittsburgh: University of Pittsburgh Press, p. 191.

California State Dept. of Health (1973). Special Study on Community Care in Santa Clara County. Sacramento, Dec. 30.

Coulton, C. J., V. Fitch, and T. P. Holland (1985). A typology of social environments in community care homes. *Hospital and Community Psychiatry* 36:373.

Cournos, F. (1987). The impact of environmental factors on outcome in residential programs. *Hospital and Community Psychiatry* 38:848.

Crystal, S., and M. Goldstein (1984). Correlates of shelter utilization. New York: City of New York Human Resources Administration.

Cumming, E., and J. Cumming (1959). *Closed Ranks: An Experiment in Mental Health Education.* Cambridge, Mass.: Harvard University Press.

Cumming, J. H., and E. Cumming (1962). *Ego and Milieu: Theory and Practice of Environmental Therapy.* New York: Atherton.

Cupaiuolo, A. A. (1980). Zoning issues in the planning of community residences, in *The Community Imperative: Proceedings in Overcoming Public Opposition to Community Care for the Mentally Ill* (R. C. Baron, I. D. Rutman, and B. Klaczynska, eds.). Philadelphia: Horizon House, p. 355.

Daggett, S. R. (1971). The lodge program: a peer group treatment program for rehabilitation of chronic mental patients. *Rehab. Rec.* 12:31.

Dear, M. (1977). Impact of mental health facilities on property values. *Community Mental Health J.* 13:150.

Dear, M., and S. M. Taylor (1979). Community attitudes toward neighborhood public facilities: a study of mental health services in metro Toronto. Hamilton, Ont.: Department of Geography, McMaster University.

Doninger, J., N. D. Rothwell, and R. Cohen (1963). Case study of a halfway house. *Mental Hos.* 14:191.

Edelson, M. D. (1976). Alternative living arrangements, in *Community Survival for Long-Term Patients* (H. R. Lamb, ed.). San Francisco: Jossey-Bass, Vol. 11, p. 33.

Emerson, R. M., E. B. Rochford, and L. L. Shaw (1981). Economics and enterprise in board and care homes for the mentally ill. *Am. Behavioral Scientist* 24:771.

Fairweather, G. W. (1980). The Fairweather lodge: a twenty-five-year retrospective, in *New Directions for Mental Health Services* (G. W. Fairweather, ed.). San Francisco: Jossey-Bass, Vol. 7, p. 3.

Fairweather, G. W., D. H. Sanders, H. Maynard, and D. L. Cressler (1969). *Community Life for the Mentally Ill: An Alternative to Institutional Care.* New York: Aldine.

Garr, D. (1973). Mental health and the community: San Jose, a preliminary assessment. Unpublished paper, San Jose State University, San Jose, Calif.

Glasscote, R. M., J. E. Gudeman, and J. R. Elpers (1971). Halfway houses for the mentally ill: a study of programs and problems. Washington, D.C.: Joint Information Services, APA and NAMH.

Goldmeier, J., F. V. Mannino, and M. F. Shore (eds.) (1978). *New Directions in Mental Health Care; Cooperative Apartments.* Adelphi, Md.: HEW Monograph ADM 78-685, National Institute of Mental Health.

Grob, M. C., and J. Singer (1974). *Adolescent Patients in Transition: Impact and Outcome of Psychiatric Hospitalization.* New York: Behavioral Publications.

Gumruku, P. (1968). The efficacy of a psychiatric halfway house: a three-year study of a therapeutic residence. *Sociological Q.* 9:374.

Hazelton, N., D. Mandell, and S. Stern (1975). *A Survey and Education Plan Around the Issue of Community Care for the Mentally Ill: The Santa Clara*

County Experience. Sacramento: California State Department of Health, July.

Hopper, K., E. Baxter, and S. Cox (1982). Not making it crazy: the young homeless patients in New York City, in *The Young Adult Chronic Patient, New Directions for Mental Health Services* (B. Pepper and H. Ryglewicz, eds.). San Francisco: Jossey-Bass, Vol. 14, p. 35.

Hull, J. T., and J. C. Thompson (1981). Factors which contribute to normalization in residential facilities for the mentally ill. *Community Mental Health J.* 17:107.

Kantor, D., and M. Greenblatt (1962). Wellmet: halfway to community rehabilitation. *Mental Hos.* 13:146.

Keskiner, A., and M. Zalcman (1974). Returning to community life: the foster community model. *Dis. Nerv. Sys.* 35:419.

Kresky, M., E. M. Maeda, and N. D. Rothwell (1976). The apartment living program: a community living option for halfway house residents. *Hospital and Community Psychiatry* 27:153.

Lamb, H. R. (1981). Maximizing the potential of board-and-care homes, in *Issues in Community Residential Care, New Directions for Mental Health Services* (R. D. Budson, ed.). San Francisco: Jossey-Bass, Vol. 11, p. 19.

Lamb, H. R., and V. Goertzel (1972). High expectations of long-term ex-state hospital patients. *Am. J. Psychiat.* 129:471.

Lamb, H. R., and V. Goertzel (1977). The long-term patient in the era of community treatment. *Arch. Gen. Psychiat.* 34:679.

Landy, D., and M. Greenblatt (1965). *Halfway House: A Socio-Cultural and Clinical Study of Rutland Corner House, a Transitional Aftercare Residence for Former Psychiatric Patients.* Washington, D.C.: Dept. HEW, Vocational Rehabilitation Administration.

Levy, P. R. (1980). Coexistence implies reciprocity, in *The Community Imperative: Proceedings in Overcoming Public Opposition to Community Care for the Mentally Ill* (R. C. Baron, I. D. Rutman, and B. Klaczynska, eds.). Philadelphia: Horizon House, p. 323.

Linn, M. W. (1981). Can foster care survive? in *Issues in Community Residential Care, New Directions for Mental Health Services* (R. D. Budson, ed.). San Francisco: Jossey-Bass, Vol. 11, p. 35.

Linn, M. W., E. M. Caffey, C. J. Klett, and G. Hogarty (1977). Hospital vs. community (foster) care for psychiatric patients. *Arch. Gen. Psychiat.* 34:78.

Linn, M. W., J. Klett, and E. M. Caffey (1980). Foster home characteristics and psychiatric patient outcome. *Arch. Gen. Psychiat.* 37:129.

Lipton, F. R., S. Nutt, and A. Sabatini (1988). Housing the homeless mentally ill: a longitudinal study of a treatment approach. *Hospital and Community Psychiatry* 39:40.

Lipton, F. R., and A. Sabatini (1984). Constructing support systems for homeless chronic patients, in *The Homeless Mentally Ill* (H. R. Lamb, ed.). Washington, D.C.: American Psychiatric Association, Ch. 8, p. 153.

May, P. R. A. (1976). When, what, and why? psychopharmacology and other treatments in schizophrenia. *Comp. Psychiat.* 26:599.

Meenach, L. (1964). The stepping stone: a report of residential rehabilitation houses for the mentally ill. Frankfort, Ky.: VRA Grant RD36660, State Department of Education, Bureau of Rehabilitation Services.

Milosak, A., and M. Basic (1981). Prolonged hospital treatment of patients in families other than their own. *Int. J. Social Psychiat.* 27:129.

Moos, R., and J. Otto (1972). The community-oriented programs environmental scale: a methodology for the facilitation and evaluation of social change. *Community Mental Health J.* 8:28.

Murphy, H. B. M., F. Englesmann, and F. Tcheng-Laroche (1976). The influences of foster home care on psychiatric patients. *Arch. Gen. Psychiat.* 33:179.

New York Times (1983). More rent money for the poor (Editorial). Sept. 9, 1983.

Ozarin, L. D., and M. J. Witkin (1975). Halfway houses for the mentally ill and alcoholics: a 1973 survey. *Hospital and Community Psychiatry* 26:101.

Phillips, M. H., D. Kronenfeld, V. Middleton-Jeter, A. Jacoby, M. Pla-Brown, N. DeChillo, and M. Allan (1981). The forgotten ones: treatment of single parent multi-problem families in a residential setting. New York: Henry Street Settlement Urban Life Center, February 1981.

Pierloot, R. A., and M. Demarsin (1981). Family care versus hospital stay for chronic psychiatric patients. *Int. J. Social Psychiat.* 27:217.

Pollock, H. M. (1936). *Family Care of Mental Patients.* Utica, N.Y.: Utica State Hospital.

Rabkin, J. G., G. Muhlin, and P. W. Cohen (1984). What the neighbors think: community attitudes toward local psychiatric facilities. *Community Mental Health Journal* 20:304.

Raush, H. L., and C. L. Raush (1968). *The Halfway House Movement: A Search for Sanity.* New York: Appleton-Century-Crofts.

Reik, L. E. (1953). The halfway house: the role of laymen's organizations in the rehabilitation of the mentally ill. *Mental Hyg.* 37:615.

Report to the President from the President's Commission on Mental Health (1978). Washington, D.C.: Vol. 1.

Richmond, C. (1969). Expanding the concepts of the halfway house: a satellite housing program. *Int. J. Social Psychiat.* 16:96.

Rog, D. J., and H. L. Raush (1975). The psychiatric halfway house: how is it measuring up? *Community Mental Health J.* 11:155.

Rossi, P. H., G. A. Fisher, and G. Willis (1986). *The Condition of the Homeless of Chicago.* Amherst: University of Massachusetts Social and Demographic Research Institute, September.

Rothwell, N. D., and J. M. Doninger (1966). *The Psychiatric Halfway House: A Case Study.* Springfield, Ill.: Charles C. Thomas.

Sandhall, H., T. T. Hawley, and G. C. Gordon (1975). The St. Louis community homes program: graduated support for long-term care. *Am. J. Psychiat.* 132:617.

Segal, S. P., and U. Aviram (1978). *The Mentally Ill in Community-based Sheltered Care: A Study of Community Care and Social Integration.* New York: Wiley.

Sheffer, E. (1980). The siting of residential facilities: the Upper West Side's point of view, in *The Community Imperative: Proceedings in Overcoming Public Opposition to Community Care for the Mentally Ill* (R. C. Baron, I. D. Rutman, and B. Klaczynska, eds.). Philadelphia: Horizon House.

Shenon, P. (1983). Welfare hotel families: life on the edge. The *New York Times,* Aug. 31, 1983, p. B1.

Sosowsky, L. (1974). Putting state mental hospitals out of business: the community approach to treating mental illness in San Mateo County. Unpublished paper, University of California Graduate School of Public Policy, Berkeley.

Srole, L. (1977). Geel, Belgium: the natural therapeutic community 1475–1975, in *New Trends of Psychiatry in the Community* (G. Serban, ed.). Cambridge, Mass.: Ballinger, p. 111.

Starr, S. (1955). The public's ideas about mental illness. Paper presented at Annual Meeting of National Association for Mental Health, Indianapolis, November.

Stickney, P. (1980). Siting residential facilities strategies for gaining community acceptance, in *The Community Imperative: Proceedings in Overcoming Public Opposition to Community Care for the Mentally Ill* (R. C. Baron, I. D. Rutman, and B. Klaczynska, eds.). Philadelphia: Horizon House, p. 331.

Turner, J. E. C., and W. J. Tenhoor (1978). The NIMH community support program: pilot approach to needed social reform. *Schizophrenia Bull.* 4:319.

U.S. Department of Health and Human Services Steering Committee on the Chronically Mentally Ill (1980). *Toward a National Plan for the Chronically Mentally Ill.* Washington, D.C.: U.S. Dept. HHS, December.

U.S. Department of Housing and Urban Development (1984). A report to the Secretary on the homeless and emergency shelters. Washington, D.C.: Office of Policy Development and Research.

Van Putten, T. G., and J. E. Spar (1979). The board-and-care home: does it deserve a bad press? *Hospital and Community Psychiatry* 30:461.

Venables, P. H., and J. F. Wing (1962). Level of arousal and the subclassification of schizophrenia. *Arch. Gen. Psychiat.* 7:114.

White, H. S. (1981). Managing the difficult patient in the community residence, in *Issues in Community Residential Care, New Directions for Mental Health Services* (R. D. Budson, ed.). San Francisco: Jossey-Bass, Vol. 11, p. 517.

Zitrin, A. A., S. Hardesty, E. I. Burdock, and A. K. Drossman (1976). Crime and violence among mental patients. *Am. J. Psychiat.* 133:142.

Chapter 7

Achtenberg, E. P., and P. Marcuse (1986). Toward the decommodification of housing, in *Critical Perspectives on Housing* (Bratt et al., eds.). Philadelphia: Temple University Press, pp. 474–83.

Appelbaum, R. (1984). Testimony before the Subcommittee on Housing and Community Development, Committee on Banking, Finance and Urban Affairs, and Subcommittee on Manpower and Housing, Committee on Government Operations, May 24, reprinted in Erikson and Wilhelm.

Baer, V., and T. Mendez (1985). *Homeless Families in New York City Emergency Housing: A Longitudinal Study*. New York: Human Resources Administration.

Beard, R. (ed.) (1987). *On Being Homeless: Historical Perspectives*. New York: Museum of the City of New York.

Blau, J. (1987). The homeless of New York: a case study of social welfare policy. Ph.D. dissertation, Columbia University, School of Social Work.

Bluestone, B., and B. Harrison (1982). *The Deindustrialization of America*. New York: Basic Books.

Bratt, R. G., C. Hartman, and A. Meyerson (1986). *Critical Perspectives on Housing*. Philadelphia: Temple University Press.

Caplow, T. (1968). Homelessness, in *International Encyclopaedia of the Social Services*. New York: Crowell, Collier.

Coalition for the Homeless, Community Action for Legal Services, and New York Lawyers for the Public Interest. (1986). *Stemming the Tide of Displacement: Housing Policies for Preventing Homelessness*. New York: mimeographed.

Council of Large Public Housing Authorities (1988). *Public Housing Tomorrow*. Boston: The Council of Large Public Housing Authorities.

Cuomo, M. M. (1983). 1933–1983—Never Again. Report to the National Governor's Association Task Force on the Homeless, Portland, Me.

Dolbeare, C. (1983). The low-income crisis, in *America's Housing Crisis* (C. Hartman, ed.). Boston: Routledge Kegan Paul.

Erickson, J., and C. Wilhelm (1986). *Housing the Homeless*. New Brunswick, N.J.: Center for Urban Policy Research.

Fabricant, M., and M. Kelly (1986). *Radical America* 20(2, 3).

Harloe, M. (1984). Social housing in the OECD countries—A selective review of developments and problems. University of Essex, mimeograph.

Hartman, C. (ed.) (1983). *America's Housing Crisis*. Boston: Routledge Kegan Paul.

Hartman, C. (1984). *The Transformation of San Francisco*. Ottowa, N.J.: Rowman and Allanheld.

Hartman, C. (1986). The housing part of the homelessness problem, in *The Mental Health Needs of Homeless Persons* (E. L. Bassuk, ed.). San Francisco: Jossey-Bass.

Hope, M., and J. Young (1986). *The Faces of Homelessness*. Lexington, Mass.: Lexington Books, p. 19.

Hopper, K., and L. S. Cox (1982). Litigation in advocacy for the homeless: the case of New York City. *Development: Seeds of Change* 2:57–62.

Hopper, K., and J. Hamberg (1984). The making of America's homeless: from skid row to new poor, 1945–1984, in *Critical Perspectives on Housing* (Bratt et al., eds.). Philadelphia: Temple University Press.

Hopper, K., E. Susser, and S. Conover (1986). Economies of Makeshift: deindustrialization and homelessness in New York City. *Urban Anthropology* 14 (1–3):183–236.

HUD News Release No. 85-163, Nov. 7, 1985.

Hulchanski, J. D. (1987). Who are the homeless? What is homelessness? The politics of defining an emerging policy issue. Vancouver, British Columbia, typescript.

Institute for Policy Studies, Working Group on Housing (1969). *The Right to Housing*. Washington, D.C.: Institute for Policy Studies.

Kasinitz, P. (1984). Gentrification and homelessness: the single room occupancy and inner city revival. *Urban & Social Change Review* 17(1):9–14.

Kirchheimer, D. W. (1987). Determinants of New York City policy on homeless families. Paper delivered at the annual meeting of the New York State Political Science Association, April 3.

Lawson, R., and M. Naison (1986). *The Tenant Movement in New York City, 1904–1985*. New Brunswick, N.J.: Rutgers University Press.

Marcuse, P. (1972). The legal attributes of home ownership. Washington, D.C.: The Urban Institute, Working Paper #209-1-1.

Marcuse, P. (1975). Residential alienation, home ownership and the limits of shelter policy. *Journal of Sociology and Social Welfare* 3(2):181–203.

Marcuse, P. (1985). Gentrification, abandonment, and displacement: connections, causes, and policy responses in New York City. *Journal of Urban and Contemporary Law* 28:195–240.

Marcuse, P. (1986). *The Uses and Limits of Rent Control: A Report with Recommendations*. State of New York, Division of Housing and Community Renewal.

Marcuse, P. (1987). Why are they homeless? *The Nation,* April 4, 244 (13).

Marcuse, P. (1988a). Neutralizing homelessness. *Socialist Review* 88:1:69–97.

Marcuse, P. (1988b). Do cities have a future? in *The Imperiled Economy.* Vol. 2. *Through the Safety Net,* Robert Cherry et al. (eds.). New York: Union for Radical Political Economics.

Marcuse, P. (1989). The pitfalls of specialism: special groups and the general problem of housing, in *Housing Issues of the 90s* (Sara Rosenberry and Chester Hartman, eds.). Westport, Conn.: Praeger.

Moberg, D. (1987). *In These Times,* Jan. 28.

National Coalition for the Homeless (1987). *Safety Network.* May.

New York City Crisis Intervention Services. 1984, 1986. *Report.* November.

New York City Human Resources Administration. 1986. *Project Bulletin 86-3.*

New York State Department of Social Services (1984). *Homelessness in New York State.*

New York Times. Jan. 12, 1986, p. 14.

New York Times. Nov. 17, 1986.

Partnership for the Homeless, Inc. (1989). *Assisting the Homeless in New York City.* New York: The Partnership, January 26.

Peddie, R. (1987). Homeless in a cold climate. Toronto, mimeograph.

Physicians' Task Force on Hunger in America (1985). *Hunger in America: The Growing Epidemic.* Cambridge, Mass.: Harvard University School of Public Health.

Riordan, T. (1987). Housekeeping at HUD: why the homeless problem could get much, much worse. *Common Cause Magazine,* March/April, pp. 26–31.

Rivlin, L. G. (1986). A new look at the homeless. *Social Policy,* Spring.

Roisman, F. et al. (Undated). Housing the homeless. mimeograph.

Rossi, P. H. et al. (1987). The urban homeless: estimating composition and size. Typescript.

Roth, D. et al. (1985). *Homeless in Ohio: A Study of People in Need.* Columbus: Ohio Department of Mental Health.

Sanjek, R. (1986). Federal housing programs and their impact on homelessness, in *Housing the Homeless* (J. Erickson and C. Wilhelm, eds.). New Brunswick, N.J.: Center for Urban Policy Research.

Schwab, J. (1986). Sheltering the homeless. *Planning,* December.

Sharman, B. (1986). The eviction epidemic. *City Limits,* December, p. 12.

Spagnolo, J. (1987). A coherent policy to stall the trend toward homelessness. Iona College. Typescript.

Statistical Abstracts of the United States, 1985, p. 417.

Stearns, M. E. (1929). Correlation between lodgings of homeless men and employment in New York City. *Journal of the American Statistical Association,* March Supplement.

Stegman, M. (1985). *The Dynamics of Housing in New York.* New York: New York City Department of Housing, Preservation, and Development.

Stegman, M. (1987). *Housing and Vacancy Report*. New York City, Department of Housing Preservation and Development.

U.S. Bureau of Labor Statistics (1987). *Employment and Earnings*. Washington, D.C.: U.S. Government Printing Office.

U.S. Department of Commerce, Bureau of the Census. (1987). *Statistical Abstract of the United States*. Washington, D.C.: U.S. Government Printing Office.

U.S. Department of Housing and Urban Development (1984). *Report to the Secretary on the Homeless and Emergency Shelters*. Washington, D.C.: U.S. Government Printing Office.

U.S. General Accounting Office (1985). *Homelessness: A Complex Problem and the Federal Response*. Washington, D.C.: U.S. Government Printing Office.

Village Voice, April 1, 1986, p. 32.

Watchman, P. Q., and P. Robson (1983). *Homelessness and the Law*. Glasgow: The Planning Exchange.

Watson, S., with H. Austerberry (1986). *Housing and Homelessness: A Feminist Perspective*. London: Routledge and Kegan Paul.

Wright, J. D., and J. Lam (1987). Homelessness and the low-income housing supply. *Social Policy* 17(4):48–53.

Yale Social Policy and Research Review. 1984.

Chapter 8

Agee, J., and W. Evans, *Let Us Now Praise Famous Men*. New York: Ballantine.

Commonwealth of Pennsylvania (1984). *A Study of Act 75: The Impact of Welfare Reform*. Harrisburg, Pa.

Cuomo, M. M. (1987). The state's role: New York State's approach to homelessness, in *The Homeless in Contemporary Society* (R. D. Bingham, P.E. Green, S. B. White, eds.). Beverly Hills: Sage.

Gudeman, J. E., W. F. Shore, and B. Dickey (1983). Day hospital and an inn instead of inpatient care. *New Eng. J. Med.* 308:749–753.

Hayes, R. M. (ed.) (1987). *The Rights of the Homeless*. New York: Practising Law Institute.

Heckler, M. (1984). Statement of Secretary of Health and Human Services Margaret Heckler, in "Shelter" (television broadcast), KCTS-Seattle, May.

Hopper, K. (1987). A bed for the night: homeless men in New York City, past and present. Ph.D. diss. Columbia University.

Hopper, K., and J. Hamberg (1986). The making of America's homeless: from skid row to new poor, 1945–1984, in *Critical Perspectives on Housing* (R. Bratt, C. Hartman, A. Meyerson, eds.). Philadelphia: Temple University Press, pp. 12–40.

Hopper, K., E. Susser, and S. Conover (1986). Economies of makeshift: deindustrialization and homelessness in New York City. *Urban Anthropology* 14:183–236.

Josephson, M. (1933). The other nation. *New Republic* 17(May): 15–17.

Kozol, J. *Rachel and Her Children*. New York: Fawcett, 1988.

Lamb, H. R. (ed.) (1984). *The Homeless Mentally Ill*. Washington, D.C.: American Psychiatric Association.

Marcuse, P. (1985). Gentrification, abandonment, and displacement: connections, causes, and policy response in New York City. *Washington Univ. J. of Urban and Contemp. Law* 28:195–240.

Mashibini, D. (ed.) (1987). *Forgotten Voices, Unforgettable Dreams*. New York: Coalition for the Homeless.

Quindlen, A. Life in the 30s. *New York Times,* Jan. 7, 1987.

Segal, S. P., and H. Specht (1983). A poorhouse in California, 1983: oddity or prelude? *Social Work* 25:358–365.

Stern, M. (1984). The emergence of homelessness as a public problem. *Social Service Rev.* 58:291–301.

Stott, W. (1973). *Documentary Expression in Thirties America*. New York: Oxford University Press.

Thompson, E. P. (1971). The moral economy of the English crowd in the eighteenth century. *Past and Present* 50:76.

U.S. Conference of Mayors (1986a). The growth of hunger, homelessness and poverty in America's cities in 1985. Washington, D.C. January.

U.S. Conference of Mayors (1986b). Responding to homelessness in America's cities. Washington, D.C. June.

U.S. Department of Housing and Urban Development (1984). Report to the Secretary on the homeless and emergency shelters. Washington, D.C.

Chapter 9

Bachrach, L. L. (1980). Overview: model programs for chronic mental patients. *Am. J. Psychiat.* 137:1023.

Barbanel, J. (1988). Number of homeless far below shelter forecasts. The *New York Times,* Jan. 26, 1988, p. B1.

Bassuk, E. L. (1984). The homelessness problem. *Scientific American* 251:40.

Bassuk, E. L., and H. R. Lamb (1986). Homelessness and the implementation of deinstitutionalization, in *New Directions in Mental Health Service* (E. L. Bassuk, ed.). San Francisco: Jossey-Bass, Vol. 30, p. 7.

Bassuk, E. L., and A. Lauriat (1986). Are emergency shelters the solution? *Int. J. Mental Health* 14:125.

Bassuk, E. L., L. Rubin, and A. Lauriat (1984). Is homelessness a mental health problem? *Am. J. Psychiat.* 141:1546.

Baxter, E., and K. Hopper (1981). *Private Lives/Public Spaces: Mentally Disabled Adults on the Streets of New York City,* Interim Report #2. New York: Community Services Society Institute for Social Welfare Research.

Campbell, D. T., and J. C. Stanley (1963). Experimental and quasi-experimental designs for research on teaching, in *Handbook of Research on Teaching* (N. L. Gage, ed.). Chicago: Rand-McNally.

Cronbach, L. J. (1983). *Designing Evaluations of Educational and Social Programs.* San Francisco: Jossey-Bass.

Crystal, S., S. Ladner, R. Towber, B. Callender, and J. Calhoun (1986). *Project Future.* New York: Human Resources Administration.

Cuomo, M. M. (1983). *1933/1983—Never Again. A Report to the National Governor's Association.* Portland, Me.: Task Force on the Homeless.

Gardner, M. (1988). Families with no place to call home. *Christian Science Monitor,* April 1, p. B4.

Goleman, D. (1987). Mentally ill poorly supervised, experts say. The *New York Times,* Sept. 11, 1987, p. 1.

Goleman, D. (1988). Shifting tactics, New York plans closer supervision of mentally ill. The *New York Times,* Jan. 18, 1988, p. 1.

Gudeman, J. E., and M. E. Shore (1985). Public care for the chronically mentally ill: a new model, in *The New Economics and Psychiatric Care* (S. S. Sharfstein and A. Beigel, eds.). Washington, D.C.: American Psychiatric Press, p. 191.

Holden, C., Homelessness: experts differ in root causes. (editorial) (1986). *Science* 232:569, May 2, 1986.

Hopper, K., E. Baxter, S. Cox, and L. Klein (1982). *One Year Later: The Homeless Poor in New York City, 1982.* New York: Community Services Society, June.

House Committee on Banking, Finance, and Urban Affairs, Subcommittee on Housing and Community Development (1982). *Homelessness in America,* Dec. 15.

House Committee on Banking, Finance, and Urban Affairs, Subcommittee on Housing and Community Development (1984). *Homelessness in America,* II, Jan. 25.

House Committee on Banking, Finance, and Urban Affairs, Subcommittee on Housing and Community Development (1987). *Homelessness in America,* Feb. 4.

House Select Committee on Aging, Subcommittee on Housing and Consumer

Interests (1984). *Homeless Older Americans* (Comm. Pub. No. 98-461), 98th Congress, May 2, 1984.

Judd, C. M., and D. A. Kenny (1981). *Estimating the Effects of Social Interventions*. Cambridge, U.K.: Cambridge University Press.

Lamb, H. R. (1984). Deinstitutionalization and the homeless mentally ill, in *The Homeless Mentally Ill* (H. R. Lamb, ed.). Washington, D.C.: American Psychiatric Association, Ch. 3, p. 55.

Leepson, M. (1982). The homeless: a growing national problem. *Editorial Research Reports,* Vol. II, No. 16, Oct. 29.

Linn, M. W., E. M. Caffey, J. Klett, and G. E. Hogarty (1979). Day treatment and psychotropic drugs in the aftercare of schizophrenic patients. *Arch. Gen. Psychiat.* 36:1055.

Lipton, F. R., S. Nutt, and A. Sabatini (1988). Housing the homeless mentally ill: a longitudinal study of a treatment approach. *Hospital and Community Psychiatry* 39:40.

May, P. R. A. (1974). Psychotherapy research in schizophrenics: another view of present reality. *Schizophrenia Bull.* 9:126.

Mechanic, D. (1978). Alternatives to mental hospital treatment: a sociological perspective, in *Alternatives to Mental Hospital Treatment* (L. I. Stein and M. A. Test, eds.). New York: Plenum, p. 309.

Mechanic, D., and L. H. Aiken (1987). Improving the care of patients with chronic mental illness. *NEJM* 317:1634.

Mehta, G. (1988). Don't look now (public shelters in New York). *Vogue* 178:498, March.

Miller, M., J. Foote, P. King, M. Gosnell, and T. Mathews (1988). What can be done? *Newsweek,* Vol. 111, March 21, p. 57.

New York Times. Officials oppose U.S. cut in aid to homeless families. March 29, 1988, p. B3.

New York Times. July 4, 1988, p. 27.

Notes from CHAMP (1988). *Workshop on Self-Help Programs for Homeless Mentally Ill Persons.* Silver Springs, Md.: Clearinghouse on Homelessness Among Mentally Ill People, July, p. 1.

Paul, G. L., and R. J. Lentz (1977). *Psychosocial Treatment of Chronic Mental Patients: Milieu Versus Social Learning Programs.* Cambridge, Mass.: Harvard University Press.

Phoenix South Community Mental Health Center (1983). *The Homeless of Phoenix: Who Are They and What Should Be Done?* Phoenix: Phoenix South Community Mental Health Center, June.

Piasecki, J. R., J. E. Pittinger, and I. D. Rutman (1978). *Determining Costs of Community Residential Services for the Psychosocially Disabled.* Rockville, Md.: NIMH, DHEW, PHS (Publ. #(ADM) 77-504).

Rossi, P. H., J. D. Wright, G. A. Fisher, and G. Willis (1987). The urban homeless: estimating composition and size. *Science* 235:1336.

Roth, D., and G. J. Bean (1986). New perspectives on homelessness: findings from a statewide epidemiological study. *Hospital and Community Psychiatry* 37:712.

Rousseau, A. M., and A. K. Shulman (1982). *Shopping Bag Ladies: Homeless Women Speak About Their Lives*. New York: Pilgrim.

Salerno, D., K. Hopper, and E. Baxter (1984). *Hardship in the Heartland: Homelessness in Eight U.S. Cities*. New York: Community Service Society of New York.

Stein, L. I., and M. A. Test (1980). Alternatives to mental hospital treatment: I. Conceptual model, treatment program, and clinical evaluation. *Arch. Gen. Psychiat.* 37:392.

Suchman, E. A. (1967). *Evaluative Research*. New York: Russell Sage Foundation.

Taintor, Z., P. Widem, and S. A. Barrett (1984). *Cost Considerations in Mental Health Treatment: Settings, Modalities, and Providers*. Rockville, Md.: NIMH, USDHHS, Division of Biometry and Epidemiology.

Talbott, J. A. (1979). Deinstitutionalization: avoiding the disasters of the past. *Hospital and Community Psychiatry* 30:621.

U.S. Conference of Mayors (1986). The growth of hunger, homelessness and poverty in America's cities in 1985. Washington, D.C.: U.S. Conference of Mayors, January.

U.S. Conference of Mayors (1986). Responding to homelessness in America's cities. Washington, D.C.: U.S. Conference of Mayors, June.

U.S. Conference of Mayors (1987). The continuing growth of hunger, homelessness, and poverty in America's cities, 1987. Washington, D.C.: U.S. Conference of Mayors, December.

U.S. Department of Housing and Urban Development (1984). A report to the Secretary on the homeless and emergency shelters. Washington, D.C.: Office of Policy Development and Research.

U.S. Department of Housing and Urban Development (1987). Report on homeless activities required by section 203(c)(1) of the Stewart B. McKinney Homeless Assistance Act. Washington, D.C.: Office of Policy Development and Research, Oct. 20.

U.S. General Accounting Office (1985). *Homelessness: A Complex Problem and the Federal Response*. Washington, D.C.: U.S. General Accounting Office.

Whitman, D. (1988). Hope for the homeless. *U.S. News & World Report,* Vol. 104, Feb. 29, p. 24.

Wyatt, R. J., and E. G. DeRenzo (1986). Scienceless to homeless (editorial). *Science* 234:1309, Dec. 12.

About the Authors

Carol L. M. Caton, Ph.D., is a medical sociologist who trained at Yale University. Currently Associate Clinical Professor of Social Sciences (Psychiatry and Public Health) at the College of Physicians and Surgeons of Columbia University, Dr. Caton has an extensive research background on homelessness and mental illness. She is involved in a socioepidemiological study of homelessness and schizophrenia and has conducted an evaluation of a shelter-based mental health program for homeless men. Among her publications is *Management of Chronic Schizophrenia*, published by Oxford University Press in 1984.

Arnold Drapkin, M.D., is Associate Clinical Professor of Medicine at the Albert Einstein College of Medicine and for over 30 years has treated indigent men and women at the Jacobi Hospital, a large city hospital in New York. He practices internal medicine in New York City and recently joined the attending staff and faculty of the Mount Sinai Medical Center.

Paula F. Eagle, M.D., is the Associate Director of Psychiatry at Columbia Presbyterian Medical Center. She founded a day treatment program for homeless men in the Fort Washington Armory Men's Shelter.

Jeffrey Grunberg, M.A., is currently working as Director of a day treatment program for the homeless mentally ill at Columbia Presbyterian Medical Center. He is also on the faculty of Columbia University as an instructor of psychology and serves as a consultant for business groups throughout New York City on matters related to the homeless.

Kim Hopper, Ph.D., is currently Assistant Professor of Medical Anthropology at CUNY Medical School in New York. He is author or co-author of a number of articles and monographs on homelessness, including *Private Lives/Public Spaces* with Ellen Baxter (1981). He is active with both New York and national coalitions for the homeless and is completing a book of homeless men in New York, past and present.

Peter Marcuse, Ph.D., is Professor of Urban Planning at the School of Architecture and Planning at Columbia University and is actively involved in housing policy issues in New York City and in national legislative issues. He has written widely on housing planning questions and has been a consultant to a number of government agencies and community groups.

David Schaffer, M.D., is Irving Philips Professor of Child Psychiatry at the College of Physicians and Surgeons of Columbia University. He is also Director of the Division of Child Psychiatry in the Department of Psychiatry at Columbia. Among his many research accomplishments was directing the New York City Study of Runaway and Homeless Youth in collaboration with Carol L. M. Caton, Ph.D.

Lois C. Wolf, C.S.W., Ph.D., moved from a career of over two decades in education, acting as a senior graduate faculty member at Bank Street College, to a second career in social work. She currently directs a day treatment program for the homeless mentally ill elderly and has a private practice in psychotherapy.

Reference Index

General Index